Policy Development
in Sport Management

POLICY DEVELOPMENT IN SPORT MANAGEMENT

SECOND EDITION

Harold J. VanderZwaag

Westport, Connecticut
London

Library of Congress Cataloging-in-Publication Data

VanderZwaag, Harold J.
    Policy development in sport management / Harold J. VanderZwaag.—
2nd ed.
      p. cm.
    Includes bibliographical references and index.
    ISBN 0–275–96089–7 (alk. paper)
    1. Sports administration—United States. I. Title.
GV713.V35   1998
796'.06'073—dc21   98–4973

British Library Cataloguing in Publication Data is available.

Library of Congress Catalog Card Number: 98–4973
ISBN: 0–275–96089–7

First published in 1998

Praeger Publishers, 88 Post Road West, Westport, CT 06881
An imprint of Greenwood Publishing Group, Inc.

Printed in the United States of America

The paper used in this book complies with the
Permanent Paper Standard issued by the National
Information Standards Organization (Z39.48–1984).

10 9 8 7 6 5 4 3 2 1

Contents

Part II.   PROGRAM   **123**

Preface

Since the first edition of this book was published in 1988, academic preparation for work in sport management has developed into a professional training ground for today's emerging sport managers. Although there were relatively few colleges and universities offering the study of sport management when the field first came into existence almost 30 years ago, today there are over 200 recognized graduate and undergraduate sport management programs in this country. This development is manifested not only in the proliferation of such programs, but by the kind of course work considered most applicable or appropriate for students in this field.

As with the first edition, the latter aspect generated the idea for writing this book. Many sport management programs tend to be initiated within the physical education department where students take a core of the more traditional physical education courses before being "farmed out" to schools or departments of business administration for preparation in the business aspect of managing a sport program. However, an increasing number of institutions are offering a more specific curriculum that is designed for sport management per se.

To accommodate the curriculum needs of these programs, there is a need for more textbooks aimed at undergraduate and graduate students who are studying sport management. For those students who are preparing for careers in either college athletics or professional sport, this book provides an in-depth analysis of a wide variety of issues and problems they will be facing.

A policy course of the type suggested by this book is highly recommended for inclusion in a sport management curriculum. There is little doubt that the success or effectiveness of a sport organization will be largely determined by the kind of policies that are developed and the degree to which these policies are carried out. Students should have an understanding of the major policy considerations among sport organizations. They should also understand the various issues and problems that confront sport managers when they are faced with the need to formulate policies for the management of a sport program.

The various policy topics, while by no means exhaustive of the potential areas for policy development in sport management, represent areas wherein significant issues and/or problems can be identified. That is not to say that each issue or problem is of equal magnitude or that the need for policies is self-evident in all cases. While much of the focus is on the personnel policies regarding athletes—on both the collegiate and professional levels—this book includes an exploration of the contemporary issues facing today's sport managers, to wit: NCAA mainstreaming policies, college football playoffs, free agency in professional sports, franchise expansion and relocation, and professional sport playoffs. A quick scan of newspaper and magazine accounts will indicate that there is some justification for establishing that emphasis.

This book begins by setting forth a perspective from which the title of the book, *Policy Development in Sport Management*, emanates. This provides the frame of reference from which this book is written. Within this discussion are answers to key questions, including: What is sport? What is sport management? What is policy development in sport management? What is the scope of sport enterprise? What is the policy domain? What are the basic techniques of case method analysis that can be used to develop a policy regarding either an issue or problem in sport management? Part I is devoted to personnel policies, particularly those policies involving athletes. Most of the chapters are on policies concerning college athletes. However, there is a chapter on free agency in professional sport.

The selected areas included in Part II have been designated as program policies. Essentially they represent policy considerations that more or less affect the entire program and yet fall outside the realm of personnel policies as such. In addition to the heavy emphasis on personnel policies, a few other factors are instrumental in the selection of certain issues and problems as a preliminary basis of policy development in sport management. One of these is that college sport seems to have more than its share of issues and problems. Consequently, a large portion of the policy area is devoted to collegiate sport. Beyond that, contemporary issues facing professional sports managers, including free agency and franchise expansion and relocation, are also addressed.

Acknowledgments

V arious people have contributed somewhat to the production of this book. However, I particularly wish to thank two people. Without their assistance the book would probably not have materialized.

The first is Maureen Kocot, who did the vast majority of the work in preparing the original manuscript. The second is Robert Fleischman, who originally planned to co-author the book with me. Robert did much of the initial research in planning for this second edition. The contributions of both Maureen and Robert are most appreciated.

Chapter 1

Introduction: The Perspective

What is covered under the title "policy development in sport management"? There is good reason to suspect that the various components of the title may well convey different messages to various people. Consequently, it seems desirable to begin by setting forth a perspective, the frame of reference from which this book is written. Key questions require answers before proceeding. What is sport? What is management? What is policy development? Answers to these questions still yield a fairly broad territory. We will also consider the need for policy development in sport management.

SPORT

Most of what we know about sport as a generic activity comes from a recognition of the specific activities that contribute to the whole enterprise. We are able to identify sports—baseball, golf, tennis, football, and bowling—the kinds of activities one reads or hears about in the media. Thus, even though we may not give much thought to the parameters of sport as a collective enterprise, we have little difficulty identifying most of the parts.

When one examines the parts (the sports) more carefully, certain common denominators emerge. First and foremost, every sport is *physical* in nature. That is not to say that it is exclusively physical. One must think to physically act in a controlled context. One of the principal challenges in sport is to effect the necessary union between the mind and the body. Physical demands also vary considerably from sport to sport. Football is not the same as golf or bowling in terms of the physical abilities that are required for effective performance. If one had to identify a single physical performance attribute pervasive among sports it would probably be coordination. The bottom line is that each sport tests the physical abilities of the participants in one way or another.

Another prime characteristic of sport is that it is *competitive*, at least in the more typical or developed form. The reason for the qualification is that there are certain basic sport skills that can also be considered part of the total sport domain. Examples would be running, kicking, throwing, hitting, skating, skiing, swimming, and surfing. By and large these activities lead up to full-fledged participation in sport. In the more fully developed form, sport is competitive because it involves a contest. This may be a struggle between two or more individuals or two or more teams for supremacy or victory. Thus we end up with the common notion of winners and losers in sport.

Certain other concepts have also been widely associated with the idea of sport. Perhaps foremost among these are *play*, *games*, and *athletics*. Volumes have been written in an effort to sort out the relationship among these concepts. It hardly seems necessary here to rehash the various analyses. However, a few thoughts may be worthy of attention.

Play is a much broader concept than that of sport. There are many forms of play that are not sport. By the same token, sport may or may not be play for the participant. Games are a form of play, but again play is the broader activity or idea. At the same time, we note physical contests (sports) that are not games (e.g., gymnastics and swimming races). In the United States, the tendency has been to use the term athletics more or less interchangeably with sport. The one distinction may be that interscholastic or intercollegiate sport is commonly referred to as athletics in the United States. On the other hand, internationally, athletics is more or less synonymous with track and field events.

A couple of other characteristics of sport are worthy of attention. One of these is that sport tends to have a unique *dependence on specialized equipment and facilities*. The equipment and facilities for golf are unique to golf. The same can be said about tennis, baseball, football, and most other sports. There is no magic behind the recognition that modern sport has developed through the medium of the sporting goods business. The implications of this for those in sport management positions are extensive. In most cases a sport program is only as good as the quality of the facilities and equipment that can be made available. The relative importance of a high-quality facility is particularly evident in the realm of highly organized, commercial sport, specifically aimed at attracting spectators.

Each sport also has its particular and unique dimensions of time and space. Game time is very different from the local standard time. In some sports the game clock is a most determining factor. There are certain special dimensions of time. This may be the last two minutes in the half of a football game or the last four minutes of a basketball game. The "shot clock" has also emerged as a key element in basketball. On the other hand, sports such as baseball, tennis, and golf are not governed by special time considerations. The unique space characteristics are even more evident in all sports. This ties in with the high importance of facilities in the sport realm. Whether it is a football field, baseball diamond, a golf course, or a swimming pool, there is no exact counterpart outside the environment of the sport. Again, the implications here for policy development in sport management are considerable.

At least one other distinguishing characteristic of sport should be mentioned. This is the relative importance of records in sport. The records are essentially of two types: those that indicate current standing in relationship to other teams or participants, or those that indicate the highest level of achievement in a given activity. This is the feature of sport that provides much of the content for the news media.

> Sport is a competitive physical activity, utilizing specialized equipment and facilities, with unique dimensions of time and space, in which the quest for records is of high significance. (Note: This definition assumes that there are various lead-up activities to the full-fledged sport participation as outlined in the definition.)

Other characteristics of sport could also be noted. During the past 20 years numerous authors of books or articles on sport theory have advanced theses about the nature of sport. However, with the foregoing characteristics we have some of the key elements to present a definition to use in understanding what is meant by sport in the context of this text.

Scope of the Sport Enterprise

Having examined the general nature of sport, we should now be somewhat more specific about identifying the scope of the sport enterprise. This is the realm wherein managers will have to develop policies for the conduct of sport activities. Where do we find programs that sponsor or promote this activity of sport as it has been delineated? At least 16 sources can be identified.

1. *School and College Sport Programs:* This is one of the prime sources for sport sponsorship in the United States. From a quantitative standpoint, high school sport programs are the single most significant dimension in the entire sport enterprise. Generally speaking, there are three components of the total sport program in schools and colleges: interscholastic or intercollegiate sport, intramural sport, and sport instruction through physical education classes.

2. *Professional Sport:* Here we include the commonly recognized professional teams and individual sports such as golf and tennis in which the promoters and participants are closely involved in a commercial activity aimed at making a profit through a large audience. This is not the place to debate the obvious overlap with a segment of college sport and so-called amateur competition in international sport.

3. *Amateur Sport Organizations:* This category includes sport organizations established to facilitate national and international competition outside the realm of collegiate sport. The various sport federations and Olympic Committees are prime examples. Again, whether or not these are truly amateur organizations can be debated and will be a topic for consideration under the issues and problems discussed in this text. Here it is only necessary to identify these organizations as another component of the sport enterprise.

4. *Private Club Sport:* Prime examples in this category are tennis, golf, swimming, gymnastics, and racquetball clubs, which can be found throughout the United States and other parts of the world. The trend toward the multiuse facility, particularly involving various forms of weight equipment, should also be noted. In this component one finds an extension beyond sport per se, but the dimension of sport is still at the forefront.

5. *Other Commercialized Sport Establishments:* In addition to private club sport, there are other forms of commercial sport aimed at mass participation in lieu of spectatorship. Bowling alleys, ski resorts, and public golf courses are some of the prime examples in this segment of the sport enterprise.

6. *Arenas, Coliseums, Civic Centers, and Stadia:* In this area of large facility management, the overlap outside the sport enterprise is most evident. Nevertheless, many of these facilities have been built primarily for the purpose of offering one or more sports, and some are used almost exclusively for that purpose. Here we also note some overlap with the professional sport component of the total sport enterprise. In some cases, the facilities are owned by the professional sport teams. In others, the facilities are made available to sport teams on a lease basis.

7. *Sport Programs under Community Recreation:* The very title indicates that sport is only one aspect of this broader category. However, the numerous sport programs are most visible in this realm. The array of youth sport programs outside school are prime examples. Beyond that, community recreation programs also sponsor many sport opportunities for adults.

8. *Industrial Sport Programs:* Large industries typically offer various sport programs for employees. In some cases a corporation sponsors a sport team for competition outside the company. However, in general this is another one of the large segments of participant sport. The parallel with community recreation programs is evident in that sport is but a part of all recreational opportunities for employees.

9. *Sport Programs in Social Agencies:* This category again includes a host of possibilities wherein sports are offered as part of a larger recreational program. Some prime sources are the YMCA, YWCA, Jewish Community Centers, CYO, Boy Scouts, Girl Scouts, and Boys' Clubs.

10. *Military Sport Programs:* Every relatively large military establishment offers a diversified sport program extending from highly organized, competitive teams to participant sport on a recreational basis for military personnel. The existence of specialty military positions in sport testifies to the significance of sport programs in this sector.

11. *Sport Marketing and Consulting Firms:* These companies exist outside sport organizations as such and offer promotional and placement services. Some examples are the International Management Group, Athletic and Sports Consulting Service, Louis Zahn Data, Service Corporation, and Charles J. Brotman and Associates. This aspect of the total sport industry has experienced rapid growth in recent years.

12. *Developmental Programs for Sport:* Here again is another broad and somewhat elusive category. Nevertheless, it has to be taken into account when assessing the scope of the total sport enterprise. These organizations

serve to develop existing sport programs in several ways. Many of these programs work from an educational context. Examples are the United States Sport Academy, the Athlete Institute, The Women's Sport Foundation, the American Sports Education Institute, the President's Council on Physical Fitness and Sport, the National Golf Foundation, and the Tennis Foundation of North America.

13. *Corporate Advertising through Sport Tournaments:* Some sports, principally tennis and golf, are promoted through the sponsorship of tournaments. Some of the early examples were Avon Tennis, Virginia Slims Tennis, and the Volvo International Tennis Tournament. In more recent years, most of the PGA Tour golf tournaments have acquired a title corporate sponsor.

14. *Sporting Goods Industry:* In one sense, this broad area is peripheral to the sport enterprise per se. Yet, in another sense the production and distribution of sporting goods is the key to all sport development. In many cases the relative success and popularity of a sport can be directly traced to the design and production of its equipment. The relationship between the sport of skiing and ski equipment is a clear example.

15. *Sports News Media:* Here we are including newspaper, magazine, radio, and television coverage of sport. The situation is roughly analogous to that noted with regard to the sporting good industry. The difference is found in the news media's almost exclusive impact on spectator sport. In that regard there is a mutual support relationship between the news media and the heart of the sport enterprise.

16. *Academic Programs in Sport Management:* This is another of the more recent developments. Basically, these are academic programs, at the bachelor's and master's degree levels, to prepare students for positions in most of the 15 components of the sport enterprise noted above. The relative success and future for these programs is at least twofold. The extensive scope of the sport enterprise offers an extensive market for management positions, and the overall popularity of sport stimulates an abundant supply of students.

One can be assured that these 16 sources of sport sponsorship do not cover the entire scope of the sport enterprise. There are so many facets and loose ends in the enterprise that it is almost impossible to account for all of the diverse dimensions. It may also be true that these categories are not the most representative of the total structure. Nevertheless, we trust that they are sufficient to provide the parameters for the territory involved when assessing the potential for sport management.

MANAGEMENT

In many respects the problems with defining management are not unlike those noted in regard to sport. Management is more easily identified as an activity than it is understood. We hear about, read about, see, and sometimes work for or with people who are considered to be effective managers. Ineffective managers are also readily identified. Often overlooked are those characteristics that determine the quality of management. Before examining some of these characteristics, it might be helpful to distinguish among the terms management, administration, leadership, and supervision.

The distinction between management and administration is quite significant. Management is the much broader of the two concepts. All administrators are managers, but not all managers are administrators. Administration is that part of the management process that is institutionalized. Be they full-time or part-time, administrators are appointed with distinct managerial responsibilities, often involving budgetary control. Personnel with other primary roles report to an administrator. In many cases, these other personnel are also managers, but they are not administrators; for example, teachers and coaches (particularly head coaches) are managers. They are not administrators unless they have also been assigned to that role as one of their major responsibilities. The fact that teachers and coaches are managers will be clearer when we consider the characteristics of management.

The distinction between management and leadership is also significant. Leadership is a component of management. Once again, management is a much more inclusive concept. Leadership is actually an ability that is particularly evident in carrying out the directing function of management. Essentially a leader is one who provides the external motivation for carrying out assigned tasks. The effective manager must provide leadership. However, one can be a fine leader and yet fall short in terms of other managerial responsibilities.

Like leadership, supervision is another aspect of management that is clearly linked to the directing function. Supervisors carry out certain functions under the managerial domain, but they are not involved with all the functions of management. To supervise is to oversee the direction of at least one component of the program.

We have noted that management is related to administration, leadership, and supervision. In one way or another, management is more inclusive than the related concepts. What, then, are the characteristics that enable one to identify the parameters of management? In considering these characteristics, it should be noted that the basic characteristics of effective management are being identified. Needless to say, there are many management situations that somehow fall short in meeting the criteria of being completely effective.

First and foremost, management is goal oriented. Management works within the context of a purposeful organization. Those who manage within such an organization must agree on clearly defined, realistic goals and direct the activities of the group toward the realization of those goals. Goals, objectives, aims, and similar ideas are all used interchangeably in this context. Everything else in the management process is likely to fall short of expectations if management cannot agree on and successfully communicate the objectives to those who work for the organization. Such objectives or goals are both institutional and individual. Managers are careful to distinguish between the two sets of goals and are interested in maintaining the proper balance between the two.

Management also involves the selection of appropriate strategies to meet objectives. Managers consider alternative strategies and choose those which are most promising. First of all there must be agreement on priorities. Personnel strategies and physical resource strategies are two general categories from which more specific strategies are developed. The former includes the means to attain staff and subsequently to assign staff duties. The latter includes the efficient utilization of facilities as well as strategies for all forms of financial procurement, expenditure, and control.

The most direct manifestation of management is found in actions taken to carry out the strategies. This involves the issuance of orders and instructions. It is at this point that we particularly observe the leadership and supervisory components of management.

Finally, management also involves the responsibility for objectively judging the progress and results of the work. At this point the direct consideration of objectives again comes to the forefront. Evaluation should be carried out only in relation to the objectives established as part of the planning process. A complete evaluation will also make provision for arriving at new goals or adjusting previous ones. Management is a continuous process; it does not cease when one concludes the assessment phase.

After considering these characteristics of management, five distinct managerial functions can be identified, although there is obviously overlap among these functions:

Planning—determining a course of action;

Organizing—providing a structure for the work of the organization;

Staffing—selecting and assigning personnel to carry out the work;

Directing—making provisions for the actual conduct of the work;

Controlling—evaluating the progress of the work and taking steps to change or modify the future plans and actions.

> Management is a goal-oriented social process involving selection of appropriate strategies, provisions for directing the work of the enterprise, and the control of performance in an effort to meet the objectives of the organization.

POLICY DEVELOPMENT

If sport and management are both somewhat elusive in their meanings, this is even more true of policy. There is a tendency to use the term "policy" in a variety of senses, some of which do little to explain how policy fits into the total managerial spectrum. Policy is often confused with philosophy, objectives, strategy, and procedures.

Various characteristics of policies can be noted. To begin with, policies have wide ramifications. They are related to the total system or organization. A policy is not established to guide the work of only an individual or part of a group. This feature distinguishes a policy from a procedure. Policies also tend to have external as well as internal implications. Even though they are developed to guide activities within the organization, they are often directed at affairs with external import.

Policies are also extended from a time perspective. Essentially they involve standing decisions on important, recurring matters. They are designed to have an effect over an extended period of time. This is why it is appropriate to think in terms of policy development.

The idea of development also has an extended time connotation. Basically, development represents change in a continuous direction. Such is the basic design of policy formation. The import of policies indicates that they should evolve. Although we may begin with certain initial policy decisions, it is safe to say that sound policy has to stand the test of time.

Policies are also aimed at those activities in the organization that involve the critical resources, classified as either human or financial. Thus we typically find a whole array of personnel policies involving matters such as recruitment, selection, retention, advancement, discipline, and various forms of reward. Public relation policies also reflect the crucial human resource. The critical nature of the financial resource is reflected in policies guiding financial acquisition and financial control, as well as the entire domain of facilities and equipment.

Significant decision making is at the heart of the policy development process. The real basis for decision making is to be found in the existence of numerous alternatives and the selection from among those alternatives. If an alternative does not exist, there really is no need to have a policy as such. This is where issues and problems come into the picture. It is also why issues and problems have been selected as the pillars of policy development in sport management. Suffice to say that the decision making aspect of policy development is either directed to taking a stand on an issue or to solving a problem. The footnote would be that this might also be an anticipated issue or problem.

A final characteristic of policy development is that it is directed toward a dynamic social process in a changing environment. In some respects this characteristic is closely related to the extended time perspective and the fact that policies evolve. Even though policies involve standing decisions, this does not mean that they lack the flexibility

> Policy development is the continuous process of making significant decisions on recurring matters resulting from issues or problems involving the use of critical resources from the standpoint of a long-term perspective.

to meet changes involving the critical human and material resources.

Sequential Program Development

Thus far we have noted at least five principal characteristics of policy development. Further insight regarding the nature of policies may be gained by considering how they fit into total, sequential program development and the total managerial picture.

1. *Basic Mission*: This is the raison d'être of the program. For what basic purpose does the program exist? In the broadest sense, a statement of mission specifies the scope of operations. Usually, this is expressed either in terms of product and market or service and client.

2. *Objectives*: As noted earlier, other terms could be used in place of objectives. These might be goals, aims, targets, or desired results. Whatever the particular label, the intent of this step in program development is the same: what does the organization hope to accomplish toward meeting the mission? These objectives or goals may be fairly general or relatively specific. In either case they are a refinement or breakdown of the mission.

3. *Policies:* Here is the precise place when policies fit into the total scheme of things. Summarizing what was said earlier, policies are broad guidelines for the achievement of objectives. They naturally have to be developed after the objectives are established, and they provide the parameters for the specifics that follow.

4. *Strategies*: These are the specific major actions or patterns of action for reaching objectives and carrying out policies. One of the real tests for coherence in a program is whether the strategies are consistent with the objectives and policies.

5. *Program or Structure:* This is the composite of generalized procedures for the actual conduct of affairs. The program or structure is the direct answer to the question: What is offered? If it is not consistent with the mission, a disparity is most evident. This is the point in which policies may be revealed as the key link. If the organization lacks sound policies, difficulty may be encountered in offering a program that is consistent with the mission.

6. *Roles:* These are the particular behavior patterns of the individuals that are necessary to carry out the program. Each role must be clarified in the relationship to the objectives, policies, and strategies that have been developed for the organization. The role of an individual on a sport team is a vivid example of how role definition is the culminating component in sequential program development.

The following examples (Exhibits 1.A and 1.B) from the field of sport management illustrate the nature of sequential program development and how policy fits into the total structures. High school sport programs and professional sport programs offer interesting comparisons.

Exhibit I.A: Professional Football Team

1. *Basic Mission:* To make a profit through the entertainment business for football spectators.
2. *Objectives:*
   a. To win the NFL championship.
   b. To develop individual player excellence.
3. *Policies:*
   a. A sound public relation program will be established.
   b. Efforts will be directed toward gradually building the program through player development.
   c. An attractive, comfortable, and safe facility will be maintained.
   d. The front office and field operations will be closely coordinated.
   e. The club will work closely with the NFL office to maintain integrity of the game.
4. *Strategies:*
   a. The club will work to strengthen the various relations with the news media.
   b. The draft will be used to develop younger players in lieu of obtaining veterans through trades.
   c. The stadium will be well maintained and clean at all times.
   d. Facility staff members will be well trained in effective crowd management procedures.
   e. Crowd management techniques will be periodically reviewed for effectiveness.
   f. Organizational relationships will be carefully delineated.
   g. Considerable attention will be given to the legal orientation for all employees.
   h. There will be a set procedure for determination of salaries and the renegotiation of existing contracts.
5. *Program:* A competitive but developing team.
6. *Roles:*
   a. General Manager—success in signing young players.
   b. Head Coach—leadership ability in developing young players.

c. Public Relations Director—success in carrying out marketing techniques.

d. Players—willingness to work on development.

Exhibit I.B: High School Sports Program

1. *Basic Mission:* To provide a sport program that will contribute to the education of the student body and serve as a means of developing interest in and support for the school.

2. *Objectives:*
   a. To be competitive in all sports in the interscholastic league competition.
   b. To provide a means of recreation for the student body.
   c. To contribute to the social development of students.
   d. To develop skills in various forms of sports participation.
   e. To enhance the image of the school through the sport program.

3. *Policies:*
   a. An integrated sport program will be offered involving interscholastic competition, intramural sport, and instruction.
   b. A diversified program will be offered for both boys and girls.
   c. Academic standards for interscholastic participants will receive high priority.
   d. Continued effort will be made to affiliate with a conference that offers balanced competition.
   e. The physical conditioning of participants will receive high priority.

4. *Strategies:*
   a. The focus will be on interscholastic sport and intramural sport for those students who do not qualify for the former.
   b. Sport instruction will be offered only in sports that are new to the students involved.
   c. Approximately the same number of sports for girls as for boys will be offered.
   d. Booster club support will contribute to the total budget for the sport program.
   e. A nucleus of a full-time sport staff will be maintained.
   f. Additional coaches will be employed as part-time coaches with major responsibility as classroom teachers.
   g. Two full-time trainers will be employed.
   h. There will be a director for the intramural sport program.

5. *Program:* Diversified sport offerings with balanced competition in all sports.

6. *Roles:*

   a. Athletic Director—success in developing and maintaining an integrated and well-balanced sport program that is consistent with the educational objectives of the school.

   b. Coaches—success in developing the participants as students and athletes.

   c. Trainers—success in contributing to the total physical conditioning of all participants.

   d. Intramural Sport Director—success in developing a viable attractive program that meets the needs and interests of all students.

The Policy Domain

Thus far we have briefly considered the nature of policy development, including how policy fits into the total picture of sequential program development. Before making further application to the sport enterprise, it might be advantageous to further specify the territory of policy. What is the basis for development of policies? Or, why are policies really needed? Could we not move directly from objectives to strategies for carrying out those objectives? The answer to any one of these questions is found in two related and yet quite different concepts: issues and problems. Essentially a policy is required either to take a stand on an issue or to provide direction toward the solution of a problem. Consequently, the policy domain largely revolves around issues and problems. These will be used as the guidelines for the policy development in sport management as set forth in this text.

An issue is an idea or activity about which there is debate. The parties involved tend to hold contrasting positions either in their understanding of the idea or with regard to the conduct of the activity. Furthermore, there are legitimate grounds for each position. A policy is needed to decide the approach that will be taken by the group. This may result from either mutual consensus or compromise. Regardless of the means taken to arrive at the policy, the need was dictated by the contrast in positions. The issues leading to policies are major. It was noted earlier that policy development is the process of making significant decisions on recurring matters. There will always be varying opinions on a host of minor issues. Such is not the basis for policy development.

Issues frequently lead to problems but the differentiation between the two is significant. Essentially a problem is an obstacle to overcome. When an organization has a problem, something stands in the way of the ability to achieve an objective or at least some aspect of that objective. Thus problem solving is aimed at eliminating the obstacle. A problem may also be expressed in terms of deep-seated dissatisfaction with one or more particulars of the current situation. As noted below, the difference between the current situation and the desired situation is the extent or size of the problem.

Facts = Current Situation

Goal = Desired Situation

Problem = Difference between the Two

The primary difference between a problem and an issue is that a problem does not necessarily reflect a difference of opinion about the way things should be or the goal that is sought. There may be considerable differences of opinion about how the problem can be solved. However, such differences involve the means and not the desired results.

Whether it be to resolve an issue or solve a problem, policy development is the key stage in an attempt to reach the objectives of the program. Policy regarding either an issue or a problem can be developed by using the basic techniques of case method analysis.

Case Method Analysis

1. *Situational Analysis*: This begins by recognizing the existence of either an issue or a problem. Are there legitimate grounds for debate, or does something stand in the way of mutual interests in reaching a goal? Why did the issue or problem arise? Who is concerned? How critical is the situation?

2. *Analysis and Use of Evidence:*
   a. Quantitative Data—What kind and amount of data are available? What is the applicability of the data to the problem or issue at hand? How appropriate is the data in terms of precision or estimation?
   b. Other Evidence:

1. Is there an adequate accumulation of other evidence to support the idea that there is a legitimate issue or that a real problem exists? These must be definite instances, not just generalizations.

2. What is the balance in terms of evidence? Considerable support from both sides indicates that there is a real issue.

3. How valid is the evidence? This is determined by weighing the facts against opinions.

4. What is the effect of such evidence on the problem or issue at hand?

5. How objective is the evidence? This is aimed at the attempt to avoid bias or prejudice.

6. What is the thoroughness of reasoning? How important or controversial is a particular point?

3. *Identification and Evaluation of Action Alternatives:*

   Basically the identification step consists of providing an answer to one of these questions:

   a. What are the possible solutions to the problem?

   b. What are the alternatives of action for resolving an issue? Evaluation of action alternatives is accomplished by considering such factors as feasibility, time involved, and the possible contribution in either solving the problem or resolving the issue.

4. *Conclusions and/or Recommendations:*

   a. Must show a relationship to the analysis.

   b. Details of development should be set forth.

   c. What is the action decision? (Note: This is essentially the policy.)

SELECTED TOPICS

Thus far we have considered the scope of the potential territory for policy development in sport management. The question now is where does one begin? What kind of policies are needed within the framework? Since issues and problems more or less point to the policy domain, one could begin by selecting issues and problems that are relatively pervasive or critical in the sport enterprise. Here the news media can be of some assistance. Many of the larger issues and problems are regularly presented by the news media. These point to the need for personnel policies.

Among the major personnel components, the athlete is the bottom line. When searching for an initial basis for policy development in sport management, the athlete is a logical place to begin. It is not too much of an exaggeration to suggest that when things are right with the athlete, the program is all right. The reverse is also true. Consequently, the selected areas are heavily aimed at policies regarding athletes.

Next to the athletes, the coaches represent a primary consideration. Of course, policy regarding athletes and coaches represents a mutually dependent relationship. Quality athletes are the key factor in the success of a coach. On the other hand, a good coach is just as essential in obtaining and developing the right kind of athlete.

The selected areas included in Part II have been designated as program policies. Essentially they represent policy considerations that more or less affect the entire program and yet fall outside the realm of personnel policies as such. In addition to the heavy emphasis on personnel problems, a few other factors are instrumental in the selection of certain issues and problems as a preliminary basis for policy development in sport management. One of these is that college sport seems to have more than its share of issues and problems. Consequently, the bulk of the policy area is in collegiate sport. Beyond that, it is easy to recognize that finances, facilities, public relations, and promotion are principal concerns in the sport enterprise generally. Some of these concerns are addressed under program policies in Part II.

Part I

Personnel

Chapter 2

Athletes: College Recruiting Violations

THE PROBLEM

The problem of recruiting violations in college athletics is far from being a recent development. It is generally well known that these violations have occurred ever since the *National Collegiate Athletic Association Manual* was first published. The immediate concern is that this problem only becomes more serious both in number and severity of reported cases. It is also evident that the leaders in college athletics have become increasingly frustrated in their efforts to solve the problem.

The reason for these violations at the Division I level is plain and simple. It is necessary to attract the best, most athletic and skillful athletes to a particular school because the bottom line in Division I college athletics is winning. Winning programs help to make money for the university; winning programs are attractive to television and media; winning programs increase the notoriety of the institution; and finally, winning programs help a coach keep his or her job. Due to these reasons, a premium has been placed on the recruitment of talented high school athletes. With this premium comes a plethora of problems involved with recruiting.

Recruiting violations are one of the major concerns of the NCAA enforcement program. The association's manual has at least 43 pages of rules and regulations on recruiting. The bulk of these rules has been instituted to combat and to react to violations that have already taken place. For example, at some point, the NCAA recognized that schools were providing excessive entertainment to prospective student-athletes while on their official visit. The NCAA created a rule that states that "an institution may provide entertainment, which may not be excessive, on the official visit only for a prospect and the prospect's parents [or legal guardian(s)] or spouse and only within a 30–mile radius of the institution's main campus. Entertainment and contact by representatives of the institution's athletics interests during the official visit are prohibited in Division I and confined to campus in Division II. It is not permissible to entertain other relatives or friends (including dates) of a prospect at any time at any site" (*NCAA Manual*, 1996–1997, p. 130). The 43 pages of recruiting rules and policies are filled with examples like these. But are these really policies? Or are they simply written to react to a much larger problem? This chapter will make an attempt to examine the larger problems that affect recruiting in college athletics today and the policies that surround these problems.

What constitutes a major recruiting violation? Should the aforementioned simple rule about entertainment for prospective student-athletes be considered a major violation? Should sending the recruited athlete a school t-shirt also be considered a violation? Or should offering a stack of $100 bills be considered a major violation?

Another policy question is who should be penalized for the recruiting violations? Is the coach responsible? or the university? the recruited athlete? the administration? or a combination of all of them?

The focus of the NCAA's Enforcement Program is on Division I football and men's basketball, as these two sports have been at the root of most of the recruiting problems in the NCAA. That is not to say that other sports have not committed violations, but it is the revenue producing sports that produce the highest percentage that need to be placed under a microscope.

There are other policy questions involving recruiting that should be considered. For example, how much money should be spent on luring recruits to campuses? Another is how special admissions and Proposition 48 factor into the recruiting problem. As each of the policy questions is raised, it is necessary to remember that the philosophy of "winning at all costs" is at the core of these issues.

History of the Problem

A look at the history of recruiting in college athletics is an important building block before examining the current policies. In fact, the recruiting of college athletes is linked with the general recruitment of students:

From the earliest times, American colleges have recruited students—if only to have enough warm bodies in attendance to justify their existence. . . . Student recruitment was woven into fabric of American higher education with the foundation of Harvard College. There is a ruling practical sense in which nobody comes to school on his own. It's "unAmerican." Furthermore, recruitment for athletic competition is a practice older than college athletics, older even than the distinction between amateur and professional. (Cady, pp. 163–165)

According to Cady, the control of intercollegiate athletics did not begin because of the recruitment of student-athletes, but rather the recruitment of "ringers." It was not unusual for coaches to seek out top athletes who would play under assumed names for colleges and universities even though they were not enrolled in that school. An example of this was the University of Michigan football team in 1893, which had at least seven members who had not bothered to enroll in the school (Cady, p. 166). As for regulations in the early days, it was a different story. "As to rules, we didn't violate any; in those days there weren't any rules," said Fielding Yost, the great Michigan coach (Cady, p. 166). It was partially because of this that the NCAA was created just after the turn of the century. And one of the founding principles of the NCAA was to regulate the recruitment of student-athletes. Over time, these rules to regulate recruiting became increasingly complex and difficult to interpret. The 43 pages that are in the current manual are an example of this complexity.

Related Factors in Recruiting

When recruiting is the subject, there are more pieces to the puzzle than just the coach and high school athlete. The university, athletic administration, parents of the athlete, academic personnel, and recruiting services can all play roles in the entire process. When an athlete is deciding which school to enroll in, it is rare that his or her family is making the decision without some outside influence pulling or pushing in one direction or another.

It is also important to note that academics is often only a minor consideration in recruits' decisions. Many student-athletes simply want to be athletes, and do not care about the student part. "Not more than 20 percent of football players go to college for an education, and that may be a high figure," said Jim Walden, the head football coach at Iowa State (Sperber, p. 229).

Another aspect of the process is the emotional impact that is felt by student-athletes, families, and coaches. It is not unusual for some of the most talented high school athletes to have their private lives invaded by college recruiters. One such athlete is Tom Kleinschmidt. A former basketball player at DePaul University, he was the recipient of over 2,100 pieces of mail from 135 schools during the recruiting process. His life was disrupted by harassing phone calls, visits from coaches, and a tremendous amount of conflicting information. One coach would tell him one thing, and the next coach the exact opposite. Basically because of his athletic talents, he was a marked man:

There was the coach from Cincinnati who Tom said refused to stop calling. Despite repeated pleas, the recruiter ended every conversation with, "Don't worry, you'll change your mind tomorrow."

Kleinschmidt found out that coaches are only a part of the recruiting ordeal. There was the high school talent scout who publicly humiliated him in the newspapers by saying he wasn't good enough to play big time college basketball. There were the neighborhood peers who, seemingly jealous of attention, spread false rumors about him. (Bissinger, p. 12)

These are only a few of the aspects of recruiting life from the athlete's point of view. But the ordeal also has a strong impact on the recruiting coach, who spends countless hours pursuing the "thoroughbreds." One of the coaches who came after Kleinschmidt, an assistant at Marquette University, seemed to understand what the process does to people. "The recruiting business is crazy," he wrote to Kleinschmidt during the summer before his senior year. "The summer is too long. You guys are under the microscope too much. I'll be glad when we can all relax when this is over" (Bissinger, p. 12).

This compassionate note to Kleinschmidt gives an inkling that many coaches dislike the process of recruiting. It has come to a point in today's college sports world that it is not necessarily the best coach who wins the game, but the best recruiter.

Another way of examining the process comes from a quote from Bobby Bowden, the longtime football coach at Florida State. "The worst part of recruiting is the cheating that goes on, along with having to inflate the egos of 17-year-old athletes" (Sperber, p. 245). Bowden's point is reinforced by Ray MacCallum, an assistant basketball coach at the University of Wisconsin. "How many people in this country base their success on whether they can persuade 17-year-olds to come to their school? This is the same 17-year-old who can't decide what television program to watch" (Sperber, p. 245).

The Major Violations

Most of the material in the *NCAA Manual* is not policy-oriented, but rather it contains specific regulations. They range from explanations of when a coach can contact and evaluate a recruit, the offers and inducements a coach can make, recruiting materials that can be sent, information on official and unofficial visits to campus and restrictions on tryouts and sports camps. Many of the rules are nebulous and confusing. At times, the NCAA has been known to give conflicting interpretations of the same rule, depending on who is making the interpretation.

In order to help coaches and administrators better learn the rules, the NCAA has developed a testing program that every coach must pass before being allowed to recruit off campus. Whether this testing program is useful or not is still in question. However, it does take away the excuse of ignorance when coaches break rules. The problem is that the testing program will not stop coaches from breaking the rules. The NCAA can legislate as many ethical rules as it wants, but it can't legislate morality into the coaches. In other words, the rules will be there, but whether an individual coach follows a rule is a different story.

What if the recruiting portion of the *NCAA Manual* had only three to four pages instead of 43? Which would be the primary policy regulations? In other words, how does one separate the forest from the trees, when it comes to the recruiting problem?

The NCAA has begun by identifying those violations that are considered to be major. Under-the-table inducements offered to athletes are thought by many to be the most serious offense. These are difficult to prove, but there have been confirmations and numerous other allegations in regard to this problem. The following quote, although humorous, probably presents the situation most accurately:

Frank Layden, former coach of the NBA's Utah Jazz, tells a story about negotiations with one of the team's top draft choices. After agreeing to an $800,000 salary, Mr. Layden recalls, "the player told me he wanted a gas card, a car, a job for his father, and four paid trips home." How did Mr. Layden respond? "I told him this was the NBA and we pay cash. No perks like in college." (Sperber, p. 264)

The hypocrisy is that the NCAA makes millions of dollars from its sports, yet it does not allow any of the member schools to entice the recruits with anything more than just a free education (which many do not care about getting anyway).

The NCAA consistently holds to its principle of amateurism: Student-athletes shall be amateurs in an intercollegiate sport, and their participation should be motivated primarily by education and by the physical, mental, and social benefits to be derived. Student participation in intercollegiate athletics is an avocation; and student-athletes should be protected from exploitation by professional and commercial enterprises. The NCAA does not want to become a pay-for-play business. Unfortunately, paying for the cost of an education does not cover daily living expenses, like going home to see family on weekends.

The NCAA has specific prohibitions contained in its manual that address the recruitment of athletes. Specifically, schools are prohibited from arranging employment for a prospect's relatives, giving gifts of clothing or equipment, co-signing or providing loans, giving cash, giving free or reduced cost housing, or other services to the prospect or his or her relatives or friends. The NCAA needs to establish a policy that allows schools to make offers to recruits over and above the scholarship in order to cover the extra costs of living. "The route is to be honest about the situation, and deal with it directly. You do that by paying outright these too-often reluctant scholars. Treat them truly as the employees of the university, which they are, employees who now, in the role of entertainers, are receiving what in many instances amounts to virtual slave wages" (Berkow, p. 47). This idea would eliminate some of the hypocrisy of the NCAA and would allow the athletes to share in the "pot of gold."

It would also help take care of many of the economically disadvantaged athletes who are competing for the university. It would pay them for being a college athlete. They need not be paid a tremendous sum, but a reasonable amount. So few of these excellent athletes ever make it to the professional level anyway.

On the other side of the spectrum, the NCAA could also take its rules and make some of them more stringent. The NCAA might require each school to hire an independent compliance officer to investigate recruiting situations. Many schools currently have compliance coordinators, but often these people work within the athletic department and do not have a direct link to the chancellor or president. For example, at one university a search was recently conducted for a compliance coordinator. In the end, the wide receivers' coach from the football staff was hired to be the compliance director. It is difficult to imagine that this individual would scrutinize the football staff as closely as it needs to be scrutinized.

Another area that should be addressed is the allowable five, official, institution-paid visits to campuses. On each of these visits in Division I football and basketball, the university makes its bid to lure the prospective athlete. Without overtly buying the recruit, universities put the recruits in impressive hotels, take them to the best restaurants in town, and basically roll out the red carpet. The president or chancellor of the school often greets the recruit and eats a meal with him or her. It is a show and a sham. Coaches and administrators put on their best faces and attempt to paint the best picture of the campus and university as possible. All of this is legal according to the NCAA. What should be examined is the excessive dollars that are spent on this type of recruiting. Many recruits fall victim to big recruiting budgets of certain programs. When an athlete is 17 years old, and gets to eat lobster, filet mignon, or shrimp cocktail on a recruiting visit, a school begins to look better and better. When the athlete is treated like a king by coaches, other athletes, administrators, and general students, it becomes easier for a recruit to say, "They really want me here."

One New York City native was aware of the recruiting process when he was being wooed a few years ago because his coach was street-wise to the recruiting ordeal. "It's all hogwash," Robert Blackwell said of the song and dance routines that the schools put on. "The best part of the trips is the eating" (Bondy, p. 6). Unfortunately not all high school seniors are as wise as Blackwell, and many fall prey to the pretty picture painted by the university.

Many schools wine and dine their prospective athletes to the tune of over $1,000 for a 48–hour trip. When a sport like football brings in nearly 100 recruits each year, the costs rise quickly. This is not a new trend, but one that has its roots in the 1960s and the 1970s. The amount of dollars that could be saved for each university would be tremendous if some policy were in place to keep these costs down. One policy could be to set a limit on how much universities can spend per recruit. This might be difficult for schools in cities that have higher costs of living, but some formula could be figured to make this idea feasible.

Who Is Responsible?

Recruiting violations occur quite frequently in college athletics. Some are minor rule breaks; others are real problems. When a violation is discovered by the NCAA, who is penalized? Is it the university, the coach, the administration, or the athlete?

Primarily today, the university is the body that is penalized the most for recruiting violations, although it is usually the coach who commits the infraction. Penalties to universities come in many different forms. They can get verbal reprimands, formal letters, or more serious sanctions by the NCAA, like loss of scholarships or limitations on recruiting travel by coaches. If the NCAA really wants to hurt the university, it hits it in the pocketbook, by forbidding television games or post-season tournament appearances. In some cases, like Southern Methodist, the NCAA issues the "death penalty" that totally eliminates the sport, in their case, football, from the institution for a period of time.

When a university is penalized, a message is sent to every other institution to "beware, this could happen to you." The penalty may act as a deterrent for other schools from making the same mistake.

Should the entire university be punished for the bad judgment or actions of a coach at the school? The NCAA takes the position that the institution must have total control over all aspects of the athletic department. If a team wins an NCAA championship, the entire school benefits from that achievement. If a coach or team commits an infraction, then by the same theory, the entire university must pay the penalty and share the blame. This is a heavy price to pay for many universities that have had recruiting violations. The entire school, including the academic program, is affected when a school receives negative publicity for recruiting violations. It may be a sad situation, but a real one, that a school can get a portion of its academic reputation from its athletic teams.

Another point of view is that the coach should be disciplined for the violation committed, not the university. It is the coach who is responsible for knowing and understanding the rules. If he violates the rules, punishment should follow. The coach often seems to get off too easily, with merely a slap on the wrist.

A problem with disciplining the coach is that it needs to come from the university, because the NCAA does not have disciplinary responsibility for the coach. It is only in extreme cases that the NCAA has attempted to punish the coach by exerting pressure on the institution. The case with Jerry Tarkanian at UNLV was perhaps the first time a coach lost his job because of NCAA pressure. The NCAA would like colleges and universities to say "no" to hiring coaches with suspect pasts. They would like the stigma of being caught committing a violation to stick with a coach for a long time and have a lasting impact. They would also like word to spread quickly within the athletic department circles. There are those who suggest that the best solution to recruiting violations is to penalize the athlete. The NCAA actually has a policy that makes provision for this, but it is seldom enforced due to time restrictions.

THE ISSUE

Thus, the problem is clearly before us, as it has been for many years: recruiting violations are the name of the game in "big time" college sport. This raises the issue: what can be done to resolve the problem? There appears to be only two real choices, and both are difficult. The first is to take further steps to control the recruiting efforts. The second is to establish a new, open division in college sport wherein some teams are recognized as having professional or semi-professional status at the collegiate level. A third choice might be to eliminate major college football and basketball programs, but that is hardly viable in light of the significance of these programs in American society. Edwin Cady, former Andrew W. Mellon professor of the humanities at Duke University, makes that point very clear:

But the American Big Game, repeated annually and often simultaneously on dozens of fields and floors, is a college game. . . .

Nevertheless, the Collegiate Big Game is different. Nothing elsewhere resembles it. Nothing in professional sport captures, for all the flattery money can buy, the same glamour or intensity of significance. . . . The difference arises from the unique involvement of major institutions of higher education and learning. It locks in symbolic combat the peoples of "sovereign states": Texas-Oklahoma; Tennessee-Kentucky; Wisconsin-Minnesota. It confronts massive regional and cultural differences: Notre Dame-UCLA; Penn State-Alabama; Virginia-DePaul. It pits lifestyles and social convictions: Stanford-USC; Duke-Carolina; Rice-Arkansas. It is symbolically fratricidal: Grambling-Florida A.M.; Yale-Harvard; Providence-Marquette. Whole spectra of the national life clash fraternally in the Big Game. (pp. 3–4)

So, we are faced with the realization that the "Big Game" (major college football and basketball) is here to stay. This leaves higher education with the first two choices. What are the arguments for each? More important, what kind of policies can be developed to carry out a decision in either direction?

Control

Perhaps the strongest argument for the control thesis is found in the idea that college administrators really have no choice. If further efforts are not made to control college sport, there will only be chaos, and the college game will eventually destroy itself and the institutions it represents. This is essentially the position taken by Cady. It is also the position manifested in the historical and current actions taken by the NCAA. The only difference is that Cady has some doubts about the NCAA legislation. (More about that will be noted shortly.)

The concept of control is the central theme of Cady's work. He discusses "internal control" and "external control," but he clearly believes any key to real success is found in the former. The burden of responsibility for controlling college athletes falls on the shoulders of college presidents, who must hire trustworthy people capable of exercising the necessary controls to keep college athletics in the necessary academic perspective. Cady introduces the last section of his book with a warning: "The president who does not steadily face the realities of his intercollegiate athletics situation puts himself in jeopardy where they play the Big Game. If he does not keep it under control, if he tries to ignore its realities, it will come and get him" (p. 143).

In terms of external control, Cady makes a specific suggestion: "A committee of one hundred ought now to prepare to put the process of constitutional renewal in motion" (p. 224). With that suggestion, he revealed remarkable foresight, in light of the fact that his book was published in 1978 and the NCAA's Presidents' Commission was established in January 1984. (More about the Commission will also be said later.)

Under the heading of "Noble Experiments," Cady presents four suggestions that might serve as guidelines for policy development if one chooses to pursue the control thesis for intercollegiate athletics:

1. "We have to clarify our intentions to ourselves" (p. 223). (Essentially, the point here is that the NCAA and the major college conferences have to rethink their structures and rules in light of the realities of the late twentieth century.)

2. "We have to find talent and free it to work" (p. 223). (Colleges and conferences should seek and train additional qualified people to administer intercollegiate athletic programs.)

3. "I would start by sending all the books of rules for the conduct of intercollegiate athletics, including the NCAA's, to archives and begin again" (p. 223). (The current legislation governing college athletics is too cumbersome and "picky." We need a few simple, clear rules aimed at a bona fide student-athlete.)

4. "I do not mean that I would destroy or even disable the present structures of people and operations through which the NCAA, for instance, provides indispensable services to the Big Game and all lesser games" (p. 224). (In spite of their difficulties with legislation and enforcement, the NCAA and conferences offer many valuable services to the colleges. Those functions should be preserved.)

External Control

The Presidents' Commission established in January 1984 is perhaps the best example of recent steps to put more teeth into the external control of intercollegiate athletics. How did the Commission come into existence, and what are the developments to date?

In August 1983, the American Council on Education's (ACE) Committee on Division I Athletics (consisting of 28 college presidents) proposed a "board of presidents" that would have had greater autonomy over college sport by having authority to veto or modify NCAA rules, as well as being able to impose new rules of its own design. The NCAA Council opposed the proposal and submitted an alternate proposal that would create a Presidents' Commission with much more limited authority than that proposed by the American Council's committee. Basically, the Commission would serve only in an advisory role to the NCAA Council.

The ACE committee slightly modified its proposal and submitted it to the NCAA convention in January 1984. However, the proposal was soundly defeated, and, in place, the convention approved the establishment of the Presidents' Commission, along the lines of the NCAA Council proposal.

As established, the Presidents' Commission had the power to review any NCAA activity; to place any topic on the agenda for a council meeting or a convention; to commission studies; to sponsor changes in rules at conventions; to demand a roll-call vote on any issue it deems important enough, thus putting members' votes on record; and to call special conventions. The proposal also stipulated that Commission members were to be chosen by a mail ballot of all NCAA members' presidents.

In April of 1984, 44 presidents were elected to the Commission and John W. Ryan, then president of Indiana University, was selected to be the first chair. One of the first actions by the commission was to conduct a confidential survey on issues dealing with the integrity and finances of college sport. The results of the survey were reported in April 1985 and showed that a majority of presidents desired stricter rules and tougher penalties for violations by coaches, players, and institutions. The Commission called a special convention for June and prepared proposed changes in the rules, based on the results of the survey.

A total of 198 presidents were among the 840 delegates who attended the special convention in New Orleans in June 1985. They passed 12 proposals by unanimous or near-unanimous votes. Collectively, these probably represent the best effort to date to develop policies aimed at external control. Following is a summary of the policy decisions that relate either directly or indirectly to recruiting violations:

1. Each member institution is required to conduct a self-study of its inter-collegiate athletic program at least once every five years as a condition and obligation of membership in the NCAA.

2. To be eligible for NCAA championships, a Division I institution is required to report annually to the NCAA, providing information on the academic status of entering freshmen, compliance with continuing eligibility requirements, and graduation rates for recruited athletes compared with other students.

3. Violations of NCAA rules are divided between "major" and "secondary" classifications. Penalties are specified and strengthened. A team that was penalized for a previous major infraction within the previous five years will be barred from all intercollegiate competition for up to two years for a second infraction.

4. All coaches in that sport are prohibited from coaching another team during the same period, even if they move to another institution.

5. Each member institution's athletic budget is to be controlled by the institution. It is to be subject to the institution's normal budgeting procedures and approved by the chancellor, president, or a designee.

6. There will be an annual audit of all expenditures for each member institution's athletic program by an individual from outside the institution, selected by the institution's chancellor or president.

The delegates also passed two resolutions aimed at the need for policies to provide external control over the conduct of intercollegiate athletic programs. The essence of these resolutions was as follows:

1. Student athletes should be held accountable for their involvement in serious rules violations and should be declared ineligible for intercollegiate competition.

2. A one term affidavit program should be established. This would require every head coach and scholarship athlete to sign a statement attesting to current compliance with specifically identified rules.

Following the special convention there were mixed reactions regarding the potential significance of the actions taken at New Orleans. One's perspective obviously made quite a difference.

NCAA president Jack Davis surveyed the audience of 840 college presidents, chancellors, and other assorted delegates at the New Orleans special convention and observed: "This is a momentous occasion," Davis said. He then urged the delegates to applaud themselves, and they did so earnestly.

But Davis and his colleagues may have been a bit overzealous. Passage of the proposals drafted by the NCAA's 44-member Presidents' Commission was a welcome first step toward a reform of college athletics, but more steps obviously are needed.

The convention's actions were mostly symbolic. Davis admitted that if a school's entire athletic budget was jeopardized by the suspension of a big-money sport as the result of the two major violations rule, "the infractions committee would probably make an exception the first time for football—that's the reality of it." He also allowed that the new legislation didn't really get at the evils of overcommercializing. But he promised that with the presidents now playing a more active role, the NCAA will no longer shrink from tackling the tougher issues. "We'll reduce pressure on coaches," he said, "and allow them to operate on a higher level of trust."

Ryan said his commission was on the "threshold of action" on these issues. He promised that more legislation would be introduced at next January's regular NCAA Convention. Never has a pledge carried more potential consequence for intercollegiate sport. If significant reform is not addressed at that time, the high-minded rhetoric of New Orleans will ring hollow. ("Scorecard," p. 9)

Internal Control

If there is to be a significant degree of success in efforts at external control, there must be consistent policies at the institutional level. Internal control is the key to solving the problem of recruiting violations through control. Only the individual institution can develop specific policies that reflect its structure and functions. However, the following ideas are suggested as policy guidelines for the internal control of college athletics:

1. The president or chancellor should appoint an athletic adviser to his or her staff. This adviser will not be a member of the athletic department but will work in conjunction with the athletic director in securing institutional control through overseeing all recruitment activities.

2. All business transactions for the express purpose of recruitment should be monitored by the president's or chancellor's athletic adviser and staff.

3. A strong and effective faculty athletic council or committee should be established. This committee should maintain close liaison with the athletic adviser, and the committee should receive regular reports on the status of recruitment practices and expenditures.

4. The chair of the athletic committee or other representatives of that committee should have an active role in conference and NCAA affairs.

5. There should be regularly scheduled meetings including individuals in the following positions to discuss the total athletic recruitment situation at the institution:

President or Chancellor

Athletic Adviser

Athletic Director

Chair of Faculty Athletic Committee

Director of Freshmen Admissions

Head Coaches of Football and Basketball

Booster Club President

Athletic Business Manager

In the final analysis the real key to internal control lies in the appointment of responsible people along with the built-in provision for continuing communication regarding the recruiting activities. Specific policies developed by the president or chancellor should reduce the gaps between the information available at the top level and the activities of the athletic department.

Professionalize College Athletics

As noted earlier, there are some who argue that the solution to the problem of recruiting violations is not to be found in further efforts at control. Their argument proceeds by pointing out that the NCAA has more or less worked at control over the past 90 years, and there is little evidence of success. Why continue to fight a losing cause?

The other possible solution to the problem would be to recognize and grant professional, or at least semi-professional, status to college football and basketball powers that are at the heart of the problem. Within the past twenty-five years, several proponents of this idea have emerged, including Howard R. Swearer, the former president of Brown University. In February 1982, the *New York Times* published the speech he delivered to the midwestern meeting of the Brown Corporation, the university's governing body. Excerpts point to the essence of Swearer's stance:

May not the time have arrived when it would be desirable to recognize openly this symbiotic relationship between the big athletic powers and professional sports, and make the necessary structural changes?

The fictions are wearing thin. I, for one, see no harm in associating a professional or semi-professional team with a university; and I do see a number of benefits. It would help clarify what is now a very murky picture. Athletes should, of course, have the opportunity to take courses and pursue a degree, if they wish; but they would be regarded as athletes first and should be paid accordingly. By so doing the regulatory and enforcement burden and the temptations for legal and unethical practices would be dramatically eased. The clear separation between the academic and athletic purposes of the university would be beneficial to both. . . .

If the big powers were to choose this course, I think it would benefit all intercollegiate athletics. High school seniors would be given a more clearly defined choice among different kinds of post-secondary athletic experience. The general public could recognize more clearly the nature of athletic competition in different leagues. The pressures toward professionalism on those institutions that chose a different course might be lessened.

The possibility I have sketched out is not a choice that I believe Ivy League and similar institutions should or would take. However, I hope that the Ivy League will also take a positive and active role in the long-term restructuring of intercollegiate sports. (Swearer, p. 2S)

Although Swearer was not the first to advocate the professionalization of a segment of college athletics, his statement prompted considerable debate because of his position. Many people consider it unrealistic to have professional sport in the college context. They contend that such action will only lead to further abuses, and that college athletics would eventually be destroyed. Their answer is to work hard at further efforts to control the situation. The reaction of Bill Atchley, former president of Clemson University, more or less typifies this counter point of view:

Brown University's president, Howard R. Swearer, proposed some time ago that big college athletic programs be turned into professional or semi-professional farm teams. . . . The idea has been batted around over the years, but not until recently has it been taken seriously. When you stop to think about the actual mechanics of professional athletic teams coexisting with a university and competing under the school's colors, the idea becomes unrealistic. . . .

Despite growing athletic budgets and lucrative television contracts, students and alumni see college athletics as amateur competition. It may not be amateur competition in the fullest sense, but that is how it is perceived. How else could the rural campus and town of Clemson, with fewer than 20,000 inhabitants, attract more than 70,000 paying fans for a Saturday afternoon of football? I can think of no professional team that has succeeded so well in such an unlikely market. A professional team representing Clemson University would eventually be overshadowed by teams from metropolitan markets like Atlanta. (Atchley, p. 2S)

The debate continued. On April 25, 1984, *USA TODAY* devoted an entire page to the debate on the central issue involving the professionalism of college athletics. An excerpt from that source reflects the opposing views:

Editorial Opinion—Colleges will lose by paying athletes—Last week Louisiana State Chancellor James Wharton said colleges may soon be hiring athletes as entertainers—they might not have to hit the books at all. Some say that's just facing the truth: College sports is already big business, so why not just start paying athletes? But turning college teams into pro teams is no way to end the abuses. Colleges would launch bidding wars for stars. Hardened pro athletes with no interest in education would be hanging around campuses. School spirit, which is the heart of student alumni support, would die. Only 2% of college athletes can make a living in pro sports. Our colleges and universities owe the 98% who can't make it an education, not exploitation. (*USA TODAY*, April 25, 1984, p. 8A)

Another Suggested Policy

Before concluding our consideration of this problem of recruiting violations, a policy proposed by well-known sportswriter Leonard Koppett is worthy of consideration. Perhaps the most unusual feature about Koppett's proposal is that he would have a professional college athlete pursuing a normal college education. In fact earlier in his book, *Sports Illusion, Sports Reality*, he bluntly makes the point that amateurism should be abolished altogether as a category for major commercial events, including college athletic and international competition. Later, in "Under Reform the NCAA" he presents his policy suggestion regarding student status:

There is, however, a simple and practical way to get the NCAA out of the policing business without weakening its other powers. Junk all the detailed restrictions concerning recruiting methods, high school grades, scholarship limits, and the rest, and zero in on the basic idea and basic problem. Call it graduation. The relevant standard for a college athlete should be his bona-fide status as a student working toward a degree.

He is being presented to the public as that, not as an achiever of certain grades, or a person with a certain income, or one who spoke with his prospective coach only 3 times. He is a student. And the measure of a student's success, as a student, is graduation. He gets his degree.

My proposal, then, would work this way. First, determine the "normal" percentage of graduates at any particular college. Then require every athletic squad to meet (or exceed, if you want to be stricter) that figure.

Any year in which the percentage isn't met, that school would go on probation (in that sport) the following year, and stay on probation until it gets back to the required percentage.

That's all. That's the whole rule. It would be self policing. It would be effective and it would be to the point. All the NCAA would have to do would be to process the graduation records submitted by the college presidents. It would collate and enforce, not judge. (Koppett, pp. 290–291)

CONCLUSION

From an ideal standpoint, I am inclined to support the attempt at control. I hope that the NCAA will be successful in its efforts to provide the necessary control. However, the reality of the situation forces one to support Howard Swearer's position that it will be necessary to recognize professional or semi-professional status for a segment of college athletics.

In terms of the professional rule, there are some attractive features to the proposal presented by Leonard Koppett. Again, ideally, one would like to see a situation in which most college athletes at the higher level of competition could receive their degrees. However, in our opinion, Koppett's proposal also lacks realism. Further problems would be created. There is too much variance in the quality of degrees from institution to institution and even within a given institution. The graduation percentage rate is only part of the total picture. Under Koppett's plan, institutions with lower academic standards would have a distinct advantage. Coaches would work even harder at pushing athletes into "soft" majors to meet degree requirements. Unfortunately, in some cases one would have to question the validity of information coming from the institutions regarding the graduation percentage rates for athletes and other students.

As we see it, this leaves the Swearer proposal as the best choice, even though one might not favor the professionalization of college athletics from an ideal perspective. If the NCAA pursued that proposal, what kind of policies might be developed?

1. There would be two basic divisions within the NCAA—one for institutions offering sport programs that are major commercial events (football, basketball, and probably ice hockey) and the other for all other institutions. It is assumed that the first division would include current Division I institutions that choose to pursue the professional route. The second division, to be called Division II, would include the current Division IAA, II, and III membership, plus current Division I schools that wish to change the direction of their programs.

2. Division I institutions (those offering major commercial sport events) would have dual membership in Division II for matters involving all other sports.

3. For Division I sports, there would be no restrictions on recruiting or financial aid for athletes in those sports. Essentially, it would be an open, competitive market. An institution would offer a prospective professional college athlete what it could afford to pay. This might prove to be financially destructive for the institution involved. In that case, it might be necessary to establish a draft system for Division I athletes.

4. Many Division I athletes would clearly be recognized as athlete-students. In other words, they are first and foremost in college for athletic purposes. Were it not for their athletic ability, they would not be college students. They would be required to take at least one course per semester or term. However, this could be a remedial course in English, mathematics, or public speaking. At the same time a sound advising system would be maintained to permit the academically qualified athletes to pursue degree work at the appropriate place. Division I athletes with first rate academic qualifications might be able to receive degrees in four years.

5. Something must be done to maintain standards regarding recruitment and academic progress for the proposed Division II athletes (by far, the bulk of the college athletes). The answer is not to be found in retention of the present *NCAA Manual*. In view of that, we would recommend that Koppett's proposal be adopted as the policy for Division II athletes.

REFERENCES

Atchley, B. L. "Keep the Pros Out of Colleges." *New York Times*, Sunday, July 4, 1982, p. 2S.

Berkow, Ira. "A Focus on 'The Light of Truth.' " *New York Times*, February 16, 1991, p. 47.

Bissinger, H. G. "Courtship of Tom Kleinschmidt: Stack of Love Letter as Tall as He Is." *Chicago Tribune*, November 13, 1991, p. 12.

Bondy, Filip. "Eating the Steak with a Grain of Salt." *New York Times*, November 3, 1991, p. 6.

Cady, Edwin H. *The Big Game: College Sports and American Life*. Knoxville: University of Tennessee Press, 1978.

Koppett, Leonard. *Sports Illusion, Sports Reality*. Boston: Houghton Mifflin Co., 1981.

NCAA Manual. Overland Park, KS, 1996–1997.

"Scorecard." *Sports Illustrated*, July 1, 1985, p. 9.

Sperber, Murray. *College Sports Inc.: The Athletic Department vs. the University*. New York: Henry Holt & Co., 1990.

Swearer, H. R. "An Ivy League President Looks at College Sports." *New York Times*, February 21, 1982, p. 2S.

Temkin, Barry, and H. G. Bissinger. "Some Just Don't Know When the Dream Is Over." *Chicago Tribune*, November 14, 1991.

"Twenty-seven Institutions under NCAA Sanctions." *Chronicle of Higher Education*, January 13, 1993, p. A35.

USA Today, April 25, 1984, p. 8A.

Chapter 3

Athletes: Academic Standards for Freshman Eligibility

Prior to 1986, freshman eligibility to participate in intercollegiate athletics was determined by this simple provision: at the time of graduation from high school a student must have "presented an accumulative six, seven, or eight semesters' minimum grade-point average of 2.0 (based on a maximum of 4.0) as certified on the high school transcript or by official correspondence" (*NCAA Manual*, 1985–1986, Bylaw 5-1-(j), p. 92).

There were no provisions for a high school core curriculum or an entrance examination standard as requirements for freshman eligibility. Some college administrators suggested that it was too easy for students to meet the standard, particularly if their college athletic aspirations were known to the high school faculty. Also, high schools vary considerably in their grading practices. An average of 2.0 at one school cannot necessarily be equated with a 2.0 at another school. Furthermore, there was speculation that some high school athletes avoided rigorous courses and took carefully selected courses to obtain the necessary overall GPA of 2.0.

PROPOSITION 48

Consequently, on January 11, 1983, delegates to the NCAA Convention in San Diego passed Proposition 48, an amendment to Bylaw 5-1–(j). This was slated to take effect on August 1, 1986. Two additional requirements for freshman eligibility were added:

1. The accumulative, minimum grade-point average of 2.0 must be in a core curriculum of at least 11 academic courses, including at least three years in English, two years in mathematics, two years in social science, and two years in natural or physical science (including at least one laboratory class, if offered by the high school).
2. The athlete must have a combined score of at least 700 on the SAT verbal and math sections or a 15 composite score on the ACT. If a freshman failed to meet both requirements, he or she would be ineligible for competition and practice at a Division I institution during the freshman year. If the student demonstrated satisfactory progress toward a degree during the freshman year, he or she would be eligible for competition in the sophomore year. However, if the ineligible freshman accepted an athletic grant-in-aid for the freshman year, he or she would lose one year of collegiate athletic eligibility.

Academic standards outlined in Proposition 48 attempted to address the limitations inherent in the existing policy. The core curriculum requirement would provide an athlete exposure to a solid base of academic work. The test score requirement would guarantee some uniformity in standards and allow institutions to better distinguish among students who report similar GPAs from different high schools. Superficially at least, it hardly seemed unreasonable to require athletes to achieve test scores that were well below the national average. However, subsequent debate would show not everyone agreed on that point.

Proposition 48 was initiated by an ad hoc committee of the American Council on Education (ACE) and passed by the NCAA for several reasons. It was a signal to the high schools that athletes with college Division I potential should pay close attention to their academic preparation if they anticipate having maximum eligibility while in college. It was designed to give these athletes a better chance of obtaining college degrees and to end the exploitation of talented athletes (primarily blacks) that had been commonplace at many Division I institutions.

Bartell et al. (1984) reported on a study of athletes who enrolled in Division I institutions in 1977. Among approximately 1,400 black males, only 14 percent graduated after four years in college and only 31 percent graduated after six years in college. By contrast, the corresponding figures for some 4,000 white males were 27 percent and 53 percent, respectively. Such data certainly support the need for Proposition 48 or similar requirements.

Although Proposition 48 was adopted as a partial solution to a legitimate problem, it was the focus of extensive controversy before and after its approval. At the San Diego convention, Pennsylvania State University football coach Joe Paterno was one of the more vocal advocates of the proposal: "We have to challenge the athlete in the classroom as well as the field. We have raped the Black athlete, as I have said, and it is time to give him everything we have to offer in college. By upgrading high school requirements, we prepare him a bit better for our challenge in the college classroom" (*New York Times*, January 16, 1983, p. 45).

Opponents objected not only to the test score standard but also to the manner in which the proposal was drafted and the negative effects it would have on certain minority groups. The most vehement opposition was spearheaded by the presidents of predominantly black institutions, who believed that the proposal was inherently discriminatory. Jesse Stone, Jr., president of Southern University, described the proposal as "patently racist."

There was outrage over the glaring lack of black representation on the ACE ad hoc committee that initiated the proposal for presentation at the 1983 NCAA Convention. After vehement objection by the presidents of predominantly black colleges, a black was finally appointed. However, the appointment of Luona I. Mishoe, president of Delaware State College, to the ad hoc committee of the ACE came only one week prior to the start of the 1983 NCAA convention. Black educators viewed the appointment as "cosmetic."

Proposition 48 also generated some debate regarding the specific standards or cut-off points for eligibility. For example, how did the committee arrive at the figures 700, 15, and 11? Could not the minimum test score requirement just as well be 650 or 800? Why not require 10 or 12 core courses? The standards seemed to be fairly arbitrary. Studies to determine the effect of such standards on athletic eligibility were not conducted until after the proposal was adopted by the NCAA.

Perhaps the most severe point of criticism was that Proposition 48 failed to take into account the vast differences among colleges and universities across the nation. Even within NCAA's Division I, these differences are readily apparent. Institutions range from relatively small universities with open admissions to large comprehensive research universities with highly selective admissions. In between, various combinations and deviations can be noted. Differences can also be identified with respect to goals or objectives, clientele, the geographic service area, and variety of programs. Critics questioned how such differences could reasonably be aggregated in a generalized standard or formula for determining freshman eligibility for athletic participation. Beyond that, Frederick Humphries, president of Tennessee State University, identified the real source of opposition: "Proposal 48 would have minimum impact on those institutions who generated it to clean up athletics and who have produced academic credibility problems, and maximum impact on those institutions in Division I, especially the historically Black colleges, who have a distinguished record of educating marginal students in higher education" (*New York Times*, January 16, 1983, p. 25).

Following the adoption of Proposition 48, 16 largely black colleges, all members of Division I, threatened to remove themselves from both the NCAA and the ACE if the new requirements were put into effect.

Modifications

Proposition 48 has been modified five times since it was originally passed in 1983. The first modification took the form of Proposition 16, which was ratified by a vote of 207 to 94 at the 1986 NCAA Convention. Proposition 16 allowed an indexing to occur for the first two years that Proposition 48 was to be in effect, so that freshmen entering college in 1986 and 1987 could compensate for a GPA below 2.0 by scoring comparatively higher than 700 on the SAT or 15 on the ACT, and vice versa. This modification, again, was only temporary; thus, the original standards of Proposition 48 applied to freshmen entering college in 1988.

The second revision to Proposition 48 took the form of Proposition 42, which was ratified at the NCAA Convention in 1989. Proposition 42 affects the Proposition 48 student-athlete's ability to receive athletic-based financial aid during his or her freshman year. Proposition 42, however, changed this rule by stating a partial qualifier: "may receive institutional financial aid that is not from an athletics source and is based on financial need only, consistent with institutional regulations, during the first academic year" (*NCAA Manual*, 1995–1996, p. 138). A nonqualifier, "shall not be eligible for . . . institutional financial aid during the first academic year" (*NCAA Manual*, 1995–1996, p. 139). If the Proposition 48 standard is not met on either count, the student-athlete is labeled a "nonqualifier," while a student-athlete who meets one of the criteria is called a "partial qualifier." In essence, Proposition 42 put a bigger bite into Proposition 48 by denying athletic-based financial aid to recruited Proposition 48 student-athletes during the freshman year. Proposition 42 remains in effect today.

Another change in the original version of Proposition 48 was made at the NCAA's 1992 Convention. This change, which went into effect on August 1, 1996, further strengthens Proposition 48 in two major ways. First, the required number of core curriculum courses is raised from 11 to 13 (two more courses in English, math, or natural science must be taken); second, the minimum GPA is raised from 2.0 to 2.5, and at the same time, a sliding test-score index has been added, which will enable a student-athlete to remain eligible despite having a GPA below 2.5 (if the SAT or ACT were comparatively higher than 700 or 18, respectively).

Further modifications were considered at the 1995 NCAA Convention. Some of these were adopted, and others were rejected. Delegates rejected an effort to provide partial qualifiers with the opportunity to earn a fourth season of athletics eligibility. They also passed a provision permitting partial qualifiers to receive institutional financial aid, including athletically related aid, effective in August 1996. Another new provision was passed that allows partial qualifiers to practice on campus, but not compete, during the first academic year in residence. A final provision permitted a nonqualifier to receive institutional financial aid that is not from an athletic source (based on financial need). The last two provisions went into effect in August 1996.

All those modifications and proposed modifications merely point to the complexity and controversy surrounding Proposition 48. It is safe to say that there is no legislation in the history of the NCAA that has sparked more controversy. Before proceeding with any recommendations, it might be useful to examine the basis for the controversy in more detail. On the surface, it would appear that Proposition 48 is just a necessary step to raise academic standards for athletes. The GPA criterion certainly seems reasonable, as does the core curriculum requirement; they both seem to go a long way toward ensuring that incoming student-athletes are adequately prepared for the rigors of higher education. The test score portion appears reasonable as well; the 700 minimum is greater than 200 points below the national average score on the SAT, and using standardized test results allows students from different schools to be judged evenly; this practice is common among college admissions offices. Yet it is important to look at Proposition 48 with a critical eye, for this NCAA policy has far-reaching implications.

Nature of the Controversy

The initial debate over Proposition 48 was sparked again in 1992, with the legislation aimed at raising the standards. Among the proponents of the new legislation were educators at the Black Athletes in America forum, most of whom supported the new standards and stressed the need for the black community to help prepare athletes to achieve them (Lederman, 1992, p. 39). Emma Best, a professor at the University of the District of Columbia, said, "In order to participate, athletes must achieve academic success" (Lederman, 1992, p. 39). Her sentiments were echoed by the likes of Howard University basketball coach Butch Beard, who said, "We have to catch the young black kids early. We have to do a better job at the high school level and the grade school level, driving home the goal of getting that degree." Similarly, Gerald Turner, chancellor of the University of Mississippi and chairman of the Presidents' Commission, stated, "This is a very significant step forward toward more actively communicating to athletes and parents and schools the kind of work that will prepare student-athletes to get college degrees" (Lederman, 1992, p. 35).

Opponents of the revised Proposition 48 legislation did not take its ratification sitting down. Among the most outspoken were Delaware State University president William DeLauder, who called the new legislation "patently racist," and Francis Rienzo, athletic director at Georgetown, who said, "I think the road to educational reform is going to be covered with the bodies of socioeconomically disadvantaged individuals. The presidents' commission is leading the way, and those individuals have no way of representing themselves" (Lederman, 1992, p. 35).

Needless to say, the highly emotional nature of Proposition 48 makes public discussion of it an open forum that is precarious at best. The best analysis of Proposition 48 is an unemotional one. While this is not always an attainable goal, the following is an attempt to present and analyze the arguments both against and in support of Proposition 48.

One of the more problematic aspects of Proposition 48 is its stipulation that student-athletes ruled ineligible must sit out their entire freshman year of college. Effectively, they are being told that for one year they must put aside the sport to which they have dedicated their lives. This layoff comes at a critical time of development for student-athletes and may permanently damage their ability to perform. They may lose the "edge" that made them such a hot commodity in high school, and they usually become hard pressed to regain their previous form. Partial qualifiers were given some relief in the 1995 legislation, which permits them to practice during their freshman year.

Probably the worst result of Proposition 48 is that once a student-athlete is ruled ineligible, he or she becomes labeled a Proposition 48 for the rest of his or her career. Everywhere this athlete goes, people will think the player lacks intelligence simply because he or she was ineligible to play during the first year of college. For most Proposition 48 casualties, this becomes a stigma that is hard to shake. This label makes a student-athlete feel academically incapable, as he or she feels the stares and hears whispers while sitting in the classroom, and suffers the condescending comments of instructors (and the instructor's surprise when the student-athlete receives a decent grade).

The SAT and the ACT reflect what students are taught in high school and how well they prepared to take the test. Unfortunately, the inner-city schools in which these student-athletes are being educated are usually of very poor quality. As a result, the students are inadequately prepared for the test.

This situation contrasts to the white, middle-class student who, though not necessarily smarter than the black student, has a better opportunity to score well on the standardized test. He or she is better prepared for the test because of the quality of the high school attended.

Originally, there was yet another problem with the Proposition 48 athlete not participating during the freshman year. When the student returned he or she had only three years of eligibility remaining. So, the Proposition 48 victim lost a year of athletic eligibility. There were several attempts to restore the fourth year of eligibility to Proposition 48 student-athletes. Proposals that would restore the fourth year of eligibility to athletes who make substantial academic progress were voted down at the NCAA Conventions in 1992, 1993, 1995, and 1996. Finally, in 1997 the NCAA Convention delegates passed Proposition 68. This restored the fourth year of eligibility to those athletes who receive their degrees in four years. These athletes have the option of either pursuing a second bachelor's degree or a graduate degree during their fourth season of competition.

Proposition 42, which limited the financial aid available to Proposition 48 student-athletes, was greatly criticized as well. It stipulated that aid given to partial qualifiers during the freshman year must be need-based, non-athletically related financial aid that is available on the same basis to students in general. It also prohibited nonqualifiers from receiving any type of financial aid during the freshman year. The effects of this legislation were potentially devastating to student-athletes. For nonqualifiers and the partial qualifiers who are not able to secure financial aid, college may become an economically unrealistic goal, as they must pay their own way for the first year; partial qualifiers are faced with the unenviable task of trying to get financial aid for which they may or may not qualify. Many believe that this was largely an economic rule voted on by the membership of the NCAA in order to save themselves from giving scholarship money to an ineligible freshman student-athlete. Athletes were again given some relief at the 1995 convention when athletic aid was extended to partial qualifiers, and institutional (financial need) aid was extended to nonqualifiers during the freshman year.

Another major criticism of Proposition 48 is that it ignores fundamental differences in the NCAA's member institutions. It applies a national standard to admissions decisions, where there should be an institutional standard. Proposition 48 fails to recognize that institutions of higher learning vary in their educational mission. For example, Temple University is a large urban school whose stated mission is to educate the masses, while Rice University is a small, highly selective, private university with a more erudite mission. These two disparate schools are judged equally in the eyes of Proposition 48.

This is unfair, for Proposition 48 has a greater negative impact on schools intent on educating marginal students than it does on schools with more lofty academic goals. The former tends to attract a number of students affected by Proposition 48; the latter does not. Is Temple a less worthy institution than Rice? The NCAA seems to be saying "yes," a value judgment that it should not be making.

The heart of all criticism of Proposition 48 lies in its use of the SAT and ACT to set minimum initial eligibility standards. George Hanford, the president of the College Board (which administers the SAT), stated, "It is an undisputed fact that minority candidates earn significantly lower scores on the average because many of them are less privileged educationally and socioeconomically than whites. The new regulation (Proposition 48) will have a differentially severe impact on the aspiring athletes among blacks, but not because of bias in the SAT, but because of the educational deficit that exists in this country" (Chu et al., p. 370). So, it is quite obvious that the use of SATs to help set minimum academic standards for freshmen is patently discriminatory and racist in its effects. Its use is a disservice to minority athletes.

A second problem with the use of the SAT minimum is that the use of this standard violates any of the scientific and philosophical principles upon which the SAT is based. For example, the designation of 700 or 900 as the minimum standard ignores the SAT's standard deviation of 50 points (Chu et al., p. 362). So statistically speaking, a 650 SAT and a 750 SAT should be treated equally; despite this, the NCAA treats them vastly different. The NCAA's lack of adherence to statistical reasoning unfairly harms the student-athlete. In addition, the NCAA is using the SAT independently to determine one's status according to Proposition 48; if the minimum 700 SAT is not achieved, the student-athlete is ineligible. Further, the SAT is meant only to help predict how well students will do academically in the first year of college. George Hanford again summarizes by stating, "Under the NCAA rule, the SAT (is) used for a purpose which it was neither intended nor designed to serve—determining athletic eligibility rather than college admissions, and . . . the way SAT scores are being used in establishing athletic eligibility is contrary to the College Board's guidelines with respect to the use of test scores in making college admissions decisions" (Chu et al., p. 368). So it is clear that the NCAA is completely misusing the SAT in associating it with Proposition 48.

It has been reported that blacks average significantly lower than whites on the SAT. Does this mean that white men are intellectually superior to black men? Of course not, for the SAT is not a test of intelligence. As previously stated, it is solely designed to predict first-year college performance by estimating how well the student takes tests (Rosser, p. 51). This is a skill with limited use, for there are no jobs in the world based solely on the ability to pick the best answer on a multiple-choice exam or on how well a person can find the synonym for a word no one ever uses. The SAT has never claimed to predict college performance beyond the freshman year, nor success in later life. Several well-known colleges, including Bates and Bowdoin, abandoned the SAT as an admission requirement because of this; many others disregard SAT scores when considering the admissions of minorities (Rosser, p. 52).

In a 1992 study done at the University of Maryland, it was found that there was essentially no correlation between the SAT scores and the first semester grades of 105 University of Maryland student-athletes. From this study, the authors concluded that SAT scores should not be used in selecting or predicting the early success of student-athletes. Proposition 48 cannot be implemented fairly using SAT scores if these results are at all true at other institutions.

An issue mentioned previously needs to be further addressed. This is the use of a student-athlete's Proposition 48 status to deny him or her admission to college. At one time, over three dozen universities, including the entire Southwestern Conference, prohibited admission to Proposition 48 student-athletes. Proposition 48 is now denying many the opportunity to attend college, and this is patently wrong. Temple basketball coach, John Chaney, explains his displeasure with this occurrence. "Proposition 48 isn't serving the youngsters it's supposed to help. It has legislated out of college those who were not dealt a fair hand at an early level of education" (Wiley, p. 33).

Finally there is the NCAA "window dressing" argument that has been levied against Proposition 48. There are those who believe that Proposition 48 was instituted just to make things "look good." They believe that the NCAA is just using Proposition 48 as a way of saying and showing that they care about academic standards, when they really do not. Explains Lee McElroy, athletic director at California State University, Sacramento, "Proposition 48 is not about standards, it's about appeasing the public. Sometimes it may force young people to fall through the cracks, but that's OK as long as the enterprise keeps going" (McElroy, p. 4).

Support for Proposition 48

Needless to say, in spite of these various arguments against Proposition 48, there continues to be much support for this policy. That is why the legislation remains in place even though there have been various modifications.

One of the most succinct, yet effective, statements in support came from E. M. Swift, in a "Point After" *Sports Illustrated* article prior to the 1995 Convention when Proposition 16, which further raised the standards for Proposition 48, was considered. Swift refers to Dr. Leroy Walker, the first black president of the United States Olympic Committee and a member of the Knight Foundation Commission on Intercollegiate Athletics. Walker came out in support of Proposition 48, even though he suspected that the SATs and ACTs are culturally biased. Swift concluded with this assessment:

If the SATs and ACTs are culturally biased against blacks, as Walker suspects they are, they are not so culturally biased that scoring 700 on the college boards is an unreasonable expectation. To claim otherwise, is to ignore the accomplishments of the 1.2 million black undergraduates now enrolled in Division I schools who have no involvement in athletics. Think about that.

The 15,000 blacks in Division I institutions who had athletic scholarships in 1992, represented only 1.2 percent of the entire black undergraduate enrollment. The message the NCAA sends our nation's young people should not be: If you're good enough on the field, we'll make a place for you. It must be: If you're good enough in the classroom, there will be a place for you—whether you are an athlete or not. (Swift, "Point After," p. 88)

Swift's position leads to another argument from those in support of Proposition 48. There are those supporters who believe that if you raise the academic standards and expectations of student-athletes, they will meet them. Students will give you what you ask of them. If the requirements demand a 2.5 grade point average, then the student-athlete will deliver and give you a 2.5 grade point average. They (student-athletes) will rise to the occasion if they want it badly enough.

If this is so, then reform needs to take place in some of our high schools and junior high schools. It will be up to our high schools and junior high schools to better prepare the students, in particular, student-athletes. "The message is simple. When you're in the eighth or ninth grade, start studying. Make sure you're ready for college. . . . It's to tell everyone to get started early," says Hunter Rawlings, president of the University of Iowa (*NCAA News*, January 8, 1992, p. 4). Steven B. Sample, president of the University of Southern California, feels that these standards need to be raised even at the elementary levels. This is "America's biggest single challenge—to raise the standards of the elementary and secondary schools, especially for the students who have traditionally performed the poorest" (*NCAA News*, January 15, 1992, p. 4). What Proposition 48 does, according to these supporters, is force our high schools to be more cognizant of preparing students academically. It forces the schools to "do a better job" at educating the students when the standards are higher.

If a student-athlete isn't sufficiently prepared academically, then the result will be a loss of one year of athletic eligibility when that student-athletes reaches a Division I college or university. To some supporters of Proposition 48, this isn't so bad. As a matter of fact, this is one of the arguments used in defense of Proposition 48. These supporters feel that sitting out a year helps the student-athlete to get "seasoned" to college life. It also gives them a chance to "catch-up" on courses they either lack or have failed in the past.

A final, and perhaps the most recent, argument in support of Proposition 48 deals with the increased graduation rates of those student-athletes first affected by the institution of Proposition 48. An NCAA study indicates that the graduation rate of student-athletes at Division I institutions increased after Proposition 48 was instituted in 1986. This first study compares a sample of student-athletes who entered Division I institutions before 1986 (prior to Proposition 48) with a sample of student-athletes who entered in August 1986 (the first class affected by Proposition 48). The graduation rates in the report are based on student-athletes graduating within six years of their enrollment. The major findings as described by the *NCAA News* (October 26, 1992) and the *Chronicle of Higher Education* (July 7, 1993) are as follows:

1. The overall graduation rate jumped from 48.1 percent for student-athletes who entered in 1984 or 1985 to 56.5 percent for those student-athletes who entered in the fall of 1986.

2. The graduation rate of scholarship athletes who entered Division I colleges in 1986 was 6 percent higher than the average graduation rate of athletes who enrolled at those same colleges in the three years before the rule took effect.

3. Graduation rates for the groups who did not achieve the minimum test score or core grade-point average (partial-qualifiers) were increased in most cases.

4. Fifty-seven percent of the athletes in the 1986 freshman class graduated within six years, compared to 51 percent of those who entered college in 1983–1984, 1984–1985, 1985–1986.

5. The overall graduation rate for black male student-athletes increased as did the rate for black male partial qualifiers.

6. The graduation rate also increased for black male partial qualifiers in the revenue-producing sports.

Findings such as these would certainly reinforce the idea that Proposition 48 is a step in the right direction.

CONCLUSION

So, where are we with regard to this most controversial legislation? As with any true issue, the arguments on both sides seem very legitimate. Thus, it is not surprising that Proposition 48 has had so many modifications and near modifications. Maybe, by the time this book is in print, a final solution will have been reached. In the meantime, the following thoughts are presented for consideration.

As long as the NCAA adheres to the concept of the student-athlete for all levels of competition, Proposition 48 (or, an appropriate substitute) is needed. What are some other possibilities to improve the academic standing of the "Big Game" athletes?

One of the much discussed possibilities is to declare all athletes ineligible their freshman year. By doing so, it will give them time to get academically and socially acclimated to college life. This seems very reasonable except for a couple of factors. One relates to the fact that many of these athletes are tagged as future recruits early in high school or, in some instances, even junior high school. Rightly or wrongly, athletics has been their life. In light of that background, what is the effect on the athlete if he or she has to sit out the freshman year?

The other factor involves athletic department finances. Can most athletic departments afford to give an athletic scholarship to a freshman who is not competing? Furthermore, if the athlete sits out the freshman year, he might still have four years of eligibility. That would mean the athletic scholarship has to be offered for five years.

Some people have suggested another way to improve the academic standards. They would base all athletic scholarships on the number of student-athletes who have actually graduated from an institution. In other words, the number of athletic scholarships allotted to an institution would be based on the number of student-athletes it has graduated. The thought here is that this would be the most equitable policy for the numerous types of institutions of higher education. For instance, the historically black colleges that have graduated the underprepared black student-athlete would benefit and wouldn't be disproportionally affected by the current standards of Proposition 48.

Both of the above possibilities are based on the assumption that the student-athlete is a viable idea for these athletes who play "the Big Game." As noted elsewhere in this text, we would suggest that the athlete-student concept is much more realistic for many Division I football and basketball players. The thought can be supported from many standpoints. An example is the $1.75 billion contract signed in December 1994 between the NCAA and CBS. This gave CBS the right to broadcast the NCAA's Division I men's basketball tournament and a few other championships for the next eight years. Even more surprising was the low-keyed reaction to the signing of such a huge contract.

In the past, such a whopper of a contract might have drawn gasps, worried cries, at least a few whistles. This time, college officials, sports fans, and television executives barely blinked. . . .

But this time few complained, as many had done after the earlier deal, about the increasing professionalism of intercollegiate athletics or the awkward fit of big time sports into the mission of higher education institutions. The loudest critics of the latest argument, in fact, took the NCAA to task for not seeking an even bigger payout.

"There's not the same soul-searching anymore," says Gary Roberts, vice-dean of the law school and faculty athletics representative at Tulane University. "The money is all part of the system that is entrenched and accepted now. The implications of the money, the compromises that might have to be made, are considered simply the cost of doing business." (Blum, p. A39)

Amid that kind of money, can one really be serious in suggesting that these Division I athletes (as a group) are truly student-athletes? Of course, there are some legitimate student-athletes playing Division I basketball and football. They are the ones who are capable enough to pursue excellence on more than one front. Yet, they are the exception rather than the norm.

This brings us to the conclusion that Proposition 48 is largely window dressing. It is not really needed unless the NCAA takes a major step in being serious about having student-athletes (as a whole) in Division I football and basketball. Should that be the case, the standards for academic and freshman eligibility should be even higher than they are today.

REFERENCES

Bartell, T., J. Keegling, L. LeBlanc, and R. V. Tombáud. *Study of Freshmen Eligibility Standards: Executive Summary*. Reston, VA: Advanced Technology, 1984.

Blum, Debra E. "All Part of the Game." *Chronicle of Higher Education*, February 24, 1995, pp. A39–40.

Chronicle of Higher Education. July 7, 1993.

Chu, D., J. O. Segrave, and B. Becker. *Sport and Higher Education*. Chicago, IL: Human Kinetics Publishers, Inc., 1985.

Lederman, Douglas. "NCAA Votes Higher Academic Standards for College Athletes." *Chronicle of Higher Education*, January 15, 1992.

McElroy, Lee. *NCAA News*, December 15, 1994, p. 4.

NCAA Manual. Article 14. Section 3. Overland Park, KS: NCAA, 1995–1996, pp. 130–141.

NCAA News. January 15, 1992, p. 4; October 26, 1992.

New York Times. January 16, 1983, pp. 25, 45.

Rawlings, Hunter. *NCAA News*, January 8, 1992, p. 4.

Rosser, Phyllis. "Girls, Boys, and the SAT: Can We Equal the Score?" *NEA Today*, January 1988, pp. 48–53.

Swift, E. M. "Propping Up Student-Athletes." *Sports Illustrated*, Vol. 81, December 5, 1994, p. 88.

Wiley, Ralph. "A Daunting Proposition." *Sports Illustrated*, Vol. 75, August 12, 1991, pp. 27–51.

Chapter 4

Mainstreaming Division I Athletes

The concept of "mainstreaming" in Division I athletics is a relatively new one. It has been brought about as part of the National Collegiate Athletic Association's response to the widespread lack of public confidence in college sports. According to the NCAA, mainstreaming encompasses the overall effort to bring the student-athlete more in context with the conditions that apply to the student body at large. Although such a policy initially seems valuable, many have wondered if it can actually be carried out. That is, is the policy just NCAA "window dressing" or is it a legitimate idea? The intent here is to respond to this and other questions surrounding the NCAA's efforts at mainstreaming. The focus will be on policies related to the following areas: Housing, Meals, Academic Support Services, Playing and Practice Seasons, and Academic Standards. Of the many arguments both for and against such mainstreaming efforts, two principal arguments can be identified:

Principal argument *for* mainstreaming: to enhance the concept of the student-athlete for Division I athletics.

Principal argument *against* mainstreaming: athletes are a special breed at the Division I level—they will never be like the rest of the student body.

Before examining this issue any further, it may be appropriate and even useful to briefly explore the history of collegiate sport and how it became what it is today.

HISTORY OF COLLEGIATE SPORT

Few of those present at the historic occasion of the nation's first intercollegiate football match (1869), in which around 200 spectators saw Princeton defeat Rutgers, could have dreamed that colleges would soon become major centers of sport. Nor did they dream that sports would contribute to the creation of a new social form, the college community. Invariably small and mostly sectarian, the pre–Civil War colleges had been largely peripheral to the mainstream of American life. But, after the war, the number of colleges and universities more than doubled, and their enrollments tripled. Students countered the heterogeneous character of the new institutions by making extracurricular activities central to their college experiences. "One of their activities, intercollegiate sports, soon exhibited a remarkable capacity to generate communal loyalties both within and outside the campus walls" (Smith, p. 34).

Unlike educational institutions elsewhere in the Western world, by the latter half of the nineteenth century sport became an integral part of American college life. Students provided the impetus for staging the games as well as for the invention of an elaborate pageantry to accompany them. Eventually, college varsity sports became a major source of commercial entertainment. Nevertheless, they were instrumental in defining college identities and in binding students, faculties, administrators, alumni, and social climbers into a single college community.

Apart from evoking the support of a burgeoning college community, college teams elsewhere also generated symbols that transcended the college themselves. Citizens in states without conspicuously significant histories, great civic monuments, or remarkable physical scenery often formed strong emotional bonds to their state university football teams. Likewise, contests between teams located in the South and the North, the East and the West evoked regional loyalties.

Yet, the popularity of intercollegiate football in the early 1900s rested on more than an intrinsic power to engender fierce loyalty. Over this period of time, custodians of the sport diverted more and more away from the amateur model in an effort to hold the fans' interest and, ultimately, to make money. For example, in a stunning understatement, the Carnegie Commission Report of 1929 concluded: "Apparently the ethical bearing of intercollegiate football contests and their scholastic aspects are of secondary importance to the winning of victories and financial success" (Rader, p. 188). In order to still such criticism, to reduce unseemly squabbling among the colleges, and to establish equal conditions of competition among the football powers, the colleges formed an association—the NCAA. Despite the NCAA's subsequent reliance upon moral persuasion to discipline its membership, commercialization, professionalization, and hypocrisy soon became endemic to big-time college football (and later, basketball).

Before World War II, only the military academies, Notre Dame, and to a lesser degree, the Ivy League schools had more than a regional following. But, in the ensuing years, this would no longer be the case. Television, jet-air travel, and massive population movements, among other forces in the post-1950 era, prompted fans and college officials to seek national standing for their teams. A team would succeed nationally only when it ranked high in the wire service polls and, by the 1960s, appeared regularly on network television. "To join the vaunted ranks of the wire service's Top Ten required large sums of money, winning coaches, fancy athletic facilities, a national recruiting system, and a burgeoning bureaucracy" (Rader, p. 273).

SCOPE OF THE PROBLEM(S)

Nowadays, as a result of the aforementioned popularization of big-game college sports, the athletic departments at most major colleges and universities are much larger in size and scope and make greater demands on their institutions than ever before. Although the fans of college sports are large in number, many have also long wondered whether and to what extent their increasing importance complements or corrupts the academic mission of their host universities.

After researching that question, one will undoubtedly arrive at some disheartening conclusions. For example, Murray Sperber concludes that:

Intercollegiate athletics, especially the big-time version, has become College Sports Inc., a huge commercial entertainment conglomerate, with operating methods and objectives totally separate from, and often opposed to, the educational aims of the schools that house its franchise. Moreover, because of its massive hypocrisy and fiscal irresponsibility, College Sports Inc. places many colleges and universities under the constant threat of scandal and other sports-induced maladies. (Sperber, p. K1)

Furthermore, according to Sperber, a situation has been created that is unknown and unthinkable in other countries. Outstanding high school football and men's basketball players in the United States, often with little interest in and preparation for higher education, are required to attend a university in order to gain an opportunity to play their sports at the pro level. In addition, American higher education has compounded the problem. Colleges and universities now take on the training of many young athletes in sports for which there are excellent minor professional leagues and circuits, particularly baseball, hockey, golf, and tennis. In essence, as college athletics grows, increasing numbers of young athletes will enter American higher education primarily for athletic, not academic training. Others have arrived at conclusions somewhat similar to those of Sperber.

Edwin Cady, author of *The Big Game: College Sports and American Life*, believes that the kind of athletes who play "the Big Game" are not like the rest of the student body. He states, "though some academic folk would prefer not to trouble themselves with thinking about it, the student-athlete has become a specialized product of contemporary culture, and that fact makes a difference which has to be taken into consideration. He, and now increasingly, she, starts as a special sort of American person" (Cady, p. 144).

The situation has grown to the point whereby the basic idea of intercollegiate athletics is in jeopardy—that is, that athletes represent their institutions as "true" members of the student body. Many Division I athletes today are far from the desired representative sample of college students, as they certainly do not even blend in very well on their own campuses. Striking at the heart of the mainstreaming issue, columnist Edward Lawry posed the question: "How are athletes 'true' members of the student body when they have special computers, special tutors, special dorms, special food, special enrollment procedures, and special counselors?" (Lawry, p. A44).

In response to such questions and cynicism, the NCAA has made the aforementioned effort to mainstream the Division I athlete—that is, to bring him or her more in context with the conditions that apply to the student body at large. As was stated before, we will be focusing on those mainstreaming efforts that appear to be at the heart of the topic. Those will include the NCAA policies regarding housing, meals, academic support services, playing and practice sessions, and academic standards. Please note that these policies, like most policies of the NCAA, have inspired countless debates in regard to their respective worth. When all is said and done, the reader alone must form his or her own opinion on the central issue involving mainstreaming.

HOUSING

The 1991 NCAA Convention adopted the following—effective August 1, 1996:

- *Athletic Housing.* The institution may not house student-athletes in athletics dormitories or athletics blocks within institutional or privately owned dormitories or apartment buildings on those days when institutional dormitories are open to the general student body.
- *Athletic Dormitories.* Athletics dormitories shall be defined as institutional dormitories in which at least 50 percent of the residents are student-athletes.
- *Athletics Blocks.* Athletics blocks shall be defined as individual blocks, wings, or floors within institutional dormitories or privately owned dormitories or apartment buildings in which at least 50 percent of the residents are student-athletes.

This new rule, in simpler terms, represents the NCAA's effort to abolish what is known to most as the typical "jock dorm." Such efforts are entirely new to the NCAA as the topic was not even considered at one time. In fact, it is the mainstreaming issue that is entirely responsible for this change.

Most critics of college athletics praise such a change as horror stories of the special housing privilege given to athletes have been rampant for years. Sperber writes, "compared to the usual small rooms, Spartan furnishings, and ordinary-to-awful food of the student dorms, jock housing tends toward the palatial" (Sperber, p. K5).

An individual unit for athletes often consists of a nicely furnished suite with large rooms and all of the fixings—television, stereo, VCR, etc. For example, the athletes' dorm at the University of Alabama is nicknamed "The Bryant Hilton" after its builder, former head football coach Paul "Bear" Bryant.

In addition to Sperber's obvious support for such changes, Edwin Cady devotes an entire chapter of his work to the subject. As the chapter is only one sentence long, his message is very clear—it reads, "THE ATHLETIC DORMITORY . . . Integrate it" (Cady, p. 189).

Although such change will undoubtedly serve to bring the athlete more in context with the student body at large, not everyone supports the change. In defense of the jock dorm, some athletes and coaches argue that the situation has more benefits than flaws. For example, it is easier for the student-athlete to study within such confines as there is a general understanding among all the athletes and a consideration for others that is unparalleled in the regular dorms. In other words, jock dorms tend to be more quiet than other dorms. If this is true, it may have something to do with the fact that Division I athletes spend a lot of time and energy at practice and simply do not have anything left to do at the end of the day but rest. Furthermore, there is no longer any off-season in most Division I sports.

In addition to a better atmosphere, the jock dorm provides athletes the opportunity to live with their closest peers (as well as those students with which they have the most in common)—other athletes. This may seem to be a weak argument, but members of a Division I team do spend most of their time together and usually form strong bonds as a result. In contrast to the new rule, the general student body is not subject to any restrictions regarding the choosing of a roommate or roommates. On another note, in assuming the complicated dual role of a Division I student-athlete, athletes grow dependent on one another. This dependency serves as a major "support" mechanism and goes as far as making sure that teammates get to class and practice on time.

It could also be argued that athletic dorms are more convenient and helpful to the university. For example, during those periods when the general student body is on vacation, the university merely has to keep the one athletic dorm open to house the athletes. Now that athletic dorms are eliminated, student-athletes have to undertake the undesirable task of moving to whichever dorm is selected to remain open during breaks in the regular sessions.

On the other hand, one might be able to see why the NCAA legislation was passed. If the NCAA is to persist in advancing the student-athlete concept, this mainstreaming attempt is necessary.

MEALS

The 1991 NCAA Convention adopted the following, effective August 1, 1996:

In Division I, an institution may provide only one training table meal per day to a student-athlete during the academic year on those days when regular institutional dining facilities are open.

This legislation simply follows along with the NCAA's other effort to limit the "extra benefits" provided to athletes. Even at those schools without jock dorms, it is common that special daily "training tables" are set up somewhere on campus for the athletes. In many cases, the free and plentiful food there is far superior to the typical dining hall meals. For example, at one institution, the "training table" was often off-campus. In fact, the men's basketball players could obtain a daily free meal at a number of local restaurants.

One of the principal arguments for training table meals is that athletes often must follow a schedule, which does not fit in well with the normal hours for dining hall meals. If they have a late practice, they may miss the meal altogether. On the other hand, the athletes may regularly arrive just prior to the closing of the cafeteria line with little left in the selection of food. Also, the frequent travel schedules of athletes often times do not work out well with the hours of food service.

Perhaps *the* principal argument against training table meals is that it is just another example of too many special benefits for athletes. Needless to say, as noted before, the special treatment may be excessive. Another argument is that athletes only further isolate themselves from other students by only eating their meals with athletic peers. In other words, training table meals work contrary to the integration or mainstreaming concept.

ACADEMIC SUPPORT SERVICES

The key NCAA policy is as follows:

- *Academic Counseling.* Division I member institutions shall make available general academic counseling and tutoring services to all recruited student-athletes. Such counseling and tutoring services may be provided by the department of athletics or through the institution's non-athletics student support services.

As a result of such legislation and to meet the minimum academic rules on playing eligibility, special academic advising has become commonplace in Division I schools. For example, some NCAA Division I athletic departments now have six full-time academic advisers, some having a staffer for each sport. In addition, the full-time personnel hire large numbers of part-time assistants to do the bulk of the tutoring and what Sperber calls "babysitting (walking athletes to class, often taking notes for them, sometimes attending class for them)" (Sperber, p. K5).

Having a separate system for academic advising is considered to be another jock privilege and is entirely outside the mainstreaming mode. Although Sperber may be exaggerating, there is little doubt that these advisory systems run counter to the mainstreaming effort. On the other hand, effective academic advising may be necessary and helpful to many student-athletes. In some cases, the system is instrumental in moving an athlete along toward graduation.

As virtually all studies indicate, proportionally more athletes survive academically and achieve degrees than their undifferentiated classmates. Of course, there is the argument that, as Cady writes, "They could hardly help it. Their motivations to stay and play, to win at any competition, to please the coaches, all help them" (Cady, p. 154). But, as Cady goes on to admit, "Tutoring and study tables help . . . our figures show that yours (referring to the athletic department's tutoring program for athletes) is the only tutoring program on campus that achieves demonstrably positive results" (Cady, p. 155).

Nevertheless, it is still unfair to the general student body if they do not have access to such services. As a compromise to the present situation, there could be an academic advising system for all those students (not just athletes) that are in need of special assistance (i.e., those who are special admissions cases or struggling). Once these students "get their feet on the ground" through the use of the system, they could be redirected into the institution's general advisory system with all the others. The only real limitation here is that a university may not be able to afford such an advising program for all students.

PLAYING AND PRACTICE SEASONS

> When you go to college, you're not a student-athlete, but an athlete-student. Your main purpose is not to be Einstein, but a ballplayer, to generate some money, put people in the stands. Eight or ten hours of your day are filled with basketball, football. The rest of your time, you've got to motivate yourself to make sure you get something back.
>
> —Isaiah Thomas
> former Indiana University basketball player and NBA star
> (Sperber, p. 287)

NCAA MANUAL ARTICLE 17—
PLAYING AND PRACTICE SEASONS

General Principles:

- *Institutional Limitations.* A member institution shall limit its organized practice activities, the length of its playing season, and the number of its regular season contests and/or dates of competition in all sports, as well as the extent of its participation in non-collegiate sponsored athletics activities, to minimize interference with the academic programs of its student-athletes.

The *NCAA Manual* extends beyond these general principles by including specific schedules and limitations for each individual sport. It seems safe to say that the limitation of playing and practice seasons may be at the heart of the mainstreaming thrust.

For football and basketball players who play the Big Game, the time and the physical and emotional demands are particularly acute. It is common knowledge now that many of these athletes are forced to neglect a meaningful education to pursue a sport full time, or, in a few cases, drop out of athletics and seriously go to school. As an example of the major time constraints on big-time college athletes, Division I-A football players are said to spend up to 60 hours a week during the season on their sport; basketball players spend 50 hours a week (Sperber, p. K4). Also, let us not overlook the unrecorded hours that athletes spend in recovery from injuries and exhaustion acquired in practices and games. This situation exists as well in many of the nonrevenue Division I sports.

Aside from the major seasonal commitment, it is important to recognize that the time required for Division I sports does not drop appreciably during the athlete's off-season. Participation in Division I athletics is now a year-round endeavor. Furthermore, it should also be noted that the athlete does not have the power to escape such time-consuming schedules. If the coach demands that the athlete spend long hours practicing, an athlete cannot refuse—unless he or she wants to drop the sport and lose the athletic scholarship. Why does the coach make such demands? The usual response is that it is necessary to keep up with the competitors.

To emphasize the unrealistic nature of this situation, "university authorities believe that a full-time student who is pursuing a meaningful degree should devote at least 40–50 hours a week to attending classes and studying—and that students who are ill-prepared for college, including large numbers of athletes, should spend significantly more time than that on their studies" (Sperber, p. K4). Some basic math will reveal that, according to university authorities, "pursuing a meaningful degree" and participating in Division I sports simply cannot occur simultaneously (not unless the athlete-student can go without sleep)! To put this situation into more perspective, consider that the federal government allows a regular student receiving a work-study grant to spend a maximum of 20 hours a week on his or her university job. The government's rationale is that more than 20 hours a week cuts into the amount of time needed for a normal course of study by a full-time student. Nevertheless, "intercollegiate athletics regularly exceed this federal guideline by as much as 200 percent" (Sperber, p. K4).

It should also be made clear that most big-time athletic programs try to finesse the time constraints on athletes by putting them in what Sperber calls special "hideaway curricula" and having them major in eligibility. Even if these athletes graduate, such course work does not constitute a real college education. And, unfortunately, for a vast majority of college athletes, this system does not work!

There seems to be little doubt that limitations on practice and playing time cannot but help if there is to be serious effort at preparing student-athletes. Only two significant questions remain: Are such restrictions realistic for those who play "the Big Game"? Also, when it comes to practice restrictions, to what extent can they really be enforced?

ACADEMIC STANDARDS

> What was allowed to become a circus—college sports—threatens to become the means by which the public believes the entire enterprise [higher education] is a sideshow.
> —A. Bartlett Giamatti
> former President of Yale University,
> former Commissioner of Major League Baseball
> (Sperber, Preface)

Following is the policy that undergirds all of the NCAA legislation involving academic standards.

NCAA MANUAL: ARTICLE 2.4

- *Principle of Sound Academic Standards.* Intercollegiate athletics programs shall be maintained as a vital component of the educational program and student-athletes shall be an integral part of the student body. The admission, academic standing, and academic progress of student-athletes shall be consistent with the policies and standards adopted by the institution for the student body in general.

The tensions between big-time athletics and academics do not represent a new crisis in higher education. The crisis and the calls for control have been growing steadily for many years. But, just as steadily, the problem has become more serious. Such a principle and its more specific by-laws (i.e., rules of eligibility, satisfactory progress, Proposition 48, etc.) represent questionable efforts by the NCAA to curb the academic problems associated with big-time college sports. Such efforts may run contrary to the mainstreaming effort, as the conditions that apply to the student-athlete should be equivalent to those that apply to the general student body. So, why allow athletes to enroll as exceptions to the general requirements? And, why make athletes subject to eligibility rules in order to participate (when John Doe can still act in a play even though he has a 1.8)?

The truth of the matter is that the NCAA is caught between the rock and the hard place. On the one hand, the NCAA works to make big-time college sports a nationally important entertainment industry by encouraging institutions to train their gifted athletes for the great prize of a national championship. On the other hand, as evidenced by the academic standards policies, the NCAA scrambles to suppress the cheating, the neglect of academic values, and the exploitation of college athletes that its own promotion of big-time winning encourages. In essence, intensifying the academic aim without de-emphasizing the aim of glory, money, and power will just exacerbate the problems facing intercollegiate athletics.

The dilemma faced by the NCAA is perhaps best manifested in the work of the Knight Foundation Commission on Intercollegiate Athletics. That commission issued its first report in March 1991 under the banner of "Keeping Faith With the Student-Athlete." A year later, the same commission reported glowingly of the progress made under the title of "A Solid Start."

Twelve months ago, the Knight Foundation Commission on Intercollegiate Athletics concluded that big-time college athletes appeared to have lost their bearings and to be veering out of control. In support of a burgeoning sports reform movement, the commission prepared a new model for intercollegiate athletics, a road map entitled "one plus three" in which the "one"—presidential control—would be directed toward the "three"—academic integrity, financial integrity, and independent certification. We believed that all of the subordinate problems and issues of college sports could be addressed responsibly within the model. . . .

As *Washington Post* columnist Thomas Boswell wrote in June, 1991, after reviewing the Presidents' Commissions new proposals to raise academic standards: Just 100 days ago, it seemed like dreamy stuff for the Knight Commission to "intone." Cutting academic corners in order to admit athletes will not be tolerated. Now it doesn't seem quite so farfetched. Today it is not at all farfetched. When the January, 1992 NCAA Convention enacted the president's proposals, significantly higher academic standards become binding on every big-time college and university athletics program. ("A Solid Start," p. 3)

The truth of the matter is that the changes in the academic standards were minimal, not nearly as earth shaking as purported by the Knight Foundation. Furthermore, several years later, the NCAA is still faced with the impossible task of trying to balance academic integrity with the big business of college athletics. In December 1994, CBS signed a contract with the NCAA to pay $1.725 billion to retain the rights to the NCAA basketball tournament through 2002. Is that not sufficient evidence of the out-sized role material wealth continues to play in college athletics? Is it possible to have financial *and* academic integrity under such a structure?

As one other example, the NCAA continues to discuss the possibility of a Division I-A football playoff to determine the true national champion. One of the arguments for the playoff game is the potential for additional significant revenue for the NCAA member institutions. But, is lengthening the season for playoffs consistent with higher academic standards for the players?

CONCLUSION

This brings us back to the major thrust of this chapter—mainstreaming Division I athletes who play the Big Game (football and basketball). Are the mainstreaming efforts for real? Possibly to some extent they are legitimate. But one would have to believe that much of it is window dressing. This is particularly true with regard to academic standards. It is difficult to imagine that many of these athletes can really be student-athletes (in light of the physical, emotional, and time demands placed on them). As a matter of fact, the very focus on academic standards for athletes seem to run contrary to the mainstreaming concept. After all, "Prop. 48" is not a factor for the student body at large.

REFERENCES

"A Solid Start: A Report on Reform of Intercollegiate Athletics." *Report of the Knight Foundation Commission on Intercollegiate Athletics*, March 1992.

Cady, Edwin H. The Big Game: College Sports and American Life. Knoxville: University of Tennessee Press, 1978.

Lawry, Edward G. "Conflicting Interests Make Reform of College Sports Impossible." *Chronicle of Higher Education*, May 1, 1991, p. A44.

NCAA Manual, Overland Park, KS, 1994–1995.

Rader, Benjamin G. *American Sports: From the Age of Folk Games to the Age of Televised Sports*. 2nd edition. Englewood Cliffs, NJ: Prentice-Hall, Inc., 1990.

Smith, Ronald A. *Sports and Freedom: The Rise of Big-Time College Athletics.* New York: University Press, Inc., 1988.

Sperber, Murray. "College Sports Inc.: The Athletic Department vs. the University." *Phi Delta Kappa*, October 1990, pp. K1–K12.

Sperber, Murray. *College Sports Inc.: The Athletic Department vs. the University.* New York: Henry Holt & Co., Inc., 1990.

Chapter 5

Evaluating Coaches

There is little doubt that the evaluation of coaches represents both an issue and a problem. As a matter of fact, evaluation, in general, poses a series of questions that generate issues and problems. (1) Why evaluate? (2) Who should evaluate? and (3) How should the evaluation be carried out? In spite of any issue or problems involving the evaluation process, some form of evaluation is necessary within any organization. Before turning to the specific topic of evaluating coaches, it seems appropriate to consider these questions generally.

Why should an organization provide for an evaluation of its members? Ideally perhaps, the principal reason for evaluating is to improve individual and/or group performance. From that perspective, evaluation can be viewed as a monitoring device. Evaluation can also be used to coordinate program development by helping to determine strengths and weaknesses. This, in turn, might lead to changes in the program. Evaluation is also used as a basis for external critique, to compare one program with another. The issue here is whether a valid standard of comparison can be established.

Perhaps the most practical need for evaluation is to make personnel decisions (promotions, retentions, dismissals, tenure, and salary increases). Here again the problem is one of finding the most valid instrument for this purpose. Finally, evaluation may also be used to fulfill a personal need involving status. Many people desire feedback regarding their performance.

Who should do the evaluation? To some extent this is situationally defined. There will be variance from organization to organization, depending on the nature of the particular organization. The traditional idea was that evaluation should be conducted by those in superior positions (e.g., the department head). In other words, evaluation is carried out through the chain of command. To a large extent this is still the case in most situations. Nevertheless, there are three other possibilities that can be and are utilized: peer evaluation, self-evaluation, and evaluation by subordinates.

Peer evaluation may actually be the most valid means of assessment, at least in certain contexts. For example, in colleges and universities, faculty evaluation usually begins with assessments by colleagues in the department. Those in favor of peer evaluations would argue that "it takes one to know one." At the same time, others contend that peer evaluation tends to be biased by popularity. Friends or those with sparkling personalities will typically get the higher ratings.

Evaluation by subordinates is a somewhat elusive category. Subordinates will always be involved in evaluation on an informal basis. The employees have their own opinions as to how well the boss does his or her job. Formal evaluation by subordinates may be a more debatable matter. Again, the particular situation will probably dictate the extent to which subordinate evaluation should be employed. Self evaluation presents less grounds for debate. It is not so much an option but rather a preliminary step in the evaluation by others. Evaluation by administrators or peers often begins with self evaluation.

How should the evaluation be done? This is probably the most difficult of the three basic questions. In most cases, evaluation is an on-going process involving observation, listening, and written documentation. There is often a quarterly, semi-annual, and/or year-end assessment of performance. This may take the form of a written report. Whatever the particular format may be, there will invariably be a need to compare the actual accomplishments with the performance standards for that job or position.

These thoughts about evaluation in general should provide the framework for the evaluation of coaches. There is probably only one factor that makes the evaluation of coaches quite unique. The coach is constantly being evaluated by parents, fans, and members of the news media whether we like it or not. Furthermore, much of this is in the form of public evaluation.

Other variables should be considered with regard to the evaluation of coaches. One is that coaches are found at different levels, extending all the way from the voluntary coach of youth sports to coaches of professional and international teams. Another significant variable is the difference between coaching a revenue producing and nonrevenue producing sport. In this chapter we will address the evaluation of high school and college coaches. Their role in the educational setting particularly points to the need for proper evaluation. This could be said for the coaches of youth sports. The one difference with the latter is that these are volunteer positions.

THE HIGH SCHOOL COACH

As noted, the process of evaluation is a complicated and controversial topic. When it comes to evaluating high school coaches, the complications are only heightened. To begin with, the coach represents different things to different people. He or she is called on to be a teacher, trainer, counselor, disciplinarian, manager, and public relations agent. All this is in addition to the up-front need to have a thorough knowledge of the sport. The coach is expected to relate well to a variety of constituencies—students, parents, administrators, other coaches, the news media, fans, and the general public.

The most complicating factor of all is that the coach is employed to win games, even at the high school level, although there may be less pressure here in some cases. Regardless of any evaluation policy employed, the matter of winning and losing is almost certain to enter the picture.

Another unique factor in the attempt to evaluate high school coaches is that they are constant subjects of public evaluation. The effectiveness of the coach is there for all to see during a game or contest. Few people in other walks of life are subjected to the same kind of public scrutiny. The coach is openly evaluated in newspapers, and on radio and television. Parents are among the foremost to assess a coach's performance.

The situation surrounding high school coaching has become even more complex in recent years. Title IX prompted a strong demand for qualified coaches in women's sports. In many cases, women coaches have lacked the qualifications of their male counterparts. The need to hire part-time coaches from outside school systems has increased dramatically due to financial restraints. In some situations, schools have been faced with state and district regulations mandating the hiring of only certified coaches. Tenured, aging teachers have sought release from coaching positions due to burn-out. Low pay for high school coaching is a persistent problem.

The net result of these conditions is that many high schools have been forced to employ coaches with marginal qualifications. It would appear that the need to evaluate high school coaches has increased. Yet, the need only points to the various issues involved. In the attempt to develop policies, a number of questions must be addressed.

1. Should a high school coach be evaluated on the same basis as any other teacher in the school system?
2. Should the performance standards for a high school coach be essentially the same as those for a college coach?
3. How much weight should be given to the won-lost record in assessing a high school coach's work?
4. Should all the coaches in the athletic program be evaluated according to the same standard (e.g., should the head football coach be evaluated on the same basis as the tennis coach)?
5. Should high school athletes be involved in evaluating the work of the coach?
6. What criteria (performance standards) should be used in the process of evaluation?
7. How should the evaluation be carried out?

Some of these questions have legal implications. For example, the Bryan Case in Alabama in 1985 related to the matter of evaluating coaches as teachers:

William Bryan taught at Weaver High School in Alabama for ten years and had achieved tenured teacher status. He was employed as a head coach for several years and received additional compensation for his coaching duties. After he was notified that his coaching duties were terminated, he contended that his tenured teaching position entitled him to a hearing before the State Tenure Commission regarding his dismissal for coaching, whether he had tenure as a coach or not.

The Court of Civil Appeals of Alabama considered numerous cases similar to the instant case and made two comments:

1. The purpose of the Teacher Tenure Act is to protect teachers from cancellation of their contracts or transfers for political, personal, or arbitrary reasons.

2. Since a coach is not a teacher, as defined in the Tenure Act, Bryan had no right to a hearing before the Tenure Commission.

It upheld the judgement of the circuit court denying Bryan's petition. (Appenzeller and Ross, p. 5)

As noted earlier, these questions provide the parameters for any policies regarding the evaluation of school coaches. Following are some thoughts that might determine the nature of these policies.

To some extent, the high school teacher has to be evaluated on the same basis as any other teacher in the school system. To begin with, in most cases the high school coach is also a teacher, be it in the classroom or the gymnasium. Furthermore, a strong proportion of high school coaching is teaching. On the other hand, the coach has many other responsibilities that extend beyond teaching. These include organization and supervision of team travel, game management, medical supervision, and relations with the news media. The coach tends to be much more of a public figure than does any other teacher. This, in itself, means that the evaluation of the coach has to extend beyond the assessment of him or her as a teacher. In other words, the coach might be an effective teacher and yet not be highly rated as a coach.

Some of the performance standards for high school coaches have to be the same as those for college coaches. For example, it is reasonable to expect that all coaches in both of these educational settings will provide leadership for the proper conduct of their athletes on and off the playing arena. The performance standard of effective teaching is also a reasonable expectation at all levels. On the other hand the performance standards for a high school coach will certainly differ in some respects from those for an NCAA Division I coach. There is no denying the fact that winning is important at both levels. However, the premium on winning has to increase as one moves from the high school level to the college Division I level. Similarly, the ability to recruit is a standard that sets apart Division I coaching from that of coaching at any other level.

From an ideal perspective, all coaches in a high school athletic program should be evaluated according to the same standard. In certain situations it may be necessary to deviate somewhat from that ideal due to the nature of the program. Regional differences often account for the variance. For example, the popularity of high school football in Texas is well documented. It would not be reasonable to expect that a high school football coach in Texas will have performance standards that are identical to that of other coaches in the school systems.

There is no doubt that high school athletes should and will be involved in evaluating their coach on an informal basis. Much the same can be said about student evaluation of a teacher. From a policy perspective, the question is largely one of the extent and nature of formal evaluation by the athletes.

The athletic director should obtain feedback from the athletes, be it written or verbal. Due to the ages of the high school athletes, the verbal feedback might be more valid and useful. Mid-season would seem like an appropriate time for the athletic director to schedule a meeting with the athletes to obtain their reactions to the coaching situation. End-of-season assessment is also a possibility. However, each assessment can be biased by team success and lack of playing time by certain team members.

Performance standards for coaches will be somewhat situationally defined. Nevertheless, regardless of specifics, the coach should be evaluated according to the following general standards:

1. *As a professional*: The coach should reflect a coaching philosophy and attitude that supports the objectives of the athletic department and the school.

2. *As an organizer and administrator*: The coach should be well prepared for practice and games. The coach should also operate within the allotted budget and be accountable to the administration.

3. *As a person*: The coach should set a good example for the players, in word, deed, and appearance. He or she should also have proper control of the team during all practice sessions and scheduled athletic events.

4. *As a teacher*: The coach should have up-to-date knowledge of his or her sport. Furthermore, the coach should be able to demonstrate and communicate the necessary knowledge and skills.

5. *As a staff member*: The coach must be able to work effectively with other members of the athletic department as well as teachers and staff in the school at large.

One final point should be made regarding the evaluation of high school coaches. Anyone who is involved with proper evaluation knows that it is a very time-consuming task. It is reasonable to assume that much of the formal evaluation of high school coaches will be done by the athletic director. Furthermore, the athletic director in most high schools is also a teacher and a coach, as well as being the high school director. As a result of such time restraints, the athletic director will have to be selective regarding the amount and mode of evaluation. It may be necessary to spend more time evaluating part-time coaches and new coaches in the department. Also, the paperwork involving evaluation may have to be kept to a minimum.

THE COLLEGE COACH

In the sports-crazy modern world the expert teacher, trainer, developer, motivator of super athletes has become a common phenomenon. But nobody elsewhere stands beside the legendary wizard of the American Big Game. He expresses and symbolizes cultural impulses swirling and conjoined to something like tornadic power: the student *virtu* which invented and evolved the games and took them into the mainstream of college life; the almost hysterical response of the constituencies; the intrusion of the public and exploitation by the media; the expertise of generations of professional sophistication; the sometimes desperate efforts of the institutions to exercise some degree of control. He stands in the eye of the storm; when it blows with him, he is exalted, bestriding the festival, godlike; when it turns and blows the other way, he is strong indeed if it does not tear him to shreds. He becomes, all dimly, the American Vegetation God, watcher of the golden bough, king today, burned tomorrow. We call him "Coach." (Cady, p. 120)

With that vivid description, Edwin Cady opens his chapter on "Coach." "The Big Game," as referred to by Cady, is American college football and basketball on the NCAA Division I level. Within that context, the evaluation of college coaches follows a simple formula: Is he a winner?

Cady contended (and I think most people would agree) that it is the need to win that accounts for many of the abuses and problems in college athletics. However, he also felt "the Big Game" must and can be controlled. His answer was to provide opportunities for tenure for those high pressured coaches: "I would begin by laying down the firm principle that, as is already largely true for the other sports, nobody among Big Game coaches can get fired for losing" (p. 136). Referring to the nine football coaches and three basketball coaches on a Division I staff, he said: "Why should those twelve apostles of the Big Game, and they only, be without job security, without reasonable expectation of continuance, vulnerable to immolation, the Cinderellas of the academic family and community? The situation is absurd and, because it negates control, disastrous" (p. 137).

Cady's work was published in 1978. Twenty years later the entire situation involving "the Big Game" and Division I coaches has only accelerated in terms of pressures on these coaches. For one thing, the money from television contracts only increases. Therefore, it is probably far from reasonable to expect that these coaches will ever be granted tenure even though there might be considerable merit in Cady's suggestion. It seems appropriate to begin by considering how coaches do or do not relate to the tenure structure in the colleges and universities.

Coaches and Tenure

The field of higher education in general has traditionally determined the status of its faculty through the terms and conditions of employment. The ultimate reward for those who achieve in teaching, scholarly research, and service to the academic community (and the primary source of status) is tenure. In a 1983 issue of *Newsweek on Campus*, Bill Barol captured the lofty position of tenure by referring to it as "academia's brass ring."

Tenure essentially guarantees employment as long as the institution has funds to pay the salaries, and the professor continues to perform in good faith, with competency, and without moral turpitude. Although circumstances such as "bona fide financial exigencies" are acceptable grounds for dismissing tenured professors, in reality, very few get fired for this reason.

Tenure is intended to facilitate the pursuit of knowledge by providing individuals with the freedom to follow intellectual inquiry wherever it may lead, without fearing dismissal for upholding unpopular thoughts or beliefs. A problem associated with tenure is that it could influence an individual's professional performance by effectively reducing motivational concerns. Nevertheless, the practice of awarding tenure has long been seen as a necessary component of the educational system. It offers the potential to attract qualified people by providing a significant degree of security, in a profession that often does not pay market value for the expertise involved.

Although the American Association of University Professors (AAUP) has set generally recognized and accepted guidelines for tenure policy, each institution is free to establish its own policy. Earlier in this century, the tone for intercollegiate athletics was directed toward integrating the role of athletics with the larger purpose of higher education by providing tenure opportunities for coaches. In accordance with the primary recommendation of a 1926 AAUP committee on the objectives of intercollegiate sport, coaches were usually full-time members of the general faculty with a seat and teaching responsibility in, but not restricted to, physical education. As faculty members directly involved in the institutions' larger purposes, coaches were afforded the same status and rewards as their academic colleagues. This included academic rank and associated compensation, the right to vote at faculty meetings and serve on elected committees, and the opportunity for tenure.

More recently most institutions have moved away from the idea of making opportunities for tenure available to coaches. The basic difficulty has been one of attempting to evaluate coaches within the framework of traditional criteria for academic achievement. The role of the teacher-coach in the academic community remains a consistent subject for debate. Much of the controversy stems from a belief that coaching is something that can be pursued in addition to academic teaching responsibilities. Furthermore, many argue that there must be this dual pursuit if a coach is to be considered for tenure.

Coaches are in a unique position in the academic community. The occupational subculture of coaches in higher education is one in which they function within the total educational organization but have little in common with the larger group. They may feel alienated from the values and lifestyle of the academic community. In most cases the coach understands that he or she is employed to produce winning teams. However, the faculty outside the coaching subculture do not face this challenge, and the majority do not fully understand a coach's position. The situation becomes more complicated when some type of academic duties are required of coaches.

Anderson (1985) pinpointed the problem when he noted that the dual roles established by appointment to teacher-coach positions carry "exceptions not among those traditionally evaluated to determine faculty performance" (p. 16). He logically explains that as each role becomes more specialized, it is more difficult for an individual to function effectively in both capacities. Under these circumstances one or the other role tends to dominate an individual's attention and energies. Those who choose to emphasize the coaching role (which is a natural choice for a coach) are still subject to the traditional criteria for promotion and tenure. However, these criteria, research, and publications are not logical extensions of the coaching position.

Anderson proposed a model that calls for a continuum of possible positions, depending on the needs of the institution and the interests of the teacher-coach. One end of the continuum represents a position where academic teaching is regarded as the primary responsibility and, consequently, the application of typical criteria for appointment, promotion, and tenure is legitimate. The other end of the continuum delineates a role where there is a major commitment to coaching.

Obviously, the middle part of the continuum, where teaching and coaching receive equal emphasis, presents the greatest difficulty for the individual and the institution. The Division I institutions have by and large stayed away from this gray area by appointing coaches to athletic positions without academic status. This practice continues to be the modus operandi, especially for the high-exposure sports of football and basketball at major institutions. Such an employment mode affords these institutions the flexibility to fire coaches who do not produce mandated results. On the other hand, it also places the coach in the kind of dilemma, as described by Cady.

The NCAA Division II and III schools are most likely to be caught in the middle territory. Traditionally the Division III colleges have been inclined to follow the policy of hiring coaches who are qualified to teach and appointing them to faculty positions with academic status. However, in recent years, an increasing number of institutions at all levels has moved away from tenure-track appointments for coaches. One reason for the change is that the relatively abundant educational resources of the 1950s and 1960s are no longer available. Declining student enrollments and concomitant financial pressures have forced institutions to re-examine their employment policies. While tenure policies in general have been affected by the changing circumstances, athletic departments are prime targets for cutbacks as the athletic and academic components compete for limited financial resources.

Recent support for the idea of providing faculty status and tenure for coaches has come from various directions. In general, the arguments proceed from the need to do something to alleviate the problems that plague intercollegiate sport. The basic thought is that a coach who isn't under constant pressure to win will be less likely to violate recruiting and eligibility regulations.

There is little doubt that a coach can be evaluated as a teacher, because the coach teaches all aspects of a sport. To be more specific, the coach can be assessed in terms of technical competence, effective communication of information, careful organization of practice sessions, and strategy development during the game. The service criteria also poses no real problem in the assessment of the coach. He or she can be evaluated on the quality of service to the profession, the institution, and the larger community. The "publish or perish" requirement and accompanying research issue pose the major roadblocks in equating the performances of coaches with the achievements of academic colleagues in decisions involving academic rank and tenure.

This much is clear: those concerned with managing college sport programs cannot seem to agree on the most appropriate relationship between athletic and academic life. The issue concerning the academic status of coaches is merely a part of the larger issue. While those institutions caught up in pursuit of "the Big Game" may have passed the point where a consideration of the academic status of coaches is relevant, the vast majority of colleges will have to seriously consider the issue if sport is to continue to be justified from the educational standpoint.

CASE STUDY: A DIVISION III COLLEGE

As a full-time member of the faculty, teacher-coaches at the College were traditionally subject to the same policies and procedures that govern the terms and conditions of employment for academic personnel. Individuals were appointed to the faculty under one of three possible scenarios: they could be hired with tenure, they could be hired to a tenure-track position with a decision concerning reappointment and tenure coming after a defined probationary period, or they could be hired to a terminal position that sets forth a specified duration of employment. In the latter two situations, no full-time member of the academic faculty would be retained in his or her teaching position for more than seven years without an appointment with tenure.

> Note: The college selected for this case is a small liberal arts college with a rich tradition of pursuing academic excellence. It is also a college that has provided leadership in recognizing the educational role of athletics by appointing coaches to regular academic appointments as faculty members. Names of the college and the individuals involved in this case are not included due to the generally sensitive nature of personnel policies of this type.

A tenure-track appointment was usually made for an initial term of three years with the possibility of attaining a second three-year contract upon reappointment. Reappointment to a second term was based on a process of review and recommendation originating in the faculty member's department. The department gathered evidence concerning the individual's teaching effectiveness, scholarly growth, and other contributions, and made a recommendation regarding reappointment or tenure. This information was then passed for review to the Committee of Six—the ruling body of the College formed by four elected faculty members, the president, and the dean of the faculty.

Following the committee's review of the evidence, a recommendation was submitted to the Board of Trustees by the president, acting on his own accord, along with the recommendations of the dean of the faculty, the Committee of Six, and the department. Although the final decision regarding reappointment or tenure rested in the hands of the board, the recommendation of the candidate's department and the considerations of the Committee of Six were the most important components of the process.

"Institutional considerations" played an important role in all decisions regarding tenure and generally weighed heavily in the deliberations of the Committee of Six and the Board of Trustees. Factors such as the rank structure of the department, the time of retirement of department members, and the fields of competence of the candidate in relation to those already represented in the department were important considerations.

During the 1970s the College experienced various changes and encountered pressures that affected the institution as a whole and had a significant impact on the athletic department. The dropping of all requirements for physical education challenged coaches to promote voluntary programs of instructional classes and intramural activities. In order to encourage a high level of participation (the backbone of the College's athletic philosophy), a wider range of intercollegiate teams was offered. This development was most pronounced by an expansion in the number of varsity and junior varsity teams, which accompanied the arrival of women through coeducation in 1975.

At the same time, like many other institutions of higher education, the College was under pressure to cut costs. Although the move to coeducation and the effects of financial constraints produced campus-wide problems, nowhere was this predicament more acutely felt than in the athletic department. The same 11 full-time coaches who supervised 26 intercollegiate teams in 1974 had become responsible for 42 varsity and junior varsity squads in 1981. This situation was mainly the result of campus-wide competition for scarce financial resources, for strictly limited faculty slots, and especially for tenure commitments at a time when retirements were low and the tenure ratio was climbing. Desperately needed new positions in the Department of Physical Education could not be justified when every academic department on campus was communicating similar needs.

A further complication centered on the issue of tenure. Understandably, the College did not wish to make too many tenure commitments during a time of financial uncertainty. Many candidates were refused tenure because of institutional considerations. The justification most often given for denying a candidate tenure was that he or she failed to satisfy the criteria. The need to meet the criteria, particularly in the area of scholarly research and publications, became a particularly critical problem for the coaches. Due to excessive coaching responsibilities the teacher-coaches had essentially been forced to abandon the role of the teacher-scholar. At the time, however, seven of the eleven full-time members in the department were protected by tenure, as a result of the policy designed to address the development of teacher-scholars among coaches. The goal had been to keep the department, both symbolically and in practice, related and responsible to the central values of the College. However, now the Committee of Six was beginning to feel uncomfortable with the institutional tradition that determined that the status of members of the Department of Physical Education should be identical to that of other academic personnel.

In 1978, following two tenure appointments in the department (the first woman and the first minority), concern was expressed about the appropriateness of continuing to apply the traditional criteria for tenure to coaches. The athletic director and the dean of the faculty (an ex-officio member of the Committee of Six) led a comprehensive review of the situation.

The resulting two-page document, titled "A Memorandum of Understanding," modified the criteria for tenure as applied to candidates from the Department of Physical Education and Athletics. The memorandum reprioritized the three components involved in tenure decisions by recognizing that "it is unusual for a coach to pursue formal academic research as an integral component of his or her professional life." Therefore, the most important criterion for the evaluation of teachers of physical education and coaches was determined to be teaching effectiveness instead of scholarly achievement. This quality was to be evidenced by the normal method of student and peer letters of assessment, which considered the teaching of skills, techniques, strategies, theories; practice and game organization and development; the ability to reach and work with students of varying abilities; analysis of the coach's own team; and analysis of opponents. In essence, the intent of the new criteria for the evaluation of coaches was to call forth a general sense of his or her effectiveness in handling the diverse responsibilities that are unique to the role of the teacher-coach.

The memorandum was presented to the faculty, not as a referendum issue, but as a topic for discussion. When its contents were not questioned, it became a matter of record in the minutes of the faculty meeting, but not as a formal policy approved by the board, and entered in the faculty handbook.

With the issue apparently resolved, the department recommended a candidate for tenure in 1981 with the understanding that the criteria set forth in the memorandum would be applied. However, a new administration had taken office, and it refused to recognize the unofficial policy. The candidate was denied tenure on the grounds that he failed to satisfy the traditional criteria.

This particular case was viewed as "a red herring" within the department. The coaches felt that the decision of the Committee of Six and the Board of Trustees to deny tenure was not due to the candidate's qualifications, but was a rejection of the practice of assigning athletic personnel to tenure-track positions. Therefore, both College administrators and athletic department personnel decided to reconsider the policy concerning the appointment of coaches. The issue no longer focused solely on the criteria that should be the means for evaluating coaches, but was extended to include the institutional desirability for tenure coaches.

Ultimately the administration decided that some changes in the traditional pattern were desirable. It was determined, however, that any new policy must preserve the sense of a common enterprise between the physical education department and the academic faculty while recognizing more accurately the necessary differences between the career paths of teacher-coaches and teacher-scholars. The range of alternative policies considered can be delineated by a continuum where one extreme represents the traditional tenure practice and the other extreme represents a complete move away from tenure-track appointments to various forms of specific contracts. The latter would allow more flexibility for accommodating the demands placed on the athletic program by increased numbers and coeducation. A contract system would serve to reduce the conflicts between the needs of athletic and academic programs by allowing for new positions in a situation where faculty seats are strictly limited. It would also make possible the retention of some younger coaches without binding the College to future commitments of tenure.

However, a contract system would seem to remove academic faculty from any significant role in the process of evaluating coaches. With the elimination of the tenure decision, there would probably be no institutional evaluation of coaches. Consequently there would seem to be no clear assurance that coaches under contract would be protected from alumni or administrative pressures to win at any cost. The parties involved argued that such a situation would be undesirable. The College sought and eventually arrived at a middle course— one that offered many of the advantages of increased flexibility through a contract system but still provided some protection for the coaches. Major elements in the new policy were three-year contracts and an extended probationary period of twelve years. A major evaluation would be made in the twelfth year. After that the coach could receive a "senior" contract, which would be a four-year "rolling contract." In other words, there was an understanding that the contract would be renewed annually for another four years unless there was a definite reason for discontinuing the contract.

SUGGESTED POLICIES AND GUIDELINES

In a division or college featuring student-athletes, there must be policies that are aimed at evaluating coaches from a broader perspective than the win-lose column. In essence, the coach has to be evaluated as one who has academic status even though that status is not identical or directly parallel to that held by faculty in the traditional academic disciplines. Using the case study as a basic model, the following policies and guidelines are suggested for evaluating coaches of student-athletes:

1. *The Gestalt* Quality of the Coach Will Be Assessed:* Due to the multifarious nature of his or her responsibilities, the coach should be assessed as a whole person. Much of the evaluation will be informal. Such informal processes would include frequent one-to-one conversations between the athletic director and the coach, during which the latter's self-appraisal is reviewed and critiqued by the athletic director and performance standards are set. Even though the focus will be on the "Gestalt," certain specifics can be identified under the general assessment. These specifics fall under three major categories: (1) coaching abilities per se (this includes abilities as a teacher); (2) managerial abilities; and (3) abilities in professional and public relations.

2. *Three-year Appointments and an Extended 12-year Probationary Period:* Unless it is a temporary or special appointment, the coach will initially be appointed under a three-year contract. Subsequently, the coach will be considered for reappointment every three years during the total probationary period of 12 years. Thus, the decision to terminate the employment of the coach can be made at the end of the third, sixth, ninth, or twelfth year if he or she does not meet the standards under the "Gestalt" assessment. Failure to receive a positive recommendation at any one of the three-year stages will result in a one-year terminal appointment.

---

* As used here, the "Gestalt" implies that the role of the coach is more than can be identified through an identification of specific responsibilities. It is the whole that transcends the particulars.

3. *Consideration for a "Senior Contract"*: The major evaluation of the coach will be conducted at the end of the twelfth year of employment at the college. The one exception to this would be that a coach could be given a period of credit time for previous collegiate coaching experience at another institution. The twelfth year is the pivotal year in the evaluation process because at this time a decision will be made as to whether the coach will be offered a "Senior Contract." This is a four-year "rolling contract," awarded with the understanding that it will be renewed unless there are valid reasons for terminating the employment. As examples, the decision may be made to drop the sport program, or the coach may decide to give up coaching. The latter would be particularly critical if other legitimate responsibilities were not available for assignment within the department. Evidence of overall coaching effectiveness, professional growth, and contribution to the college community will be major factors in considering the coach for a "Senior Contract."

4. *Modified Faculty Status:* Coaches will have faculty status except for the opportunity to obtain tenure in most cases. The exception to the latter would be in cases where the coach has achieved what Cady terms as "Artist-In-Residence" status. That is, a coach with a long and distinguished record of achievement and service to the college might be awarded tenure as a special recognition. However, coaches would have academic rank with full privileges, including comparable salaries, fringe benefits, the right to vote at faculty meetings, and the right to serve on significant college committees. Depending on the specific faculty structure of the college, the initial appointment could be made at the rank of lecturer or instructor with eligibility for appointment to assistant professor at the end of the sixth year and to associate professor when a "Senior Contract" is awarded. Appointment of a coach to full professor rank would only be made in those exceptional cases where tenure is awarded.

CONCLUSION

There are no simple answers to the question about how coaches should be evaluated. Only this is clear: the coach has to be evaluated in a way that is consistent with the objectives of the athletic program. The high school coach cannot be evaluated on the same basis as a Division IA university coach. A Division III coach is in a different situation yet, although his or her role is more like that of the high school coach. The one difference is that the teaching function is often the top priority for the high school coach. He or she is a teacher-coach whereas the roles are reversed at the college Division III level. Emphasis on the performance standard of winning also increases significantly as one moves from the high school to the Division III college level and then to the Division I level.

REFERENCES

Anderson, E. W. "The Faculty-Coach." *Journal of Physical Education, Recreation, & Dance,* August 1985, pp. 16–18.

Appenzeller, Herbert, and C. T. Ross. *Sport and the Courts: Physical Education and Sports Law Quarterly,* Vol. 7, No. 3, Summer 1986, p. 5.

Barol, Bill. "The Threat to College Teaching." *Newsweek on Campus,* October 1983.

Cady, Edwin H. *The Big Game: College Sports and American Life.* Knoxville: University of Tennessee Press, 1978.

Chapter 6

Part-Time Coaches

One of the more significant changes in staffing athletic programs during the last 25 years has been the use of part-time coaches at both the high school and collegiate levels. Obviously, the decision to employ part-time coaches is first and foremost based on financial considerations. The passage of Title IX in 1972 brought about the need to employ additional coaches for women's sports. At the same time, athletic departments were facing inflation and reduced budgets. The relative significance of salaries in budget allocations made the move toward part-time coaches a logical necessity in many situations.

Before proceeding with an analysis of the problem, it is important to note that there are various categories of part-time coaches. They share only the common characteristics of reduced responsibility and compensation. Part-time coaches range all the way from the volunteer coach, who is in an auxiliary role on a temporary basis without compensation (more likely to be found at the high school level), to the coach with a primary appointment as a coach with some other additional responsibility in the athletic department. In between those two extreme, part-time positions, one also finds other part-time coaches who may be (1) college athletic administrators who also coach, (2) university graduate assistants, (3) high school classroom teachers who also coach, (4) personnel outside the school or college who have other occupations, or (5) interns.

THE PROBLEM

When one considers the range of part-time coaching categories, it becomes difficult to generalize about the nature of any problem. However, the following dimensions of an overall problem may be evident whenever a coach is a part-time volunteer or employed for less than half time as a coach.

1. Part-time coaches may have less loyalty toward the athletic department and less respect and concern for the facilities and equipment.

2. They have a reduced time commitment to the overall program. This becomes critical in terms of carrying out certain administrative duties necessary in the management of a team (recruiting, scouting, or budget management). Of course one can also find part-time coaches who actually serve full time. That poses a problem for the coach and may lead to low morale.

3. They often have a poor understanding of the institution's position on the role of athletics and athletic policies and procedures.

4. Due to reduced availability, a severe lack of communication may develop between part-time coaches and administrators. However, part-time employment is rarely the only reason for communication problems.

5. Frequently, a part-time coach may be restricted in terms of overall qualifications. He or she may have the necessary athletic background but lack knowledge in the areas of health, athletic training, and safety.

6. Athletes may feel neglected by a part-time coach. The coach may not be available for advice and counseling mentor.

7. There tends to be a high turnover rate among part-time coaches. When the coach remains for only one season, one year, or a couple of years, there is a lack of stability on the team and a lack of continuity in the athletic department.

8. Administrators may feel less need to evaluate part-time coaches due to the turnover rate. This may lead to a general reduction in standards.

9. Due to the general lack of availability, part-time coaches are not easily integrated or accepted by the full-time staff.

THE ISSUE

When viewed from the standpoint of the administration, there are advantages as well as disadvantages in employing part-time coaches. Many of the arguments for and against are similar to those involving part-time faculty generally.

Arguments for Part-Time Coaches

1. From the viewpoint of administrators, the number-one reason to employ part-time coaches is finances. The move to part-time coaches, like part-time faculty, results from cost-benefit analysis. Faculty in a school or college and coaches within an athletic department represent the principal labor cost.

2. Part-time coaches offer greater flexibility in determining workloads and making personnel decisions such as reappointments and terminations.

3. In many situations, a part-time coach makes the difference between retaining or dropping a sport program. This may well be one of the principal arguments for employing a part-time coach.

4. Part-time coaching often provides a young person an entry into coaching or the sport management field. This sort of advantage is particularly manifested in graduate assistants and interns. Regardless of the particular form, the idea of the apprentice is very much related to part-time coaching.

5. Major studies on part-time faculty point to certain motivational advantages in part-time teaching. "Studies suggest that most individuals teach part-time for positive rather than negative reasons and find a relatively high level of job satisfaction. . . . Studies argue that part-timers experience lesser levels of dissatisfaction because their reasons for teaching are clearly defined" (Lightman et al. pp. 55, 56). There is reason to believe that those two conclusions regarding part-time teaching would apply to part-time coaching as well.

6. Part-time coaches are particularly useful as assistant coaches in many situations. As a matter of fact, if it were not for some part-time coaches, there would not be assistants. The full-time head coach would likely view the part-time assistant with considerable favor.

Arguments against Part-Time Coaches

1. Various dimensions of the problem with part-time coaches were identified earlier. Collectively these are the principal arguments against em-

ploying part-time coaches. However, the opposition to part-time coaching also comes from other directions.

2. From a conceptual or symbolic standpoint, the employment of part-time coaches (particularly as head coaches) reflects negatively on the central role of coaches in an athletic department. (This is related to the opposition to part-time faculty in light of the central role of faculty in institutions of higher education.) In essence, the part-time coach can be viewed merely as "cheap labor."

3. The gradual move toward more part-time coaches can be seen as a threat to job security in the athletic department. Beyond that, there may be an overall threat to professional advancement due to the general reduction in full-time positions at all institutions.

4. Perhaps the strongest argument against the employment of part-time coaches is that there tends to be a lack of continuity or stability in the sport program. This is particularly true when there is a part-time head coach. The athlete is most affected. He or she may feel that the sport lacks administrative support.

5. Continued and increased use of part-time coaches tends to reduce the salary base within the department. The general disparity between full- and part-time salaries is well documented. Once the shift is made to part-time positions, it is difficult to get funding for restoration of full-time positions. There is typically an erosion of the salary structure.

Sources for Part-Time Coaches

Each part-time coach presents his or her unique set of circumstances in terms of being integrated into the total structure of the department. When an athletic director has a need to make a part-time coaching appointment, what options are typically available? At the college level, at least five sources can be identified.

1. *Faculty members outside the athletic department*: These are faculty members who have primary appointments in one of the academic departments in the college or university. A history professor may have an extensive background in tennis, or a geology professor may have been a competitive skier in his or her college days. There can be considerable advantage in this kind of part-time coaching appointment. Communication may be facilitated because the faculty member has an office on campus and is likely to be more accessible to students and administrators. The fact that these individuals are already faculty members helps to alleviate the problem of orientation to the institution.

2. *Individuals from the community at large:* This category of part-time coach is not otherwise employed by the college or university, but lives nearby. The individual may have previous coaching experience or may be a former, accomplished athlete who seeks involvement with coaching. The appeal of this source of appointment is the potentially rich source of talent "out there." Limitations could include lack of orientation to the college, availability, communication, and program stability. However, if the individual is well established in the community, this type of appointment may offer some stability to the program because he or she is more likely to remain in that setting.

3. *Graduate student assistants:* Within universities this tends to be one of the more common and acceptable sources for part-time coaches, particularly as assistant coaches. Obviously, this source is limited to institutions offering graduate programs. There are distinct advantages to this form of appointment. From the perspective of the graduate student this is *the* means of entry into the coaching field and of gaining the necessary experience. This may also be the principal means for the student to finance a graduate education. For the department, the graduate assistant offers a rich source of enthusiasm and energy. The limitations to this source of appointment are the relative lack of experience of these part-time coaches and the constant turnover. This does not facilitate program continuity or stability. Also, the source is "cheap labor," which has certain negative aspects.

4. *Student interns:* This source may well offer the greatest potential for future development. By and large, the interns are college graduates who have been college athletes and are now enrolled in graduate programs (usually sport management) at other institutions. The internship is necessary to fulfill master's degree requirements. The advantages and disadvantages of this form of part-time coaching are similar to those involving graduate assistants. However, certain additional advantages can be noted. Employment of student interns is not restricted to universities that offer graduate programs. As a matter of fact, the intern may be contracted from an academic program in sport management to any collegiate athletic program. The internship gives the student contacts with at least one other institution and often provides a means of entry into the field. Furthermore, the internship often combines administrative and coaching requirements. This provides training in the complete functioning of an athletic department.

5. *Administrative staff members in the athletic department:* These are part-time coaches who hold other primary assignments within the athletic department. This could be an assistant athletic director who also coaches the golf team or the ticket manager who coaches the tennis team. The clear advantage is that the individual is likely to understand department and

institution policies and procedures. The most apparent disadvantage may be time commitment to the sport and the team. Depending on the particular arrangement, there could also be problems with administrative partiality and relationships with other coaches.

In the spring of 1985, 21 of 50 randomly selected Division I institutions responded to a survey regarding the sources for part-time coaches and the reasons for this type of employment. Sources for part-time coaches are described in Table 6.1.

Information from this limited survey pointed to the following conclusions and reactions to part-time coaching.

1. Among the available sources, athletic directors rely most heavily on employing part-time coaches (both head coaches and assistant coaches) from the community at large. Athletic directors who responded said they preferred these individuals because they did not have conflicting commitments to the athletic department and were more stable. The athletic directors also noted a "larger opportunity for unearthing new talent." One institution indicated its best type of part-time coach was the independent businessman or woman who did not wish and could not afford to be full time. The next most popular choice is the young, "just give me an opportunity to get started" type, who understands that the position is, and will remain, part time.

2. The survey showed that a relatively large number of faculty members were part-time head coaches. The athletic directors often preferred this source of part-time coaching because the faculty tended to have organizational skills that allowed accommodations for reduced time. In general, the athletic directors also felt these faculty coaches were more "in

Table 6.1
Sources of Part-Time Coaches

Source	Part-Time Head Coaches	Part-Time Assistant Coaches
1. Faculty member outside the department	19	9
2. From the community (outside the college)	41	95
3. Student assistants	4	48
4. Interns	0	18
5. Athletic staff (administrative)	0	4
TOTALS	64	174

tune" with college philosophies, more reliable, and easily accessible. On the other hand, the available pool of faculty for part-time coaching positions tends to be very limited.

3. Students and interns are employed rather extensively as assistant coaches. The basic reasons are in line with the advantages of these sources noted earlier. However, the survey revealed that work/study funds, as a supplement to regular budget allocations, were another significant reason for employing students as assistant coaches.

DIFFERENCES BETWEEN THE HIGH SCHOOL AND COLLEGE SITUATIONS

Thus far we have considered the subject of part-time coaches in general. However, it is important to note that the utilization of coaches is really quite different between the high school and college levels.

Most high school coaches are part-time coaches. In many cases they are physical education or classroom teachers who also coach one or more sports. Sometimes (increasingly so in recent years) they are people who hold other jobs in the community (mailcarriers, sales persons, etc.). The need for policies providing for effective supervision may be particularly critical for the latter group.

Within college and university athletic departments the situation involving part-time coaches has to be contrasted with full-time coaches. This is particularly true at the large university level. Most of the part-time coaches are young graduate assistants or interns who seek part-time coaching to "get their foot in the door." In actuality, they are full-time coaches with part-time pay. It is a form of apprenticeship. Today this is the way in which most of these coaches eventually obtain full-time positions. From there they go on to become full-time assistants with full pay, and then some become head coaches at some point. Policies to facilitate development are particularly needed for this group of coaches.

POLICIES AND POLICY GUIDELINES FOR PART-TIME COLLEGE COACHES

Due to the fact that part-time coaching is now an integral component of the collegiate athletic structure, it seems desirable and necessary to facilitate the integration of these coaches. The following policies and guidelines are suggested for college athletic departments in general, recognizing that there will always be variations from institution to institution due to local and periodic exigencies.

1. *Policy: Selecting and Hiring*

   The screening process for selecting and hiring part-time coaches will be comparable to that employed in obtaining full-time staff members.

   Guidelines

   a. General, minimum qualifications for all coaches should include: (1) a thorough knowledge of the sport, including the rules and regulations; (2) a demonstrated ability to teach the skills for the sport; (3) a knowledge of safety procedures; and (4) the ability to relate to athletes, coaching peers, and administrators.

   b. Whenever possible, part-time staff members should be selected from among individuals who are already established in the community. This enhances the possibility of having stability in the program. It would be highly preferable to recruit qualified coaches from other academic departments because these individuals already understand the institution orientation.

   c. When considering individuals for assistant coaching positions, particular attention should be given to internship candidates who generally comprise an available pool of young, enthusiastic coaches with great potential for development.

2. *Policy: Orientation*

   Due to the general problem of communication, special attention will be given to a structured orientation program for all coaches, including those who are employed part time.

   Guidelines

   a. All new coaches should have a thorough tour of the athletic facilities as well as other college facilities that may be utilized.

   b. Information about institutional philosophy and athletic policies should be presented.

   c. Each coach should receive written copies of departmental procedures (e.g., team travel arrangements, equipment distribution, and laundry procedures) as well as applicable conference rules and regulations.

   d. Whenever possible, another coach should be appointed to serve as a mentor to the new coach, particularly for the part-time employee.

   e. In an early meeting between the athletic director and the new coach, the responsibilities and expectations for the position should be clearly defined, preferably in a written agreement, signed by both parties.

3. *Policy: Communication*

Specific steps will be taken to facilitate continued communication with and among coaches in the department.

Guidelines

a. Every coach would be expected to attend a regularly scheduled departmental meeting on at least a monthly basis.

b. The athletic director should follow an open-door policy on an available basis.

4. *Policy: Evaluation*

The basic format for coaches' evaluations will be management by objectives.

Guidelines

a. Evaluation should be based on performance standards determined by the athletic director and coach prior to the sport season.

b. In a regularly scheduled meeting between the athletic director and coach, the performance of the latter will be assessed at the conclusion of each season and prior to any reappointment.

c. Any extenuating circumstances or unexpected variables should be taken into account when making the evaluation.

d. The evaluation meeting should be followed by some form of formal, written evaluation signed by both the athletic director and coach. It becomes a part of the employee's record.

5. *Policy: Reward*

The department will take steps to recognize that reward for professional accomplishments involves more than pay increases and promotions.

Guidelines

a. Part-time coaches should be invited to all departmental functions that are attended by full-time staff members.

b. Whenever possible, there should be an annual dinner or luncheon to recognize part-time coaches.

c. The sports information director should be alerted to the need to publicize the achievements and success of part-time coaches.

d. Part-time coaches should also have the opportunity and encouragement to grow professionally through attendance at workshops, clinics, and other professional meetings.

e. The athletic director should attend selected home games and practices for all coaches, including those who are employed part-time.

REFERENCE

Lightman, M., E. Katz, and D. D. Helly. "The Literature on Part-Time Faculty." *Thought & Action: The NEA Higher Education Journal*, Vol. 3, No. 1, Spring 1987.

Chapter 7

Title IX and Gender Equity

No person in the United States shall, on the basis of sex, be excluded from participation in, be denied the benefits of, or be subjected to discrimination under any education program or activity receiving Federal financial assistance. (Section 901 (a) of Title IX of the Education Amendments of 1972)

On July 1, 1972, the above provision of Title IX became Public Law 92–318. In the ensuing years this legislation has had a major impact on athletic programs for women in the United States. However, the effect was not immediate. There have been various stages of development as well as one temporary setback.

As noted above, athletic programs are not specifically referred to under the original Title IX legislation. As a matter of fact, there was strong opposition to the inclusion of athletics due to the revenue producing element in certain intercollegiate athletic programs. As a result of the efforts of the Department of Health, Education, and Welfare (HEW), athletics was included in 1974 under the contention that sports and physical education are integral parts of education. The Education Amendments of 1974 specifically stated that:

The Secretary (of HEW) shall prepare and publish . . . proposed regulations implementing the provision of Title IX of the Education Amendments of 1972 relating to the prohibition of sex discrimination in Federally-assisted education programs which shall include with respect to intercollegiate athletic activities reasonable provisions considering the nature of particular sports.

These regulations to implement Title IX became effective July 21, 1975. Institutions were required to complete self evaluations of their programs and activities by July 21, 1976. However, they had an "adjustment period" until July 21, 1978, to bring their athletic programs fully in line with the regulation. Also, the Title IX regulation did not mandate a specific process for evaluating or modifying athletic programs to ensure equal opportunity for women.

In response to criticism about the vagueness of the regulations, the Office for Civil Rights (under HEW) finally released the policy interpretation for Title IX in December 1979. The amended Title IX regulation provided a broad mandate for equal athletic opportunity for both sexes. In determining whether equal opportunities are available, the Office for Civil Rights would consider the following 11 factors:

1. *Selecting Sports and Levels of Competition*: Should be based on effectively accommodating the interests and abilities of both sexes.

2. *Equipment and Supplies*: There should not be widely different standards for purchasing or replacing equipment.

3. *Games and Practice Times*: Should be centralized in one institutional office, and women's teams and men's teams should have equal opportunity for the most "desirable" times.

4. *Travel and Per Diem Allowance*: Buses, cars, and other vehicles should be equally available to women's and men's teams. Also, female and male athletes should receive the same per diem allowances for lodging, meals, and other expenses.

5. *Coaching and Academic Tutoring*: The number of coaches per team must be determined by objective standards, such as the nature of the sports or the number of participants in a particular athletic program. Also, institutions must ensure that female and male athletes have equal access to academic tutoring or other academic services.

6. *Locker Rooms, Practice, and Competitive Facilities*: All facilities must generally be available without discrimination on the basis of sex. Locker

rooms, toilets, showers, and other facilities available to women and men must be comparable.

7. *Medical and Training Facilities and Services*: An institution should have a single standard for both female and male athletes regarding the type, nature, and extent of medical, health, and training facilities. This also includes equal and comprehensive medical insurance programs.

8. *Housing and Dining Facilities and Services*: If those available to female athletes are not comparable to those available to male athletes, an institution is required to evaluate how equal opportunity can best be provided.

9. *Publicity*: Institutions are expected to centralize and closely coordinate the publicity and/or public relations services to ensure that women's teams and men's teams have equal access to these services.

10. *Assignment and Compensation of Coaches*: A number of other prior federal and state regulations prohibits any employment discrimination on the basis of sex. In terms of this section of Title IX, an important point was that the three-year "adjustment period" that applied to athletic programs affecting students did not apply to employment discrimination. At the outset, the assignment and compensation of coaches was one of the factors that would be considered in determining whether or not an institution is providing female and male athletes with overall equal opportunity.

11. *Financial Aid to Athletes: Athletic Scholarships*: Essentially, an institution must provide reasonable opportunities for such awards for members of each sex in proportion to the number of students of each sex participating in intercollegiate athletics. (*Note*: From the beginning this was one of the principal "bones of contention" as to whether or not football should be exempt from this equation.)

Basically, the Title IX legislation was first and foremost aimed at providing equal opportunity for both women and men. At the same time it recognized certain exceptions that related to the very nature of athletics programs. The policy interpretation outlined certain nondiscriminating factors that were to be considered when assessing Title IX compliance. These included differences that may result from the unique nature of particular sports, special circumstances of a temporary nature, the need for greater funding for crowd control at more popular athletic events, and differences that have not yet been remedied but that an institution is voluntarily working to correct. In the area of compensation for men's and women's coaches, OCR also took into account experience, nature of duties, number of assistants supervised, number of participants, and level of competition.

THE GROVE CITY COLLEGE CASE

A decade of progress in achieving equality between men's and women's athletics was slowed by the Grove City College case, legally identified as *Grove City College v. Bell*. On February 24, 1984, the U.S. Supreme Court ruled that Title IX was intended to apply only to education "programs and activities that receive direct federal aid."

The case began in 1977 when Grove City College, a small, Presbyterian, liberal arts college in Pennsylvania, filed suit in district court against HEW. Terrel H. Bell was the commissioner of education in HEW at that time; thus, the suit was officially identified as *Grove City College v. Bell*.

HEW had requested that the college execute an "assurance of compliance" with Title IX as a recipient of federal funds. The college argued that it should not be subject to Title IX because it received no direct federal funds. However, the college did enroll students who received funds under Pell Grants. The college had no control over such disbursements. When Grove City College refused to execute the assurance of compliance, HEW initiated proceedings that declared the college and its students ineligible to receive Pell Grants. The college and four of its students then filed the suit in district court. The court ruled that the student aid could not be terminated even though the Pell Grants constituted federal financial aid. Later, the decision was reversed by a court of appeals, which held that indirect as well as direct aid was covered under Title IX. However, in the 1984 decision, the Supreme Court disagreed, ruling that only those programs *directly* receiving federal funds were subject to the regulation of Title IX. This meant that at Grove City College, Title IX jurisdiction was limited to the financial aid office.

Overall, the Grove City College case pointed to a major issue regarding Title IX, namely, the scope of the legislation and the programs to which it is applicable. Debate over the issue centered largely on the programmatic approach vs. the institutional approach. In other words, does Title IX apply only to specific departments that receive direct funding or to any department in an institution that benefits from federal assistance? In the Grove City case, the Supreme

Court decision was for the former, that Title IX is program-specific. Consequently, receipt of federal money by one college department does not mean that the entire institution has to comply.

In the final analysis, neither side really won. Grove City College was hurt by losing the Pell Grants for its students. (The college responded with private financial aid through what it called the Student Freedom Fund.) The college was also sensitive about a common perception that it discriminated against women in its athletic programs. It should be noted that from the beginning the intent of Grove City College was to resist federal interference, not to denounce equal opportunity for women.

Following the Grove City case there were mixed but generally pessimistic reactions concerning the future prospects for further development of women's sport programs. Some of the women leaders in the sport field expressed the idea that the implementation of Title IX had taken two steps forward and one step back. There was consensus that the Office of Civil Rights' enforcement mechanism had been severely weakened by Grove City. Supporters of Title IX were waiting for the U.S. Congress to make the next move to put teeth into the legislation.

THE CIVIL RIGHTS RESTORATION ACT OF 1987

A few years later, congressional action regarding Title IX did materialize. Leaders in women's sport programs joined a broad coalition of civil rights groups in lobbying for passage of the Civil Rights Restoration Act of 1987. This was passed by Congress on March 22, 1988, over President Reagan's veto. The Restoration Act was passed to restore the institution-wide requirement of Title IX. It essentially reversed the Grove City decision by providing that any institution receiving federal funding must not discriminate in any program offered by that institution. As a result, the focus of litigation shifted from the scope of Title IX jurisdiction to the real issue of determining whether sex discrimination exists and finding ways to correct it. By enacting the statute, Congress focused on correcting the programs of gender-based inequity.

Even though the Civil Rights Restoration Act restored the original power to Title IX, this does not mean that all institutions can be found to be in compliance, even today. In the years since 1988, various female athletes have brought law suits against their respective institutions, alleging violations of Title IX. At least two of those cases, Brown University and Louisiana State University, are worthy of special note. The Brown case was the first to be heard, but an appeals process extended the case. Therefore, we will begin with the LSU lawsuit and decision.

THE LSU CASE

The Louisiana State case began in March 1994. Three female students sued the university, demanding that the athletic department start women's soccer by that fall and softball by the following spring. The women argued that the institution had failed to follow through on organizing the teams it said it planned to start. In 1995, two other female students who played softball filed separate suits against the university. The lawsuits were considered and tried together in the fall of 1995. Federal District Judge Rebecca Doherty found in favor of the two softball players in the latter suit, but dropped the claims of the soccer players in the earlier suit. More significant was Judge Doherty's interpretation regarding Title IX compliance. To be judged in compliance with Title IX, a collegiate athletic program must meet at least one of three criteria or "prongs": (1) proportionally having the same percentage of female athletes and female undergraduates, (2) a continuing history of expanding athletic opportunities for women, or (3) demonstrating success in meeting the "interests and abilities" of female students.

Much of the on-going debate about Title IX has centered on the first prong—the "substantial proportionality" provision. There have been different legal interpretations. In the LSU case, Judge Doherty rejected this particular test. "To accept proportionality as a measure of equity," she wrote, "one must assume that interest and ability to participate in sports is equal between all men and women on all campuses. She said there is no basis for such an assumption" (Blum, p. A33).

In spite of her interpretation, Judge Doherty did find Louisiana State in violation of Title IX with reference to the softball players. Her decision was based on the conclusion that LSU failed to provide adequate opportunities for female athletes due to "arrogant ignorance" and an outdated view of women and athletes. Nevertheless, the proportionality part of her decision triggered much speculation about the future in determining Title IX compliance.

As one might expect, Judge Doherty's decision was greeted with much enthusiasm by those who opposed earlier court decisions. Some felt that the LSU decision could stop the trend to cut men's sport programs when college athletic programs face sex-discrimination complaints. Lawyers for Brown University were also encouraged that the LSU case might be a factor in reversing a lower-court ruling that Brown violated Title IX in 1991 when it cut financial support for two women's sports teams. However, as we shall see, that was not the case with the Brown decision.

THE BROWN UNIVERSITY CASE

In April 1991 Brown University cut its women's gymnastics and volleyball teams as well as its men's golf and water-polo teams. Amy Cohen, a gymnast, and eight other female athletes filed suit against the university in *Cohen v. Brown University* in April 1992.

At the time of the cuts, Brown had one of the largest athletic programs in the country with 16 women's sports. However, the expansion of its women's sport programs had occurred basically in the years soon after 1971 when Pembroke College, an all-female institution, was merged with Brown, which was then all-male. When the cuts were made in 1991, roughly 40 percent of the university's athletes were women, compared with more than 50 percent women among all the undergraduates at Brown. Thus, when the case was initially heard in late 1994, U.S. District Court Judge Raymond Pettine ruled that the university had not met the "proportionality" prong (as explained under the LSU case). He also ruled that Brown did not meet the second (a continuing history of expanding athletic opportunities for women) and third (demonstrated success in meeting the "interests and abilities" of female students) criteria. The judge noted that the sports expansion for women had ceased and then had been reversed by the cuts. Again, the judge ruled that Brown could not claim to have satisfied the interests and abilities of its female students when it had cut successful women's teams.

Brown University appealed the decision to the next level. In November 1996, in a 2 to 1 decision, the U.S. Court of Appeals for the First Circuit said that Brown had failed to meet any of the three criteria that determine a college's compliance with Title IX. In its appeal, Brown had presented a battery of statistics in an attempt to demonstrate that their support for women's sports was commensurate with the abilities and interests of its female students. The university argued that the women did not have the same degree of interest in athletics as the men did. Senior Circuit Judge Hugh Bownes and his colleague, Norman Stahl, viewed this argument with "great suspicion." Bownes wrote:

There exists the danger that, rather than providing a true measure of women's interest in sports, statistical evidence purporting to reflect women's interest instead provides only a measure of the very discrimination that is, and has been, the basis for women's lack of opportunity to participate in sports. (Naughton and Srisavasdi, p. A41)

However, the two appeals court judges did not support the compliance plan set forth by Judge Pettine in the initial 1994 decision. Brown University had drawn up a plan that called for capping the size of men's teams and creating junior-varsity squads in existing women's sports. The judge decided that the Brown plan was not drawn up in good faith. His plan called for the university to provide funds for four new women's teams.

The appeals court contended that a university could come into compliance with Title IX either by reducing athletic opportunities for men or by abandoning its athletic program. However, in his dissenting opinion, Chief Judge Juan Torruella wrote that the appeals court should have reconsidered Judge Pettine's ruling altogether. He felt that the other appeal judges had put the power to control athletics in the hands of the women and not the institution. He also expressed that this was an exception to almost every other aspect of college life.

As one might expect, the reactions to the appeals court decision were mixed. Leaders in women's athletics were elated. Christine Grant, director of women's athletics at the University of Iowa, was one who expressed satisfaction with the Brown decision. On the other hand, many of those in men's athletics were apprehensive and concerned, particularly about the proportionality provision. Particular concern was expressed by the coaches in those sports that generally produce no revenue and yet drive up the number of female athletes a university needs to achieve proportionality. Sports such as baseball, wrestling, gymnastics, cross country, and lacrosse fall into this category.

In February 1997 Brown University asked the U.S. Supreme Court to hear the case in an effort to overturn the decision made by the U.S. Court of Appeals for the First District. The university argued that a key federal anti-bias law had been interpreted incorrectly by the appeals court. According to Brown officials, the appeals court erroneously assumed that women were as interested in playing sports as men were. However, supporters of the appeals court decision argued that Brown failed to take into consideration that opportunity drives interest. If women are given the opportunity, they are just as interested in sports as are the men.

On April 21, 1997, the U.S. Supreme Court announced that it would not hear the appeal. This elated the advocates for female athletes who viewed the *Cohen vs. Brown* case as the most significant legal challenge involving Title IX compliance.

THE FINANCIAL FACTOR

When all is said and done, financial considerations continue to loom as the overriding factor in institutional attempts at achieving gender equity. In that regard, football remains at the center of the debate. Major college football coaches have seen their number of scholarships reduced from 120 to 85. Women's sports leaders have suggested that the number should be reduced much further, even to 55. At the same time they would give the other 30 scholarships to women's sports.

On the other side, football coaches and some athletic directors argue that football provides most of the revenue to support women's sports and other men's sports. At one I-A football school, the athletic director estimated that football provides 85 percent of the revenue in the budget. Yet, the financial value of a football program is also subject to debate, with conflicting, available data. In 1995, the *USA Today* reported that 80 percent of the 668 collegiate football programs lose money. On the other hand, some of the more successful I-A programs show considerable profits through football. The NCAA published a financial survey in 1994. Among the 85 responding I-A members, 67 percent averaged profits of $3.9 million in 1993.

Another most significant financial consideration is the expenditures for men's and women's athletic programs. The Equity in Athletics Disclosure Act of 1995 became effective on October 1, 1996. Under that federal law, the athletic expenditures must be made public. After the new law went into effect, the *Chronicle of Higher Education* collected data from the Big 12 Conference for the academic year 1995–1996. Following are selected data from the total report:

1. The proportion of athletes at Oklahoma State was 76 percent men and 24 percent women. At the University of Kansas it was 53 percent men and 47 percent women.

2. Eighty-two percent of the recruiting expenses at Oklahoma State were for men. At the University of Oklahoma the figure was 78 percent for men. By contrast the proportion at Texas A&M was 62 percent to 38 percent.

3. At Kansas State University, men received 73 percent of the sports-related financial aid.

4. At Kansas State, the head coaches' average salary for men's teams was $99,146. For women's teams it was $44,972.

5. Only the University of Kansas had more than 200 female athletes. Each of the Big 12 institutions had at least 215 male athletes.

6. All of the institutions reported a loss on women's athletics—most lost more than $1.7 million for the year.

7. Only Iowa State reported a loss on men's athletics—roughly $44,000 for the year. (Naughton and Srisivasdi, pp. A45–46)

In the final analysis, the complications involving the financial factor in gender-equity relate primarily to the differences between revenue and nonrevenue sports. What can or should be done to change the situation? Differences of opinion are most apparent.

John Weistart, a law professor at Duke University, notes the "upward spiral" or "athletic arms race" in revenue sports. He says "you have to spend more to win more." He proposes that the NCAA cap expenditures on revenue producing sports.

"Many college presidents are asking the question, How do we tame this beast?" Mr. Weistart says. "Yes, it is generating a lot of revenue—but it is consuming most of that money."

But Mr. Neinas, of the College Football Association, says capping expenditures would decrease revenues and thereby harm women's sports.

Besides, he says, it is not college coaches but college presidents who are intent on maximizing football revenues. "The football coaches voted unanimously against having a Big 12 Conference playoff," he says. "But the presidents voted it in." (Naughton and Srisivasdi, p. A46)

The financial impact of Title IX has also been a factor in the decision to drop certain men's sports, as noted earlier. In January 1997, Michigan State University demoted the men's lacrosse team and the men's fencing team to club status. The same month, Syracuse

University cut wrestling and men's gymnastics. Officials at both institutions said that Title IX had prompted these decisions. They were not alone in having to make such difficult decisions. In 1982 there were 59 intercollegiate, men's gymnastics teams, contrasted with 27 in 1997. Similarly, more than one-third of the universities dropped their wrestling teams during that period. Chancellor Kenneth A. Shaw at Syracuse University described their situation, which was much like that faced by other Division I institutions:

Chancellor Shaw says he and other officials reached their decision to add softball while cutting wrestling and men's gymnastics, by asking themselves a series of questions:

"Should we provide more opportunity for female students now and in the future? The answer to that is yes," he says.

"The next question: Is there somebody out there who is going to provide the money for the expansion? The answer to that was, that somebody was the athletics department. It is a self-sustaining enterprise. We were not going to raise tuition to pay for this. We were not going to take it out of the library or out of salaries.

"Then we asked whether we should cut everybody a little bit. We said no. If we do that, than everybody is watered down. And it is not fair to a student-athlete not to be able to compete on a national level.

"Do you cut your big spenders (football and men's basketball)? Well they provide all the money for our program. If you do that, you are not going to have a winning tradition, and you are not going to raise the revenue you need."

Cutting wrestling and gymnastics will save the university roughly $700,000, Dr. Shaw says. "It is one of those unfortunate things you hate to do." (Naughton and Srisivasdi, pp. A39–40)

TWENTY-FIVE YEARS LATER

A quarter of a century has elapsed since Title IX was passed. One wonders how much progress has been made in achieving gender equity in college athletics over that span of time. In March 1997, the *USA Today* published the results of a survey of 303 NCAA Division I schools. Only two schools were excluded: The Citadel and Virginia Military Institute. Data were available for all 303 schools because the Equity in Athletics Disclosure Act now requires colleges to make participation and financial data public. Following are excerpts from this data for the 1995–1996 academic year.

- The number of female athletes in Division I schools is up 22 percent since 1992.

- The number of women participating in college sports has increased fourfold since 1972.

- Almost two-thirds of the athletes at Division I schools are men, while more than half of the undergraduates at these schools are women.

- Female athletes came within five percentage points of women enrolled at only 9 percent of the Division I schools. In Division 1–A these schools were Air Force, Navy, Army, Georgia Tech, Washington State, Virginia Tech, Kansas, Utah, and Washington.

- The money spent on men's sports is three times that spent on women's sports.

- Female athletes receive 25 percent of the operating budget, 27 percent of the funds for recruiting, and 38 percent of the scholarship money.

- Women's soccer is the big winner in terms of growth in women's sports. For example, the number of NCAA Division I teams in women's soccer has increased from 22 in 1982 to 211 in 1997.

- Only 51 Division I schools offer women's crew. However, at those schools the women's participation figures tend to be much higher. The average size of a team is 52. Several schools have squads twice that size.

- In 1995–1996, men's sports teams generated $13 for every $1 for women. Women's sports brought in only 2 percent of the total revenue. On the other hand, football brought in 37 percent of the total.

- Division I schools had $2 billion in expenses for that year—43 percent went to men's programs and 20 percent to the women's programs.

- The football revenue in Division I schools was $653 million. However, 25 schools accounted for half of that revenue.

- Ninety-eight percent of the coaches of men's teams are men. By contrast, 50 percent of the coaches of women's teams are men.

- In 1995–1996 there were 78 1-AAA schools (those with basketball but no football)—the gender gap tends to be less in those schools. For example, women's teams received 49 percent of the athletic scholarships, 37 percent of the athletic recruiting funds, and 38 percent of the total athletic operating budget.

- The percentage of 1-AAA schools that meets the proportionality test is twice that of 1-A schools—16 percent vs. 8 percent. (*USA Today*, March 3, 1997, pp. 1C, 4C; March 4, 1997, pp. 1C, 6C; March 5, 1997, p. 9C)

CONCLUSION

It is safe to say that Title IX has had a tremendous impact on the recent history of college athletics. The number of women's teams and participants has increased significantly. Nevertheless, a gender gap is still apparent, at least in certain situations. The above data more or less tell the story. When it comes to finances, women are still well behind the men in support for their teams. However, the variance between larger and smaller schools should also be noted. What will the future bring? As difficult as it is to speculate, one would have to think that the gender gap will continue to be reduced. Financial equity, at least in Division I, is another matter. Football and men's basketball represent a unique dimension in college athletics.

REFERENCES

Albert, Tanya. "1-AAA Women Get Bigger Cut of Budget." *USA Today*, March 5, 1997, p. 9C.

Becker, Debbie, and Tom Witosky. "Number of Women Playing Sports Rises." *USA Today*, March 4, 1997, pp. 1C, 6C.

Blum, Debra E. "Measuring Equity." *Chronicle of Higher Education*, January 26, 1996, pp. A33–A34.

Brady, Erik, and Tom Witosky. "Title IX Improves Women's Participation." *USA Today*, March 3, 1997, pp. 1C, 4C.

Naughton, Jim. "Appeals Court Affirms Ruling That Cohen v. Brown Discriminated Against Female Athletes." *Chronicle of Higher Education*, November 29, 1996, pp. A41–A44.

Naughton, Jim. "More Colleges Cut Men's Teams to Shift Money to Women's Athletics." *Chronicle of Higher Education*, February 21, 1997, pp. A39–A40.

Naughton, Jim, and Rachanee Srisavasdi. "Data on Funds for Men's and Women's Sports Become Available as New Law Takes Effect." *Chronicle of Higher Education*, October 25, 1996, pp. A45–A46.

Chapter 8

Free Agency in Professional Sport

The profitability of a professional sport team depends largely on the difference between the expense of player salaries and the revenues from gate receipts and television contracts. Ironically, free agency can affect either side of that equation. On the negative side for an owner's profit, free agency has historically resulted in rapid salary increases for players. As one example, the average salary in Major League Baseball increased from $29,303 in 1970 to $1,028,000 in 1992. On the other hand, the positive effect is that free agency can make a team more talented and more competitive, resulting in higher gate receipts and better bargaining power for local television contracts. There is also a third consideration, which is subject to debate. That is whether free agency improves or damages the competitive balance of the league. Some would argue that parity has a positive effect on television ratings and thus increases national broadcast revenues.

Aside from any financial considerations, there is a basic argument in favor of free agency. This is the idea that to limit player movement is unique to the sports industry. Why should players have to play where they don't want to when other employees get to choose their place of employment whenever they are offered a position? In any other industry, an employee is free to move from company to company, accepting the most attractive offer, location, working environment, colleagues, or whatever is most important to him or her.

Those who would restrict free agency agree that it is unique to the sports industry, but they also point out the equally unique characteristics of the employment situation in the sport leagues. To begin with, the players' associations do not have the homogeneous qualities of industrial bargaining units due to contrasting interests of superstars and marginal players. The relatively short careers and high turnover rate of players are also unique to the sports industry. Finally, there are varying degrees of revenue sharing in each of the professional sport leagues. This practice is certainly not characteristic of other industries.

Another argument against free agency is that given complete freedom, players will flock to the most desirable cities with large television markets. For example, New York, Los Angeles, Chicago, and Boston might be able to attract all the top players. Franchises in these cities would dominate the league, and games would become less competitive with the outcomes relatively predictable. As a result, attendance for the weaker teams would suffer, television ratings and hence broadcast revenues would decrease, and the economic stability of the entire league would be in question.

There are also those who oppose free agency on the grounds that it works against fan loyalty. Owners and players might agree with that, but the bottom line is that each side must look out for its own best interests. There are fans who are upset when one or more of their favorite players leaves to play with another team. Yet, there may be many more fans who are first and foremost concerned with winning. They can identify with and root for any player who performs well for the team.

Regardless of the arguments for and against free agency, there is no doubt that this is one of the driving forces in professional sport today. It is also fairly safe to say that free agency, in one form or another, is not about to disappear in the near future. To better understand the current situation involving free agency it might be useful to begin by looking at how each of the major professional sport leagues has arrived at this point. Major league baseball is a good place to begin because of the long tradition of that sport.

MAJOR LEAGUE BASEBALL

The efforts to restrict player movement in baseball can be traced back to 1879 when the National League (formed in 1876) secretly established a "player reservation rule" to cope with the financial consequences of unrestricted competition.

Under this collusive agreement, exclusive property rights to five players (about one-half of the roster) were assigned to each club. Clubs were forbidden to compete for the contracts of the reserved players; players who jumped their contracts were blacklisted, and clubs that employed such players were boycotted. Reserved players thus either played on the club that held their reservation rights or they did not play professional baseball at all. (Scully, p. 2)

By 1883, this practice was extended to protect the entire player roster under what was later called the reserve clause. This reserve clause was part of the Standard Player Contract. If the player refused to sign the contract for the next playing season, the club was empowered to unilaterally renew and extend the Standard Player Contract for one year under the same terms and conditions including salary. The player was effectively bound to one team for his entire career, but he could also be sold or traded, and he would be bound to his new club.

A lawsuit was the logical means to challenge this collusive practice in baseball. However, it was not until 1922 that the reserve clause reached the Supreme Court of the United States. In the *Federal Baseball Club of Baltimore v. National League*, the court established an antitrust exemption unique only to baseball. Following that decision there were two other major legal challenges to the reserve clause: *Toolson v. New York Yankees* in 1953 and *Flood v. Kuhn* in 1972. In the latter case, the majority opinion concluded that the exemption of the baseball reserve clause was an aberration. However, Justice Blackman, who wrote the majority opinion, concluded that it was an aberration that had lasted five decades. Therefore, previous decisions should be upheld.

In 1974, Jim "Catfish" Hunter became the first free agent in baseball. However, this was accomplished through arbitration, not through any legal action involving the reserve clause. Earlier, the Major League Baseball Players Association had negotiated a provision for grievance arbitration in the collective bargaining agreement with the leagues. Hunter was the first player to take advantage of that provision. He had an agreement with Oakland A's owner, Charles Finley, that half of his 1974 salary would be placed into an insurance trust. Later, Finley reneged on the agreement, and Hunter filed a grievance. The arbitrator ruled in favor of Hunter and declared him a free agent. Although this case did not deal directly with the reserve clause, it established a precedent for players' rights in contract negotiations.

In 1975, another arbitration decision dealt directly with the reserve clause. The case involved pitchers Andy Messersmith of the Los Angeles Dodgers and Dave McNally of the Montreal Expos. The Players Association claimed that since the two players had completed the renewal year of their contracts, they were no longer under contract to their clubs. Accordingly, they should be free to negotiate with any other club in the league. The arbitrator once again agreed with the players, declaring them free agents. In essence, this decision had the effect of eliminating the reserve system.

During the 1976 negotiations for a new collective bargaining agreement, the owners were intent on regaining some limitation on the players' right to free agency. Successful in that regard, the owners obtained a provision that players must have had at least six years of major league service before they could become free agents. There would also be a re-entry draft for free agents, with teams choosing in reverse order of team standings. Under this system, free agents were not high in numbers, but their salaries escalated rapidly. Free agents did not necessarily have to sign with another team to get a higher salary. In some cases, owners were willing to match other offers. Compensation for losing a free agent was an extra choice in the amateur draft.

In the 1982 collective bargaining agreement, the free agency system remained essentially the same; however, the compensation rules were altered. Free agents were ranked as either "A" or "B" players, depending on performance. If a team signed an "A" free agent (ranked in the top 20 percent at his position), compensation was an unprotected roster player from the compensation pool and an extra choice in the amateur draft for the team losing the player. Twenty-four players from each team were protected. If a team signed a "B" free agent (ranked in the top 21–30 percent at his position), the former team got two extra choices in the amateur draft. Players who had gone through the re-entry draft before or had 12 years experience were exempt from the rankings.

The 1982 rules were complex and, at times, inequitable. As a result the 1985 negotiations lifted almost all of the impediments for a player to become a free agent after six years. The re-entry draft was eliminated. If a club wanted to retain the rights to a player, it was required to offer the player final-offer arbitration by December 7. Compensation was only required if the player left before December 7 or if final-offer arbitration was offered and the player refused.

The 1989 collective bargaining agreement left the free agency structure relatively unchanged. All players with six or more seasons of service are eligible to become a free agent at the completion of their contract. Eligible players can declare free agency within 15 days after the conclusion of the World Series. In order to keep the player, the club must agree to final-offer salary arbitration before December 7. If they do not do so, they lose all rights to that player until May 1. If the player accepts arbitration, he must do so before December 19. If he refuses, the club has no rights to him from January 8 to May 1. If a club loses a free agent to another team, compensation is only given if arbitration was offered before December 7 or if the player signed with another team prior to December 7.

NATIONAL FOOTBALL LEAGUE

Prior to 1976, the National Football League also operated under the reserve system. The player contract contained a reserve clause that bound the player to the same club for his entire career unless he was traded, sold, or waived. As a result, the players had little bargaining power. There were no choices for the players, and there was rarely movement of players between teams.

Some of the earlier challenges to the reserve system were relatively unsuccessful. In 1957, through *Radovich v. NFL*, the court did establish the principle that the NFL falls under the coverage of antitrust law. However, the court also found for the NFL, as the defendant, and awarded no damages to the player. In 1962, R. C. Owens of the San Francisco 49ers played out his option and signed with the Baltimore Colts. Although this move was encouraging to the players, the owners quickly established the Rozelle Rule. When a player became a free agent and signed with a new team, the NFL Commissioner, Pete Rozelle, was permitted to award compensation in the form of players, draft choices, money, or any combination thereof to the former team. Due to the uncertainty of what they might lose, teams were very reluctant to sign free agents. Consequently, from 1963 through 1967, only four players played out their options and signed with new teams.

In 1976 the NFL players took further legal action to gain more freedom of movement from team to team. John Mackey of the Baltimore Colts, in *Mackey v. NFL*, argued that the Rozelle Rule violated the Sherman Antitrust Act by denying players the opportunity to contract freely for their services. The court agreed, finding the rule to be an unreasonable restraint of trade because it acted as a prohibitive deterrent to player movement in the NFL. As a result of this decision, players were free agents after the option year of their contract, and there was no compensation penalty to the signing club.

During the 1977 negotiations for a new contract, the NFL Players Union bargained away their rights in order to gain other concessions from management. The result was the establishment of the Right of First Refusal/Compensation (RFR/C) system. If a player received an offer from another club, his club had the opportunity to exercise its right of first refusal or receive compensation. Draft choice compensation for free agents was a function of the salary and the years of experience of the player signed. The same provisions, with a modified compensation table, were also included in the 1982 collective bargaining agreement.

In 1987, several players challenged the legality of the Right of Refusal/Compensation system in *Powell v. NFL*. At the same time, the players association was refusing to meet with the NFL to bargain over a new agreement. Later the district court ruled that an impasse had occurred in the negotiations. After this impasse decision, the NFL presented two new free agency plans to the union. Plan A called for a continuation of the RFR/C system with some minimal enhancements to nonsalary benefits. Plan B slashed the benefits but granted free agency to a limited number of players. Each club was allowed to protect 37 players, and these players were still subject to the RFR/C system. The union rejected both plans, but the NFL unilaterally implemented Plan B on February 1, 1989.

Later that year the players decided to give up their right to collectively bargain with the NFL and decertify the union. Their status was changed from a labor union to a professional association. This cleared the way for the players to challenge the system embodied under Plan B. Under that plan the restricted players received virtually no offers, and they lost a substantial portion of their nonsalary benefits. Furthermore, unrestricted back ups, free to market their services to the highest bidder, were often being paid more than starters at the same position. In April 1990 several players led by Freeman McNeil filed suit arguing that Plan B was a violation of antitrust law.

In 1992, the court ruled that Plan B was an illegal restraint of trade, and that the NFL must develop a less restrictive system. Subsequently, players with four years of service or less with expired contracts are restricted free agents. They are subject to the RFR/C system in which the compensation is much less prohibitive. Players with five or more years of service and expired contracts are unrestricted free agents and are not subject to compensation. An exception is that each team can designate one "franchise" player who is protected and tied to the club for the life of his contract. He is guaranteed to be paid either 120 percent of his previous year's salary or the average salary of the top five players at his position within the league, whichever is greater. Another initial exception involved "transitional players." Each team was allowed to protect two players under this category in 1993 and one in 1995. They were subject to the right of first refusal system and had to be offered at least the average salary of the top ten players at their position. Transitional players ceased to exist in 1995. There is also an effort to somewhat control salaries. If player salaries add up to 67 percent of the league's "designated gross revenue," a salary cap of 64 percent of gross revenue is placed into effect the next year. The cap is lifted once salaries fall below a certain level.

NATIONAL BASKETBALL ASSOCIATION

Prior to 1975 the NBA players were subject to the same type of reserve clause found in the other professional sports. However, in 1975 a group of players led by Oscar Robertson of the Milwaukee Bucks charged that the reserve clause was a violation of the Sherman Antitrust Act. In *Robertson v. NBA*, they argued that the reserve clause was a conspiracy in restraint of trade. The players alleged that if a player refused to sign with the same team year after year and sought to negotiate with another team, he would be subject to a boycott or blacklisting. In addition, the offending team was subject to penalty by the league. The players also sought to prevent the NBA-ABA merger, which could eliminate what little competition existed for players' services. In 1975, the court did find the reserve system to be a per se violation of the Sherman Act. Also the court stated that the merger would have the effect of restraining trade by eliminating competition between leagues for players.

As a result of the Robertson case, the owners and players negotiated a new free agency system in the 1976 collective bargaining agreement. There was a right of first refusal and a compensation system. During the 1978–1979 season a controversy arose over the compensation system. Morris Webster of Seattle signed as a free agent with the New York Knicks. Commissioner Larry O'Brien awarded Seattle a first round draft choice and $450,000 as compensation. As a result of the effect of such compensation on the market for free agents, the players association appealed the decision to federal court. The court ruled that the O'Brien decision should be overturned, and that compensation should not be as much a penalty for signing a free agent as it should be reimbursement for the loss of a player. Subsequently, the compensation system was eliminated after the 1980–1981 season.

In 1988, the right of first refusal provision was modified at the bargaining table. From that point on there were two types of players—restricted and unrestricted free agents. Unrestricted free agents are players with four or more years of service. These players are free to negotiate with any team and are subject to no restrictions or compensation. Restricted free agents (those with less than four years of service in the NBA) are subject to the right of first refusal if they agree to a one-time extension of the first player contract.

NATIONAL HOCKEY LEAGUE

As with the other major professional sport leagues, there was no free agency in the National Hockey League for many years. The change came with the establishment of the World Hockey Association in 1972. As a result of litigation involving players jumping from the NHL to the WHA, the NHL unilaterally adopted a policy of retaining players for only one year beyond the expiration of their contract. In 1975 the policy was incorporated into the collective bargaining agreement.

A compensation system was established within the 1975 agreement. When a player signed with another club, the two clubs had to agree on compensation. If they could not agree, the dispute was submitted to final-offer arbitration, where the arbitrator had to choose one side without amendment. Due to the uncertainty of compensation, there was relatively little movement of players. Nevertheless, there was an advantage over the NFL's Rozelle Rule. A neutral arbitrator made the decision, not a league official.

In 1982 union and management decided on a system wherein the compensation was definite. The compensation was based on the salary of the player involved. For example, if the player's salary was over $200,000, there were two choices for compensation: two first round draft choices or a player from the new club with four players protected, including the player signed. A player over 33 years of age could change teams without the compensation requirement. A player under the age of 24 or who had less than five years of service in the league was subject to the 1975 system of teams agreeing on compensation or going to final-offer arbitration. As a result of this 1982 agreement, there were no upper-level players who changed clubs.

Three groups of players were defined in the 1986 negotiations: (1) players who at the expiration of their contract have neither reached 24 years of age nor played five years of professional hockey—subject to the same right of first refusal and compensation system as before. If the clubs could not agree on compensation, the dispute was submitted to final-offer arbitration; (2) players whose contracts expired after having reached age 24 or having played five years as a professional—subject to the same right of first refusal compensation system as in 1982, with the salary amounts modified; (3) players whose contracts had expired after having reached age 31 could change teams without the compensation requirement—which was lowered from the age of 33 in the 1982 agreement. As a result of the 1986 agreement, the players still did not move freely.

In 1992, the NHL players went on strike, with free agency being one of the major issues. As a result, the league was forced to make some concessions. However, the three groups of players in the 1986 agreement still existed. Further modification was made in 1995 when a new agreement established three groups of unrestricted free agents and three groups of restricted free agents. Of particular note are the players with fewer than three years of professional experience. A player in that group has no right of free agency except if he does not receive a "qualifying offer" from the club to whom he was last under contract. Although the current system is somewhat less restrictive, there is relatively little player movement. Consequently, the salaries continue to be relatively low compared to the other three major professional sport leagues.

CONCLUSION

As noted earlier, whether or not there will be free agency in professional sport is now a moot question. The only remaining question is how free is free, or what are the limits of free agency? Differences among the sport leagues will continue to exist. This is primarily due to the fact that no two sports are the same. There are variables related to relationships between union and management, player positions, and potential of one or a few players to dominate a team or league. The best-known factor is that policies regarding free agency will be made at the collective bargaining table.

Another remaining question is how far salaries will continue to escalate as a result of free agency. Is there a limit beyond which salaries cannot get any higher? To date it would appear that the limit is only that which owners are able and willing to pay.

REFERENCE

Scully, Gerald W. *The Business of Major League Baseball.* Chicago: University of Chicago Press, 1989.

Part II

Program

Chapter 9

Dropping and Adding College Sport Programs

One of the more difficult decisions to be made by a college athletic director involves the dropping or adding of sports. Of the two, the former is particularly difficult. Yet, every year athletic departments throughout the nation are forced to eliminate sports from their programs.

This matter is a vivid example of the need to manage change. The environment surrounding college sport is constantly changing. Economic conditions, legal requirements, and NCAA regulations have all changed rapidly in recent years. The difference between an effective manager and an ineffective one is often seen in the ability to manage change. The latter tends to manage reactively. Crisis management becomes the name of the game. In essence, situations are dealt with after they become problems.

Economic conditions are the principal factor in any decision to drop sports from all athletic programs. During the past 15 years, most of the sports dropped have been men's sports. By and large this is an economic decision resulting from the need to add women's sports to bring institutions in fuller compliance with the provisions of Title IX.

Gender equity has received renewed emphasis in recent years. The number of women's sport programs increased significantly in the 1970s and early 1980s. Then, there was a lull in terms of further progress in that regard. In March 1992, NCAA Executive Director Richard Schultz established a Gender Equity Task Force. This was in response to an NCAA gender equity study that revealed that 69.5 percent of the participants in intercollegiate athletics were men, while undergraduate enrollments were roughly evenly divided by sex. In August 1993, the task force issued its final report. One of the key guidelines in that report is as follows:

Institutions should support intercollegiate athletics participation opportunities for males and females in an equitable manner. The ultimate goal for each institution should be that the numbers of male and female athletes are substantially proportionate to their numbers in the institution's undergraduate student population. (*NCAA News*, August 4, 1993, p. 14)

Needless to say, there is basically one way institutions can reach this objective, and that is by adding more sports for female participants. In that line, the task force report also identified nine "emerging sports" for women that could be added in the effort to reach the objective.

In a time of steady, if not dwindling, economic resources, it is also obvious that something must go if there are additions to a program. Thus, the result in college athletics was to drop various nonrevenue sports for men. In the fall of 1994, several coaches associations in men's nonrevenue sports appealed to the U.S. Congress for assistance in their efforts to preserve their sports:

What the coaches associations seek is a hearing with officials from the U.S. Department of Education Office for Civil Rights, which investigates institutions to determine if adequate and equitable opportunities are present for women in athletics under Title IX guidelines. . . .

Perhaps no nonrevenue men's programs is at a more critical point than men's gymnastics, which is in danger of losing its NCAA championship because of a deficient number of institutions sponsoring the sport.

"That's really not fair in the atmosphere of college athletics today," said Roy Johnson, men's gymnastic coach at the University of Massachusetts at Amherst and president of the National Association of Collegiate Gymnastics Coaches (Men).

"I would hope (OCR) would look at developing a protected status for endangered sports," he said. The OCR has that ability. What has slowly happened is the elimination of men's [O]lympic sports. I think that is an unintended consequence of Title IX. . . .

Anne Goodman James, women's swimming coach at Northern Michigan University and president of the College Swimming Coaches Association of America, said that women athletics administrators and coaches of women's sports are just as concerned that men's nonrevenue sports are being eliminated in the name of gender equity. . . .

"We've got to ask institutions to do some creative thinking. Take a look first. Don't just drop the sport." (Mott, pp. 1, 21)

NCAA legislation regarding sports sponsorship has been another important factor in the decision to add or drop sports. Until 1986, Division I member institutions were required to sponsor a minimum of eight men's sport programs and three women's sport programs. During the 1984 NCAA Convention, the association voted to require Division I members to sponsor six women's sport teams by 1986 and eight by 1988. At the 1985 convention, this was further modified to require eight sports for women as well as men by 1986 for all Division I-A football playing institutions. In 1991, this was changed to seven and seven, effective September 1, 1994. Then in January 1994 there was yet another revision. At this writing, a Division I institution must sponsor at least seven men's sports and seven women's sports or six men's sports and eight women's sports.

All of the above considerations point to the fact that the adding and dropping of college sport programs is a volatile situation. Far too often, such decisions are made from a crisis basis. This is precisely why there is a need for policy development in this area.

THE ISSUE

A basic philosophical question beyond any legal requirement must be faced when an athletic department considers the addition or elimination of a sports program. Is it more desirable to strive for excellence in selected sports or to offer a more comprehensive and diversified program? One's initial response might be to wonder why this has to be an either-or consideration. Is it not possible to proceed from the assumption that a department should attempt to pursue excellence in all sports? The answer again is found in finances. If there are sufficient funds to do both, there will be no problem and no issue. However, most institutions are not in that kind of comfortable situation today. Basic choices about the direction of the total program have to be made.

The answer to the key question can be found by considering the objectives set forth for the athletic program. However they may be worded, the possible objectives essentially fall into one of the two categories: image objectives and educational objectives.

The image, status, or reputation objectives are first and foremost aimed at gaining external support for the institution even though the internal effects may also be extensive. Quite clearly, most Division I football and basketball powers operate from this stance. Just think of the visibility that basketball has provided for Villanova and Georgetown and that football has provided for Alabama and Oklahoma. Lacrosse, a so-called minor sport, has enhanced the image of Johns Hopkins. This kind of externally directed objective points to the choice of striving for excellence in selected sports.

The other category of objectives might be called educational. These are directed internally, aimed at broadening the educational opportunity through sport for the entire student body. The objectives proceed from the assumption that participation in a sport program is an integral part of the educational process. In contrast with the image category, the educational objectives require a more comprehensive and diversified program so that more students can benefit from the intercollegiate sport experience.

A survey of institutions throughout the country will reveal that a few are in the fortunate position of being able to pursue excellence in selected sports *and* offer a comprehensive program. However, a growing majority face decisions about dropping sport programs. In such cases, policy is needed to determine what should be dropped. Legislative requirements to add sports dictate the same need for established policy.

THE PROBLEM

The problem is particularly manifested when a decision is made to drop certain sports. Generally speaking, it is always easier to increase than it is to delete. The exception, of course, is that financial restraints may prohibit any additions. Nevertheless, once a program is in place it is a most sensitive matter to get it removed without offending parties with vested interests. Up front the problem in dropping a sport is acute with regard to the direct impact on athletes and coaches. Neither of those groups can be expected to be objective when a decision is made to drop their sport. Beyond that, the political ramifications involving the reactions of alumni, boosters, trustees, and various other supporters are almost certain to be extensive. As with the overall issue, the problem also points to the need for sound policy. There must be a basis on which to make and justify critical decisions. A consideration of criteria for adding, dropping, or retaining sports is a logical place to begin.

CRITERIA

The criteria actually provides the basis for policy development in this area. A criterion is a standard for correct judgment. As an administrator, how does one know whether he or she has made the correct decision? Furthermore, how can that decision be justified? The absence of criteria or questionable criteria will receive most of the criticism when a decision to add or drop a program is announced. Any sign of arbitrary decision making will prompt an outcry that will reflect poorly on the athletic department. Predetermined criteria should be used as the basis for any decision. Sound criteria, based on program objectives, will go a long way toward minimizing negative reactions and possible legal complications.

Following are criteria that might be used as a basis for policy development regarding the addition or deletion of sports. Except for the first, these are not necessarily listed in order of importance. The relative weight of the criteria will have to be determined within the context of the given institution. That is the first step in establishing policy.

1. *Legal Concerns:* One must start with this criterion. NCAA bylaws set forth sponsorship requirements regarding the minimum number of sports that must be offered for men and women. As noted earlier, this has been an important factor in many Division I sport additions in recent years. Both the bylaws and Title IX are aimed at promoting balanced programs for men and women. In terms of specific implementation, the ensuing becomes one of determining equity versus equality.

2. *Needs and Interests of the Students:* Ideally, this would rank as an important criterion for most institutions. However, it is perhaps the most elusive among the various standards. A form of market research can be done with the students viewed as the consumers of the athletic department's programs. Such research would include the use of surveys, informal feedback, and continuous observation.

3. *Current/Potential Cost/Success Ratio:* This is a complicated criterion that ranks near the top of the list for many institutions. Basically it involves an assessment of what has been achieved in relation to the funds spent on the program. Determination of success is a judgment call. Nevertheless, a .500 or better record over a five-year period is a place to begin. For conference schools, relative cost might be assessed within the budget range of conference competitors. Potential cost/success ratio is likely to be based on the current ratio unless there are significant changes that indicate a shift.

4. *Current/Potential Facilities:* Anyone close to a sport program knows that the quality of the facility is a significant factor in the success of the program. When it comes to adding or dropping sports, both the current and potential facility situations have to be taken into account. Several questions must be addressed. How do facilities compare with those of comparable institutions at the same level? What are the sub-par facilities? Is there adequate practice space? What are the possibilities for obtaining new facilities? Which sports have facilities that provide a special quality dimension to the total program? Which facilities are no longer adequate for use under current conditions?

5. *Current/Potential Staff Qualifications:* One has to assess the current staff profile. Are some of the coaches particularly well established in their present positions? In some institutions there may be a certain number of tenured coaches on the staff. In most cases it would probably make less sense to drop a sport that has a tenured coach. Based on comparable competition, what are the measures of relative success among the coaches on the staff? All other factors being equal, it is easier to drop a sport with a part-time coach. What are the financial limitations in adding new coaches to the staff? Are retirements anticipated in the near future?

6. *Regional and Climatic Considerations:* The decision to add or drop a sport can also be based on the region or climate in which the institution is located. The matter of regional popularity of certain sports should be taken into consideration. It would be unlikely for a college in the Baltimore or Long Island area to drop lacrosse. By the same token, a college in Minnesota or Massachusetts without an ice hockey program might well consider adding that sport. The climatic criterion extends beyond regional popularity. Spring sports such as baseball, softball, golf, and tennis have extensive national popularity. Yet, a decision to drop one or more of these sports could be based on the relatively short time available for the spring semester play in a northern region of the country.

7. *Current/Potential, Competitive Context:* What is the available competition in a given sport? Furthermore, what is the potential for adding new opponents? In some cases, these questions may also represent an impor-

tant criterion for decision making on the scope of the total program. Economic considerations obviously factor into this kind of assessment. Is there an adequate number of potential opponents within a reasonable distance from an economic perspective? Sports offered by other conference schools can be a significant factor. For example, if more than 50 percent of the conference schools offer a sport, this might provide a basis for retention or addition.

THE PROCESS

Well-established criteria provide the key to policy regarding changes in the total sport offerings. However, the process in implementing these changes may be just as important. Thus, once the criteria are established, there is also need for policy to control the process. In developing such policy, certain factors should be taken into account.

Most important, there is a need for political sensitivity. In particular, any decision to drop a sport program has either direct or indirect effects on a variety of interest groups, including athletes, coaches, parents, boosters, trustees, and administrators. Collegiate sport, particularly in the public sector, exists in a bureaucratic structure that tends to be hierarchically regulated. The built-in, top-down management style is a primary constraint. Policy must be directed accordingly. The athletic director is responsible for representing all parties from the trustees to the coaches and athletes. The process can be a political balancing act for the director.

Dropping or adding sports has implications for a program's public relations. How the media and the general public view the athletic department's actions can affect the overall program. Public opinion regarding athletics is a powerful force in educational institutions. It is important to maintain a positive image for the purposes of athletic recruitment, athletic contributions, and the overall welfare of the institution.

Special consideration should be given to those directly affected by the decision, specifically the coaches and athletes. Two-way communication is vital to the effectiveness of the process. Coaches and athletes should be informed in advance of the final decision, and they should have the opportunity to provide feedback. They should understand the precise reasons why their program is being dropped. There is something amiss when the coach and athletes of a sport to be dropped are the last to know. By that time, they really have no choice but to file their protests and ask for reconsideration. Whenever possible there should be ample time between the decision and implementation for those directly involved to make alternative plans.

CASE STUDY

Before proceeding to any recommended policies, we will consider the challenges faced by an institution that needed to change its sport offerings. Although this case took place in 1984, the issues, problems, and subsequent policy recommendations apply equally as well today. This is an actual case involving a state university in Division IAA with a student population of approximately 20,000. The name of the institution is disguised due to the public relations sensitivity of coping with this situation.

UNIVERSITY A

At the time the decision was made to drop seven sports from the program, this university offered 28 varsity sports. In 1981, University A was second among all NCAA Division I athletic programs in terms of the number of sports offered. Even with the drop from 28 to 21, the university would be offering a relatively high number of sports for a Division I program.

Much of the strong reaction against the decision can be attributed to the tradition and basic philosophy of the athletic department, which prided itself on offering a comprehensive and diversified program for the educational benefit of the student body at large. In addition to the extensive intercollegiate offerings, the intramural sport program was also sponsored by the athletic department. The athletic director stated that the plan to drop sports did not reflect a change in philosophy. He contended that they were simply taking into account the reality factor—the financial situation within the department.

Other people, especially coaches and athletes of the sports to be dropped, had different opinions. One of the coaches stated bluntly that a state university should not drop any sports. His opinion was supported by a journalist from his hometown newspaper who said that the department should be adding rather than dropping sports. "A state university should have everything under the sun," he stated.

On the other hand, a local sportswriters who regularly covered the university's athletic program, applauded the decision. His point was that a college athletic program in the 1980s cannot continue the "fun and games" of 20 years ago. From his perspective, the decision was overdue. The plan would put more emphasis on the revenue-producing sports and bring University A more in line with its competitors and other major college athletic programs.

The decision by University A's athletic department clearly reflects typical issues and problems. To better understand the reasons for the decision, it might be well to review the chronology of events leading to it.

A decline in University A's win-loss records was a primary cause of the problem. Not all of the teams were experiencing a decline in success level; in fact, several of the women's teams (particularly field hockey, soccer, and lacrosse) had been very successful. The problem was in the relative lack of success in the three sports that had the most spectator interest and media attention at University A: men's football, basketball, and lacrosse. The latter's popularity could be largely attributed to an exceptional record over a period of several years. However, in 1983 the lacrosse team's record fell to 5–10. Even more critical, the men's basketball team had experienced five consecutive 20-loss seasons prior to 1983. The culminating blow came in the fall of 1983 when the football team finished a poor season by losing to a state rival in the state capital city by a score of 31–14. That event caught the attention of trustees, legislators, and alumni.

During the winter of 1983–1984 a change in attitude about University A's athletic program was evident among people in power. The president informed the trustees that he was continuing to receive "expressions of unhappiness" about the status of the athletic program from alumni and legislators. He urged the trustees to find out more about the nature of the problems and determine how they might be solved.

Ironically, the athletic department had attempted to gain higher level support for needed athletic changes, but the efforts were met with apathy. Proposals for football tuition waivers and doming the stadium were not well received by the board of trustees. The latter proposal would have been particularly beneficial for the basketball program because it included provision for a major basketball arena within the stadium. Recruiting for basketball was limited by a sub-par facility. The tuition waiver proposal was predicated on the fact that the athletic scholarship fund was projected to run out of money by 1986.

Yet, in spite of the previous indifference, in the winter of 1983–1984 the trustees demanded that the athletic department develop a plan to make its major sports more competitive. What kind of options were available? One might suggest that an option would be to preserve the status quo, do nothing. Yet, that was hardly realistic under the circumstances. The more viable alternatives are described below.

1. *Obtain the necessary funds to keep all programs, while raising their competitive support.* This appeared to be the ideal solution, but according to the athletic director additional funding was unlikely from the possible sources. Student fees were already relatively high at the university, with a significant percentage going toward the support of the athletic program. Furthermore, there was considerable student reaction against recent fee hikes on the campus. Possible alumni/booster contributions merely reflected the old "chicken and the egg" problem. Contributions tend to increase as teams win more games. At any rate, University A could not look for much from this source at that time. Additional funding could not be anticipated from the state legislature through the trustees due to the need to upgrade other programs on campus. The trustees also had recently authorized an increase in athletic funding for improving the facilities. Another possibility might have been to charge admission to sport events in addition to football and basketball games. By and large this would again involve mostly students. Due to the relatively high student fee, this option was ruled out. Additional television revenue could not be projected. University A was a Division I AA football school. Television revenue had been very limited in the past. The Supreme Court television ruling against the NCAA further limited any potential in that regard. The long and short of the matter is that none of the possibilities was promising.

2. *Drop down to NCAA Division II or III.* From one standpoint this would appear to reduce the pressure to be more competitive. The university could certainly compete more successfully at a lower level. But University A was not only a large state university, it was the university of the state. It would be unthinkable for many people (trustees, alumni, boosters) to see University A drop out of Division I.

3. *Cut back administrative support.* Pursuit of this alternative would also conflict with the more competitive posture sought by the trustees. Ac-

cording to the athletic director, University A was already operating at the bare bones level. If anything, there was a need to add administrative staff members.

4. *Cut programs*. As noted in the introduction to this case study, this route was ultimately selected. Here also, options were available. The junior varsity programs could be dropped, but this option was eliminated from consideration due to the minimal savings involved. In 1982–1983, the athletic department sponsored 11 junior varsity programs at a cost of $14,000. Subsequently, the football and softball junior varsity programs were dropped, bringing the cost down to $8,000. In 1984 the number of student-athletes participating in junior varsity programs at University A was about 100. This left the choice of dropping varsity sport programs. Seven sports were selected for change from varsity to club or intramural status.

The Plan

Dropping the seven sports was only part of the total plan presented by administrators in the athletic department. The complete plan outlined below was predicated on a number of contingencies in the effort to alleviate mediocrity and bring the athletic program in line with the growing recognition of academic excellence at University A. Steps to be taken were the following:

1. Increase the number of tuition waivers.
2. Increase the football scholarships from 55 to 75.
3. Provide three levels of scholarship support with corresponding expectations.
4. Renovate the field house.
5. Build an ice skating facility.
6. Hire more staff: strength coach, academic adviser, fund-raising promoter, and more assistant coaches.
7. Reduce the number of sports offered.

The latter received the most attention because of its controversial implications, particularly in light of the other steps calling for increased expenditures. By moving the following sports from varsity to club status, $75,000 savings were projected: men's and women's golf, men's and women's tennis, men's and women's skiing, and wrestling. Critics readily pointed out that the figure represented a drop in the bucket in comparison to the funds to be spent in upgrading the major sport programs.

Criticism was also directed toward another part of the plan, that involving the administrative expectations for all sport programs with their corresponding scholarship support. In essence, three classes of athletic citizenship were established, and a fourth class was eliminated.

With regard to the seven sports dropped, one overriding theme should be noted—the relative lack of visibility in comparison with most of the other sports in the total athletic program. This was reflected in the restricted amount of media attention and spectator interest. Undoubtedly, this had an effect on the decision.

The Process

Having made the preliminary decision, the athletic administrators had to obtain approval and implement the plan. Implementation posed a new problem. Late in the winter of 1983–1984 the plan was presented to the athletic committee of the university's board of trustees and to the university's top administration. Both groups approved the plan. The coaches were the next to be informed in May 1984, when the athletic administration gave a lengthy presentation on the problem of the University A's mediocrity in athletics and the need to become more competitive. Then the coaches of the sports involved were informed that their sports were to be dropped to club status the following year.

There were two very different perspectives on the implications of that meeting. The athletic director stressed that the coaches were told that it was a "proposed" plan, not final at that time. By contrast, the coaches felt they received the word that their teams were "dead."

Following the coaches meeting the plan was announced to the news media. The timing of the announcement is also worth noting. In late May students at University A are either busy with final examinations or gone for the summer. The students' newspaper was not being published. This averted much conflict from students. However, the timing caused problems for incoming recruits and current team members of the sports to be dropped. Late May was too late to obtain scholarships from other institutions.

During the summer of 1984 there was a great deal of lobbying by the coaches, athletes, and other concerned parties. Numerous letters were received by the athletic department and the trustees of the university protesting the "change of status" plan. Pressure and concern over prior commitments and the need to give affected athletes time to relocate prompted the trustees to give the teams a temporary reprieve. The seven teams were reinstated for two years through a special trustee reserve fund. Reinstatement occurred in mid-August, soon before school was to start. The seven teams competed during the 1984–1985 academic year with terminal status in mind. The men's and women's teams of golf, tennis, and ski were scheduled to lose varsity status after their 1985–1986 seasons. Wrestling was terminated after the 1984–1985 season due to the expiration of the part-time coach's contract in June. In May 1985 students on campus, led by the athletes involved, made a further effort at reinstatement through a "save our sports" protest. However, the decision to drop the sports remained firm.

POLICY GUIDELINES

We have now arrived at the important question: What kind of policy can be developed by an athletic department to facilitate the decision-making process when there is a need to make a change in program offerings (i.e., sport sponsorship)? The case study should offer some testimony to the fact that the central issue can be resolved and the subsequent problem minimized if there is a policy in place when the decision has to be made. The case study also reveals the need for policy to guide the process.

The following points are not designed to be specific policy statements. Rather, they are guidelines for the development of policy within the context of a given athletic department. A particular policy can only be developed at the institutional level. The divergent nature of collegiate athletic programs precludes the possibility of national policy in this area:

1. There must be a strong correlation between the policy and the objectives of the athletic program. As noted earlier in this chapter, an institution basically has two choices when it comes to establishing objectives in sports programming. The sport programs are either educational in nature or they are externally directed at enhancing the image of the institution. A combination of objectives is possible when finances permit. However, most institutions will have to make a choice between a broader based program and one that is highly selective in sport offerings.

2. Definite criteria should be in place when the time comes to make a decision regarding the addition, retention, or deletion of sports. Problems are likely to occur if the criteria have to be determined at the time the decision is made or applied after the fact. The more effective policy provides a rank order listing of criteria to be considered. Legal concerns should be the number-one criterion for every college or university program. Beyond that, each institutional policy should provide a rank order identification among those possibilities described earlier:

   Current/potential, cost/success ratio

   Current/potential staff qualifications

   Regional and climatic considerations

   Current/potential, competitive context

3. A set procedure should be established for adding a sport to the intercollegiate athletic program. Once again, the specific policy to control that procedure will have to be determined within the context of the institutional structure. However, it is reasonable to expect that a sport would have met the test of being a successful club sport. The groups seeking varsity status for the sport would be required to submit a formal petition through the appropriate channels. In many institutions, the initial screening of petitions might be done by an athletic council or a similar body. A petition would include a detailed plan for implementation covering such matters as budget, facilities, competition, coaching staff, and participation base. Petitions would be considered in accordance with the pre-established criteria for determination of sport offerings.

4. A policy would also be needed to modify the procedure for adding a sport in those cases where legal requirements precipitate the addition. The NCAA legislation increasing the required minimum number of women's sports would be a prime example. In such cases, the policy might outline a procedure for soliciting petitions for varsity sport status.

5. Deletion of a sport should be controlled by a policy that sets forth the review process when an apparent need arises. In most cases the athletic director will initiate the recommendation for deletion. There should be a provision for requiring support for the recommendation. Whether the reasons are financial or based on other factors, the athletic director is most likely to have access to the necessary information. Those directly involved, particularly coaches, should have the opportunity to provide input early in the review process. Prior to submitting the recommendation through administrative channels, there should be a complete preliminary review by an appropriate advisory body, probably the athletic council in most institutions. At every step in the process, the recommendations should be assessed in accordance with the pre-established criteria for determination of sport offerings.

6. Whenever possible, there should also be a policy controlling the deletion of a sport through a phasing-out period. In most cases, this would likely be a one- or two-year extension period for any relocation of athletes and coaches. Provision must also be established for determining scholarship aid for athletes when a sport is dropped from the program.

CONCLUSION

The issue of dropping and adding sports will exist as long as there are collegiate athletic programs. This is one of the more difficult issues to be faced by an athletic director. It is important that athletic directors stand ready with the policy and competence to make the decision and carry it through in a professional manner. The initial key is the pre-established criteria for determination of the sports to be offered. Beyond that there is need for policy to control the process of change.

REFERENCES

"Gender-Equity Task Force Issues Its Final Verdict." *NCAA News*, August 4, 1993, p. 14.
Mott, Ronald D. "Men's Nonrevenue Coaches Take Case to Congress." *NCAA News*, October 24, 1994, pp. 1, 2.

Chapter 10

Promoting Nonrevenue Sports in the Colleges

Sport promotion on the collegiate level is a relatively new activity, having developed over roughly the past 20 years. Promotion includes the associated activities of marketing, fund raising, and merchandising. Don Canham, athletic director at the University of Michigan, was one of the first to recognize that sport promotion requires a multifarious approach. In addition to his efforts in enhancing football ticket sales in the 1970s, he also merchandised a variety of products identified with Michigan football. His success became a model for university athletic programs throughout the country.

Promotion of nonrevenue collegiate sports is an even more recent development. For purposes here, a nonrevenue sport is any sport that is not considered potentially profitable for the institution. There are no extensive gate receipts or television revenues, and the activity is not primarily aimed at spectator attendance and support. Basically, the nonrevenue sports are all sports other than football and men's basketball, with a few exceptions, such as ice hockey in Michigan, wrestling in Iowa, or baseball in Florida and Texas.

Much of the interest in promoting nonrevenue sports can be attributed to the expansion of women's athletics and the financial crunch that threatens the continued existence of a diversified sport program. Most women's sports are in the nonrevenue category, and men's nonrevenue sports have been caught in the squeeze between the women's expansion and the ever-growing popularity of revenue-producing sports.

THE ISSUE

The central question is this: Should an athletic department make a special effort to promote a nonrevenue sport? The rationale behind the promotion of a major revenue-producing sport is quite simple. The potential for significant financial support for the institution is great. But what is to be gained from promoting a nonrevenue sport? While the coach of any given sport might be interested in its promotion, the reasons for promotion are not always apparent from a departmental perspective. After all, there are repeated claims that sport programs should be offered purely in an educational context. What does that tell us about the desirability of making special efforts to promote nonrevenue sports?

Once a decision is made to promote nonrevenue sports, other questions also emerge. Which sports should be promoted? Does the department promote all sports, a selected few, or only one? Answers are likely to be dependent on a number of variables.

The overall consideration is the potential for development of various sports within the department. The status of facilities and staff, both present and planned, are principal determinates. The geographic location of the institution is also critical. For example, it is easy to see why Johns Hopkins University decided several years ago to promote lacrosse, and why efforts are made to promote women's basketball in Iowa. Another significant consideration is the competitive success of the various sports. Quite obviously, it is easier and more logical to promote sports that have proven records of success.

At least one other factor may influence a decision regarding the specific nature of promotion in the nonrevenue category. This revolves around the status of revenue-producing sports in the institution. It would be more difficult to promote a nonrevenue sport that is in direct competition with a major revenue producer at the same institution. This might explain why the University of Vermont chose to promote soccer where there is no intercollegiate football program.

THE PROBLEM

Deciding what to promote brings one to the problem: How can the promotion be most effectively accomplished? One way to solve the problem involves the use of management by objectives (MBO).

Deegan and Fritz (1975) identify three classes or categories of job-related goals or objectives: routine (regular), problem-solving, and innovative. Routine objectives are concerned with normal work output, and they are set forth to meet a standard. With a problem-solving objective, the current results are below par; the objective is aimed at finding a solution. An innovative objective involves something new, a change, with the intent of adding benefits (p. 160).

Any effort to promote a nonrevenue sport is both problem-solving and innovative in nature, particularly the latter. The very nature of a nonrevenue activity indicates that one is dealing with something that is not inherently promotional. Essentially, it is a new endeavor. However, at the same time, the promotion will not be easily accomplished.

Deegan and Fritz also identify nine steps in a problem-solving model:

1. Identify the problem area.
2. Determine the present unsatisfactory level.
3. Define a reasonable desired performance level.
4. Isolate the difference between the present and desired levels.
5. Brainstorm possible causes of the problem.
6. Decide which causes are the most crucial.
7. Identify alternative solutions.
8. Evaluate proposed solutions.
9. Make commitment to time and action plan. (pp. 197–198)

These steps will be applied in an analysis of a hypothetical analysis of a Division I institution's situation later in this chapter.

CASE STUDY: UNIVERSITY OF CONNECTICUT*

In 1969 when Coach Joe Morrone arrived at the University of Connecticut in Storrs, the soccer program existed in relative obscu-

---

*This case study is found in the first edition of this book, published in 1988. Since that time there have been many other changes in the University of Connecticut soccer program. Nevertheless, the principles of promoting any nonrevenue sport still apply.

rity. The schedule traditionally included the better teams in New England. However, in some 40 years of soccer at UCONN, the teams only had four or five years of significant success. No scholarships were offered to soccer players, and there was not an organized recruiting effort. Games were played in an open area without any bleachers. In Morrone's first year as coach, the team played on a field that was converted swampland. As the head coach, Morrone also found that he had to line the field. This was the status of soccer at UCONN in 1969.

Three basic choices were available to the coach. He could maintain the status quo by carrying out his coaching responsibilities without giving any special attention to promotion and development. This may well have been completely acceptable to the athletic administration at UCONN. They did not view the status of the soccer program as a particular problem. Soccer was not a priority, and there was no reason to consider promotion at that point. However, preservation of the status quo was unacceptable to Morrone.

To change the situation, he had a choice of two options. He could focus his efforts internally by working within the department and university structure to obtain support for better facilities, equipment, schedule, indoor and spring play, scholarships, and staff additions. Eventually, those developments materialized. But, Morrone basically chose a third action alternative—to embark on a long-term development program by working both internally and externally. Much of the external work helped in obtaining the internal support. External development included the formation and development of the Mansfield Youth Soccer Association, the Connecticut Junior Soccer Association, the Connecticut Soccer School, the Friends of UCONN Soccer Club, and the overall support to generate gate receipts.

Underlying all these public relations, promotional, and fundraising activities was the dual objective of developing soccer, in general, and UCONN soccer, in particular. Morrone realized that the soccer program would have to be built on a firm foundation to achieve a pattern of success, and that this would take time. The record shows that it took from 1969 until 1980 to establish a broad base of support. In essence, a nonrevenue sport became a revenue-producer through the promotional effort. The steps along the way are worthy of note.

1. In 1969 Morrone worked for and received an electric scoreboard and three rows of bleachers to accommodate spectators.

2. The Connecticut Junior Soccer Association was formed in 1970. This was accomplished through the combined effort of Morrone and Al Bell, who had previously organized a youth group of four teams in Hartford. Morrone recognized that the organization could improve soccer in the state, work as a potential feeder system to the UCONN soccer program, and develop spectator interest. He wrote the constitution and served as the association's first president for eight years.

3. The same year, 1970, Morrone also organized the Mansfield Youth Soccer Association. He enlisted sponsors for eight teams and worked with the recreation department to recruit parents of the participants as coaches. The teams played at the halftime of UCONN games. This resulted in more fans for UCONN soccer and contributed to goodwill in the community. This developing local support group included parents who were faculty at UCONN and business people in Storrs and Mansfield.

4. An indoor soccer tournament also was initiated by Morrone in 1970. This was the first of its kind in the nation, and subsequently it has developed into the largest. Beginning in 1981, Metropolitan Life Insurance Company agreed to sponsor the tournament. More than 50 different colleges have participated over the years, and since 1978 it has been a 32–team tournament. Tele-Media has also televised segments of the tournament in the local area. This has been another step toward increased visibility for the UCONN soccer program.

5. Spring practice, including some informal games with other colleges, was instituted in 1970.

6. Morrone began the Connecticut Soccer School in 1970. He brought in high school coaches to work at the school, which sought to improve the level of coaching, impart Morrone's philosophy of coaching, and add to the visibility of UCONN soccer. A recruiting benefit also developed. Camps were promoted through nationwide advertisements in all major soccer publications. Typically, only one-half of the campers were from Connecticut. Having campers and eventually players all over the country coincided with the UCONN schedule of intersectional games to promote a program with national scope.

7. Finally, Morrone's 1970 thrust at gaining external support for the program was manifested in the formation of the Friends of UCONN Soccer. As with most clubs of this type, the basic idea was to provide a link among former lettermen and other interested people to support the advancement of UCONN soccer. Initially the club was strictly a Morrone endeavor. Funds generated went through an account number in the

alumni association. Over the past several years the club has developed into a true "friends club," running independently of Coach Morrone's leadership. The club purchased video tape equipment (soccer was the first sport at UCONN to use video as a teaching tool and a recruiting aid) and office furniture, and laminated and mounted certificates for players awards. The club also hosts post-game dinners for both teams after Sunday games, conducts youth soccer games before and at halftime of most home games, sponsors raffles, and maintains a hospitality tent for fans during games. The club also covers the cost for the annual awards banquet, the printing of players' names on game shirts, rings for players who play in the "Senior Bowl," the stationery with UCONN soccer logo, and a newsletter, which is published four to six times per year.

8. In 1973 Morrone initiated the first intersectional soccer game in New England. St. Louis University, a perennial national power, came to Storrs to play UCONN. Since then, UCONN has scheduled intersectional games each season. Objectives of this schedule are to improve player performance through a stronger schedule, give UCONN national visibility, and to gain more consideration in the voting weekly polls and in the tournament selection at the end of the season.

9. Through the efforts of Morrone, a fence was constructed around the game field in 1976. This gave UCONN the capability to charge for attendance. Initially only intersectional games required a paid admission, and the receipts were used to pay guarantees to visiting teams. The next step was to charge for adult admission for all games. From there the move was to eventually charge all fans for all games. Paid admission has developed to a point when UCONN has gone from general admission to reserved sections to having reserved seats. The combination of the fence and admission charges appears to have helped boost the budget allocation for soccer. For example, one plane trip per year was authorized for the soccer team. Trips were made to Texas in 1983, South Carolina in 1984, and Indiana in 1985.

10. The first scholarship for soccer was offered in 1976. By 1985 the number of scholarships for the soccer program was increased to eight.

11. Although earlier there were various modified forms of a game program, the UCONN soccer program came out with its first bonafide printed game program in 1977. Costs, which have risen considerably in recent years, are largely covered by program advertisements.

12. ESPN televised five UCONN soccer games on a national basis in 1981.

13. Also in 1981, UCONN hired a full-time assistant soccer coach and a full-time secretary for the soccer program.

14. Revenue from gate receipts, parking, and concessions totaled over $100,000 in 1981.

15. To avoid scheduling conflicts with football, the weekend soccer games were moved to Sundays beginning in 1982.

16. In 1984, the UCONN soccer team played their first home game away from home—the New Britain game. This game, played on a weekday, drew 6,200 spectators.

17. All home and away games for soccer are now broadcast on the UCONN radio station.

The action alternative pursued by Coach Joe Morrone at the University of Connecticut is a vivid example of how a nonrevenue sport can be promoted. What can one conclude from this case? First, careful planning is necessary to employ a promotional strategy. To achieve any degree of success takes time, and there are many building blocks along the way. Second, staffing is a crucial factor in the decision to promote a nonrevenue sport. That is not to say that the University of Connecticut necessarily hired Coach Morrone with the promotional potential in mind. Nevertheless, it is very clear from this case that the role of the coach is pivotal if a nonrevenue sport is to be promoted. Third, real promotion takes place through persistence, patience, and a long-term developmental strategy. The chronology of events related to the UCONN soccer program is testimony to that fact. Finally, building a broad base of support through a solid public relations effort is integral in its success. UCONN soccer would not be at its present level without the support of the larger community. Tables 10.1, 10.2, and 10.3 are partial indicators of the degree of success in promoting soccer at the University of Connecticut.

SUGGESTED POLICIES FOR A DIVISION I INSTITUTION

Following the outline and guidelines for the Deegan-Fritz model, we can hypothesize the particulars in problem solving for a Division I institution and arrive at policies. To a certain extent, these policies may also be applicable for Division II and III institutions. However, in most cases the potential for significant promotion is restricted to Division I programs and efforts in that regard are more consistent with the revenue-producing thrust.

Table 10.1
Comparisons—Season Records and Tournaments

Year	Wins	Losses	Ties	Tournament Appearance
Pre-Morrone				
1962–1968	37	44	5	None
Morrone Era				
1969–1972	21	32	3	None
1973–1976	65	11	3	Four NCAA appearances
1977	9	11	1	None
1978–1981	79	16	4	Four NCAA appearances 1981 National Champions
1982–1983	31	12	8	NCAA Final Four twice
1984	14	9	1	NCAA appearance

1. *Problem Area:* The athletic department is dissatisfied with the current level of support for its nonrevenue sports.

2. *Present Unsatisfactory Level:* The lack of general support is manifested in low student participation, limited spectator appeal, and little news media coverage. Due to budgetary restrictions, the department is in a position wherein it may be forced to drop some of the nonrevenue sports due to unfavorable comparisons with other (more lucrative) sports. Part of the problem is that the developing women's sports programs have received relatively little attention from students, faculty, administrators, alumni, and the media.

3. *Reasonable Desired Level:* The department desires to retain its present level of offering 21 intercollegiate sports (12 for men and nine for women). There is a particular need to provide greater visibility for developing women's sports. However, at the same time, the promotional effort should be extended to all the nonrevenue sports, with emphasis on one or two sports that show promise for national recognition.

4. *Difference between Present and Desired Level—The Problem*: By and large the promotional effort to date has been restricted to the revenue-producing sports (men's football and basketball). Any promotion in the nonrevenue area has been more incidental than by design.

5. *Possible Causes*:
   - unfavorable comparison with popular, spectator, revenue-producing sports
   - administrative apathy in the nonrevenue area

Table 10.2
Player and Coach Recognition

Player Recognition:	
Professional Players:	16 Players
Hermann Trophy (Nation's Top Player):	One player (1980)
All American Players:	Five players (two times)
	Four players (once)
Senior Bowl (Top seniors in nation; game began in 1972):	Eleven players
All New England:	One player (four times)
	Four players (three times)
	Eight players (two times)
	Ten players (once)
All NEISL:	One player (four times)
	Five players (five times)
	Seven players (two times)
	Eleven players (once)
Coach's Recognition:	1980 NSCAA New England Coach of the Year
	1980 and 1981 Coach of the Year

- student apathy in the nonrevenue area
- athletic staff apathy in the nonrevenue area
- general lack of competitive success in the nonrevenue sports
- lack of staff orientation toward promotion
- qualifications of the coaches
- environmental restrictions (facilities)
- general apathy toward the women's sports
- lack of alumni support
- insufficient news media coverage

6. *Most Likely Causes*:
    - unfavorable comparison with popular, spectator, revenue-producing sports
    - administrative apathy in the nonrevenue area
    - qualifications of the coaches

Table 10.3
Attendance Records

Year	Number of Games	Total Home Attendance	Avg. Home Attendance
1981	18	53,900	4,146
1982	15	64,320	4,288
1983	17	64,535	3,796
1984	16	58,160	3,635
Attendance—Leading NCAA Soccer Playing Schools—1984			
School		Avg. Home Attd.	NCAA 2nd Round Attd.
Connecticut		3,635	6,948
Indiana		2,200	2,500
Duke		2,000	NA
Penn State		1,720	NA
San Francisco		1,350	NA
Fairleigh Dickinson		1,200	4,010
Columbia		1,000	1,900
Clemson		842	2,177
St. Louis		775	1,500
Virginia		750	1,855
UCLA		500	1,500
Note: Figures supplied by respective schools.			

In this hypothetical situation, we conclude that the above three causes of the problem are the most crucial because the other possible causes can ultimately be attributed to one or more of these three. The unfavorable comparison with the popular, spectator, revenue-producing sports is the overriding consideration. Consequently, any promotion of a nonrevenue sport will require a special effort. However, the record also shows that some athletic administrators are also more generally inclined toward promotion than others, and that coaches also vary considerably in the willingness to promote. In most cases, apathy on the part of students, alumni, and staff may be attributed to attitudes and actions of administrators and/or coaches. The same can be said for any general lack of competitive success. There may be a certain amount of inherent apathy toward the developing women's sports, but their situation is not that different from those of the other, nonrevenue sports. The facilities may be different from those of the other, nonrevenue sports. The facilities may also be sub-par in some cases, but that brings one back to the lack of administrative support. If facility improvement is not possible, the need to drop the sport may be justified. Any deficiency in media coverage may ultimately be attributed to all of the foregoing considerations. Reporters clearly reflect the level of the promotional effort.

7. *Alternative Solutions and Evaluation*:

a. *Reducing the emphasis on the revenue-producing sport.* This is not one of the better solutions, either from a cost or feasibility standpoint. It is doubtful whether this could be accomplished without losing considerable alumni support and having a negative effect on the image of the institution. Furthermore, the nonrevenue sports are largely financed from sports that produce revenue. Any reduction in revenue-producing sports would only magnify the problem.

b. *Analyze the products.* This is a prime step in most marketing strategies. What it means here is a careful assessment of the potential for each sport within the total program. Promotion starts with a quality product. In the case of sport, this is generally manifested in being able to successfully compete at the existing level. Having a quality coach and talented athletes are key elements. Geographical priorities and restrictions and schedules must also be taken into consideration. The product analysis may show that one or two of the nonrevenue sports should be targeted for special promotional efforts. The major limitation of this alternative is that it may only further contribute to an unbalanced program and result in the need to drop certain sports. Women's sports could be at a disadvantage because of their recent development. At any rate, women's sports will also require a special promotional effort.

c. *Set new performance standards for coaches.* Another possible way to promote nonrevenue sports is to make promotion one of the performance standards for coaches. Obviously, having a competitive team is the place to begin. Beyond that, the coach would be expected to carry out various other promotional activities, such as establishing a strong alumni network. In addition to the alumni, maintaining a larger group following is another key to success in promotion. Mike Palmisano, director of promotions, marketing, and special events at the University of Michigan, recommends building a group of alumni and interested business people. According to Palmisano, baseball is a top, nonrevenue sport at Michigan because the coach is particularly adept at public relations with the general public, groups of supporters, and the media.

There would appear to be a couple of possible limitations in this third alternative. Not all coaches have the personalities required for successful promotion. Also, some coaches may work at a disadvantage due to the absence of tradition or status in their sport.

d. *Hire a professional in marketing to organize special promotions.* A fourth, major alternative would be to hire a professional person in marketing or advertising who is specifically responsible for promoting nonrevenue sports. This requires an increase in the budget allocation for salaries, and there is no guarantee that the investment will pay off. Palmisano (1982) identifies several possible special promotions developing a theme for a team, recognition days, special clubs, alumni events, social tournaments, appreciation days, and special advertisements. Lopiano (1980) cites additional possibilities that have proven successful: establishing a support group for each sport, hosting a major annual event for each sport, hosting a minimum of one national championship a year (when feasible), and highlighting individual athletes as opposed to the entire team.

Not every Division I institution will be in a position to employ a professional solely for the purpose of promoting nonrevenue sports. The resources for various special promotion efforts will also vary considerably from one institution to another.

8. *Action Plan*:

a. *Performance standard for coaches*: Demonstrated ability to promote their sport will be one of the performance standards for the selection and evaluation of coaches. In the long run, this standard will be a measure of total coaching effectiveness because the quality product is essential for successful promotion.

b. *Special consideration for women's sports*: At least one or two women's sports will be targeted for special promotional efforts. Although women's sports will also be promoted on the basis of product analysis, there is a need to take into account the differences in the stage of development for women's sports.

CONCLUSION

We began by discussing this topic of promoting nonrevenue sports as being both an issue and a problem. In the final analysis, it would appear that the latter is the prime consideration. There is not much of an issue regarding the promotion of a nonrevenue sport, *provided* that that sport is deserving of promotion. The problem is essentially twofold: (1) determining what should be promoted, and (2) assessing how this can be most effectively accomplished. Hopefully, product analysis will contribute to solving the first part of the problem, and the second part will be approached with promotion as a performance standard for coaches. The University of Connecticut case study is a vivid testimony of the significant role of the coach in promoting a nonrevenue sport.

REFERENCES

Deegan, A. X., and R. J. Fritz. *MBO Goes to College.* Boulder: The Regents of the University of Colorado, 1975.

Lopiano, Donna A. "Selling Women's Athletics: Realities and Potentials." *Athletic Purchasing and Facilities*, Vol. 4, No. 10, October 1980, pp. 8–14.

Palmisano, M. "Promoting Your Non-Revenue Sports." *Athletic Purchasing and Facilities*, Vol. 6, No. 4, April 1982, pp. 84–86.

Chapter 11

College Football
Playoffs

The topic of college football playoffs is far from being a fresh consideration. As a matter of fact, such playoffs have existed in NCAA Divisions I-AA, II, and III for a number of years. The idea of having a I-A playoff is also far from being novel. The possibility has been kicked around for a long time. In recent years an NCAA committee was even appointed to study the feasibility of a playoff tournament. However, a playoff proposal never made it to the convention floor.

THE ISSUE

Should there be a Division I-A college football playoff? This is the key question and consequently also the heart of the issue. A secondary question follows: If there were to be a playoff, how would it be structured? We will begin by noting some pros and cons involving the first question.

On the plus side, having such a playoff would clearly be a step in the right direction in the effort to determine a true national champion in college football. Almost everyone knows that the end of the year polls are virtually useless in those years in which there are two or more teams with undefeated records. From an even more pragmatic standpoint, another reason for having playoffs is to generate additional funds for college athletics. Just the television revenue from the playoffs would add substantially to the NCAA funds for distribution to member institutions. Ironically, this may also be the reason why a playoff proposal has not reached the convention voting stage to date.

What could be right about a playoff? There is the notion that it would cure the financial ills that plague many athletic departments. Well, a playoff would make piles of money, which, in theory, would be spread throughout the NCAA membership to serve all manner of good. Maybe these dollars could save some crew or wrestling programs now being sacrificed in the name of gender equity.

But this spread-the-wealth theory is flawed. A struggle is going on in the NCAA between the schools that play I-A football and those that don't, precisely because the big schools won't agree to share potential playoff money. (That's a key reason a playoff proposal won't make it as far as the floor of the NCAA convention.) The I-A schools regard their smaller counterparts, the Muhlenbergs and the Trenton States, as parasites that feed off of their full stadiums. (Layden, p. 128)

Nevertheless, this situation could change in the near future. The new structure for the NCAA may well provide the key for changes in the way I-A programs function. The I-A schools might not need to share the wealth from I-A football playoffs. Following that line of thought some people within the NCAA structure are projecting that we will see a I-A football playoff by early in the next century.

So, determining the true champion and bringing in the additional dollars are the major pluses, but what are the drawbacks in having a playoff? There are more than one. Perhaps most significantly, a playoff would lengthen the season unless there is also a major change in the current bowl structure. As a matter of fact, the tradition of the various New Years' bowl games is also one of the principal reasons why the playoff has been so slow in materializing. The bowl committees have consistently resisted the playoff idea because it could seriously effect the significance of the bowl games. As things stand now, the New Years' Day bowl games mark the end of the college football season. A playoff would seriously detract from the significance of these games unless it is factored into the bowl structure. More about that will be said later.

There also are academic limitations involved with a Division I-A football playoff. This is particularly true if the season is to be lengthened. But, even if the January 1 closing is maintained, a playoff invariably means that there will be increased pressure to win. It is not reasonable to expect that a football player involved with a I-A playoff can give a great deal of attention to his academic pursuits during that period of time. It's a simple matter of establishing priorities. The playoff is another step toward enhancing the athlete-student concept in lieu of the student-athlete concept.

The truth of the matter is it would appear that the NCAA would like to have it both ways, so to speak. Following the theme of the Knight Foundation report, within recent years there has been much talk about academic integrity and financial integrity within the NCAA framework. Establishment of the I-A football playoff would seem to work at cross-purposes to both of those aspirations. The "big bucks" associated with the playoff certainly does not facilitate financial integrity. Likewise, the achievement of academic integrity becomes even more tenuous when athletes are faced with the time and emotional pressures of playoff competition.

Other pressures associated with big-time athletic programs are also likely to mount when the playoff structure is established. Being number one becomes that much more significant in the eyes of the alumni and public at large. This is in addition to the financial benefit from winning the national championship or even making the playoffs. These pressures will be felt by athletes, coaches, and administrators. As one example, the problem of recruiting violations will likely be only more severe.

The need for attention to compliance will increase rather than diminish. On the other hand, maybe there could be an advantage to all this. It might be the appropriate time for the NCAA to throw its manual out the window and start afresh with a few simple policies.

At least one other limitation of a playoff system should be noted. That is, it may be very difficult to determine which teams to select for the playoff. There are already problems in selecting teams for the 64–team men's I-A basketball tournament. In light of time limitations, a football playoff would have to consist of much fewer teams. Even an eight-team field would require three weeks of play, assuming only one game can be played per week. How does one select these eight teams without getting into subjectivity, which is currently criticized?

CONFERENCE REALIGNMENT AND
THE BOWL ALLIANCE

One possible point of assistance is that which is taking place in terms of conference realignment and the bowl alliance. The trend is definitely toward large conferences. A few years ago, Penn State triggered the change when it joined the Big Ten. Subsequently, there has been much discussion about another team being added to that conference. All of the major independents, with the exception of Notre Dame, are searching for conference affiliation. Also, all of the conferences, with an eye on television, are seeking to expand their markets. The Southwest Conference had its demise when Texas, Texas A&M, Texas Tech, and Baylor opted to join the Big Eight, thus making that conference the Big Twelve. Earlier, the Southeast Conference expanded and split into two divisions.

In essence, having fewer, larger conferences could facilitate the selection process for a football playoff. The reason is pure and simple: Reduction in the number of conference champions means there are fewer possibilities for a playoff spot. When a conference has two divisions, the number of playoff contenders is already reduced by 50 percent.

The bowl alliance or coalition was another step in the right direction in the effort to determine a true national champion or possibly even a playoff structure. In 1994, under pressure to alleviate a messy bowl selection process, some of the conference commissioners established the Fiesta-Orange-Sugar Alliance. This was designed to increase the chances of matching the nation's number-one and number-two teams. However, the alliance was not without its limitations, the principal one being that the Big Ten and Pac Ten were not part of the alliance. In other words, who is to say that in a given year, the number-one team is not the winner of the Rose Bowl? For example, in 1998 Michigan won the Rose Bowl. Subsequently, Michigan was voted number one in the Associated Press Poll. However, Nebraska was ranked number one in the CNN coaches' poll. In 1999 the alliance will be expanded to include the Rose Bowl. But, who is to guarantee that there will be two undefeated teams at the end of the season to compete in one of the bowls for a national championship? There could be only one undefeated team before the bowl games, or there could be three or more undefeated teams.

The alliance also signaled the demise of the 58-year-old Cotton Bowl after it failed in the effort to become part of the alliance. That bowl had been part of a tradition as one of the New Years' Day Big Four, along with the Rose, Orange, and Sugar Bowls. This merely is an example that all of the realignment of conferences and the alliance is not done without paying a price. College football has thrived in large part on tradition. Some of that tradition has been lost in the new conference affiliations.

THE PROBLEM AND A POSSIBLE SOLUTION

In spite of any limitations, some people feel that a Division I-A college football playoff is inevitable, only a matter of time. At any rate, this leads to the second question: How can the playoff be best structured to arrive as a true national champion in college football? A related consideration is how this can be done while at the same time retaining some of the traditions involving the bowls and the conferences. This points to the problem. Essentially, the problem is to determine a suitable playoff structure that will maintain the New Years' Day bowl tradition and yet not lengthen the season any more than necessary. The following is offered as a possible solution.

To begin with, the top eight teams in the country could be selected to participate in the four major bowl games on New Years' Day or near that day, depending on whether or not January 1 is on a weekend. The NCAA would still be faced with the problem of selecting these eight teams, but a similar problem exists in selecting the 64 teams for the Division I basketball tournament. For example, six teams could be automatic qualifiers as champions of the following major conferences: Atlantic Coast, Big East, Big Twelve, Big Ten, Pacific Ten, and Southeastern. That would leave two teams to be selected as at-large entries.

The next part of the larger problem would be to determine which teams play in which bowls in a given year. There are at least two possibilities for making that kind of decision. The one is to rotate the order of selection from year to year among the four bowls. For example, one year the Orange Bowl might be awarded the first selection and next year the first choice would go to the Sugar Bowl. The other possibility would be to conduct a form of lottery each year in which representatives from the four bowls would draw to determine the order of selection from among the eight teams. For example, in a given year the Rose Bowl representative might draw the number one and number six selections.

These major bowl game winners would advance to the semi-finals, probably to be scheduled the second Saturday in January at sites to be determined. The selection of sites for the semi-finals and final could be done by the NCAA in much the same way as is done for the basketball tournaments. The semi-final teams could be matched on a seeded basis, again as is done with basketball.

That would leave the final game to be scheduled on probably the third Saturday in January. This means that the college football season would be lengthened by two weeks. This is less than desirable for at least two reasons. The first is the extended time of physical and emotional demands on players and coaches. The other drawback involves the additional time away from academic pursuits, which was referred to earlier. Ideally it would be preferable to have the final game on New Years' Day with the quarter final and semi-final games scheduled earlier on consecutive Saturdays in December. That may not materialize due to the resistance on the part of the major bowl committees to move away from the traditional New Years' Day games.

One other possible limitation with extending the playoffs to the second week in January should also be noted; the conflict with the NFL playoffs. The first two weeks in January are also prime time for the NFL. The only real hope would be that the fan appetite for football playoffs is sufficient to accommodate both the NFL and college football. It is true that the NFL and college football do co-exist quite well during the regular season. On the other hand, one of the appeals of "March Madness" is that college basketball has center stage at that time as far as playoffs are concerned. At any rate, it would be interesting to compare the television ratings if the NFL and college football playoffs were both held during the first two weeks in January.

THE "X" FACTOR: ATTACK ON COLLEGE FOOTBALL

There is at least one other factor that must be taken into consideration when assessing the feasibility of Division I-A football playoffs. We will call it the "X" factor because the topic is somewhat elusive or lurking behind the scene. Generally speaking, this is the attack on college football that is in large part stimulated by gender equity considerations. Beyond that this attack also comes from men's so-called "minor" or nonrevenue sports, which have long felt threatened by the powerful influence of football and men's basketball. The topic is elusive only because one cannot be sure that this is a direct consideration in the debate about the possible playoffs.

In a three-part series (November 7–9, 1995), *USA Today* assessed the impact of Title IX 23 years after the passage of that federal statute in 1972. One part of this series focused on the role of football in the gender gap that still exists when one assesses men's and women's athletic programs. The report surveyed the 107 Division I-A football schools for the 1994–1995 academic year. Among the 94 who responded to the survey, only nine passed the proportionality test. This is the Title IX stipulation that the percentage of women athletes in a college should be equal to the percentage of that school's undergraduate female enrollment. The survey revealed that the big rosters of football players skewed the numbers in testing proportionality. However, even if football was not factored into the equation, 52 of the 85 schools would not meet the test of proportionality. Nevertheless, as some coaches state, football was still viewed as the "whipping boy."

Some leaders of women's sports including Donna Lopiano, executive director of the women's Sports Foundation, suggested that the NCAA limit of 85 I-A football scholarships should be reduced to 55. The football coaches reacted by pointing out that the number of scholarships for I-A football had already been reduced from 120. They also stressed that football provides much of the revenue that finances the other college sport programs. The bottom line is that in late 1995, the sides were clearly drawn:

Also rankling I-A football coaches is that their programs make the most money for their universities yet face the most criticism to cut expenses. While an estimated 80 percent of the USA's 668 football programs lose money, an NCAA financial survey published in 1994 showed 57 of 85 responding I-A members (67%) averaged profits of $3.9 million in 1993.

I don't know many businesses that would cut programs that help the female side of athletics, says Virginia Tech coach, Frank Beamer.

Debbie Brake, Senior Counsel for the Women's Law Center, is bothered by many football costs, "Look at the teams that stay in a hotel before a home game and these high-powered coaches who make more than university presidents." . . .

To create funds, Iowa women's athletic director Christine Grant suggests revamping the recruiting process, including the elimination of off-campus recruiting. (Brewington, p. 8C)

Such statements merely reinforce the idea that football is either the villain or the good guy, depending on one's frame of reference. Nevertheless, the possibility of having Division I-A football playoffs seems to become more remote when one considers the pressures of gender equity and cost containment in college athletics. On the other hand, such playoffs could also enrich the coffers of Division I-A schools in the restructured NCAA wherein these schools might not have to "share the wealth" with the entire NCAA membership. If that were the case maybe it would be possible to achieve gender equity without reducing the costs for football.

RELATIONSHIP TO THE BROADER PICTURE

In many respects this issue of college football playoffs cannot be viewed in isolation. The issue goes far beyond the matter of the playoffs per se. The larger issue involves the role of football in college athletics and American life.

To begin with one has to consider the historical significance and popularity of college football. Football was not the first intercollegiate athletic event in the United States. That recognition belongs to rowing, as the first Harvard–Yale Regatta in 1852 marked the beginning of American intercollegiate sports. However, from the time that the first football game was played between Rutgers and Princeton in 1869, it became clear that football would emerge as the dominating college sport. By World War I, the significance of football in American colleges was clearly established.

As the period of intercollegiate athletics between the Civil War and World War I came to a close it was clear that college athletics had reached an early stage of maturity with football leading the way. A survey by the NCAA at that time indicated that 150 colleges were spending a combined total over $1,000,000 on athletics each year, a sizable amount then. . . .

Nationally, an average of $59 was spent on each varsity athlete, while the east led by spending an average $170 per athlete—much on the one sport of football. College football had matured in many ways by World War I. It would grow profoundly in the decades which followed, but the direction, the evils, and the benefits were well established by the second decade of the twentieth century. (Lucas and Smith, p. 247)

The dominance of college football has basically continued to date with basketball as the only other college sport to make significant inroads in sharing center stage in college athletics. Ironically, basketball has achieved its high popularity through the NCAA Division I basketball tournament. One cannot help but wonder whether a Division I-A football playoff would still further enhance the popularity of that sport.

The popularity of college football extends beyond the game per se. A football weekend is a fall fiesta, an event that stirs the emotions of even those who are not real football fans. When it is homecoming weekend and the game involves traditional rivals, the fiesta is that much larger. No one better captures the spirit of the football weekend than Edwin Cady in his book, *The Big Game: College Sports and American Life*. According to Cady, the Big Game is college football, which he identifies as being "a major form of public art" (p. 4). He also has this to say about the football weekend:

Why? What is all the excitement about? For one thing, it is about something for which we seem not to have an adequate English word: the Big Game is a fiesta, a communal and ritual party, a blowout at which you are authorized to take a moral holiday from work, worry, and responsibility. . . . It has often been noted that the Big Game fiesta shares qualities with religious drama. . . . George Stoddered is said to have maintained that Americans need the football weekend because we have no other equivalent of the feast days lost with the old religion. Perhaps there are deep reasons for the placement of the football season at harvest time. At any rate, there is a lot more going on here than meets the incurious or untrained eye. (Cady, p. 62)

So, what does all this have to do with football playoffs or a post-season tournament? Some people would argue that the playoffs would be anticlimactic; that the essence of college football is found in the Saturday games during the season, capped by the New Years' Day bowl games. Others would argue that the regular season games would lose much of their significance when everyone is looking ahead toward the post-season tournament. For example, it is true in many respects that the heart of the college basketball season begins around March 1. This argument regarding the adverse effect of a playoff on the regular football season was perhaps best expressed by Tim Layden. He suggested that "A national playoff would squeeze the life out of the college football season. . . . There's not much romance left in college football or in sport itself. Autumn Saturdays are an exception. Three months of them, not three weeks" (Layden, p. 128).

Still others might oppose the playoff due to their opposition to the dominance of football generally. The line of thinking here is that the playoff would only add to the emphasis on football. If the NCAA basketball tournament is such a premier event, just think of the impact of an NCAA Division I-A football tournament. Advocates for gender equity and coaches of so-called minor sports might assess a football playoff as yet another factor in adding to the dominance of football. After all, reduction of costs for football and a post-season tournament don't exactly go hand in hand.

CONCLUSION

At the time of this writing it is a bit difficult to speculate as to whether an NCAA Division I-A football playoff will materialize. Some NCAA leaders have suggested that such a playoff is inevitable, but there is a difference of opinion as to if and when the post-season tournament will be a reality.

There are at least three obstacles to having a post-season tournament at this time. The proposal does not seem to have the support of the players due to the need to extend the season. This was determined when an NCAA committee interviewed a random selection of 300 players. The college presidents are also inclined to oppose the playoff for academic reasons, as noted earlier. Finally, there is a numbers problem. At best, only eight teams would be able to compete in the tournament, as contrasted with the 64 teams in men's basketball. The record will show that there are eight to ten I-A teams that are consistently near the top of the polls at the end of the year. That means that the playoff teams would generally be the same teams year after year, and the vast majority of the schools would never make the playoffs. Also, this larger group of schools might lose bowl opportunities. There is good reason to believe that many of the newer and less prominent bowls would be eliminated under a playoff structure.

The most likely possibility at this point is that a true playoff will not be established. As noted earlier, the alliance is scheduled to be expanded in 1999 to include the Pacific Ten and the Big Ten, thus also bringing the Rose Bowl into the alliance. However, there is also considerable opposition to the alliance by those conferences that are not part of the configuration.

Regardless of the outcome, it should be clear that the idea of having a tournament or playoff for Division I-A college football is truly an issue. The media would lead one to believe that the playoff must be established. However, to put it in place would be a major policy decision by the NCAA for all the reasons noted earlier. Furthermore, establishing the most appropriate structure for such a playoff would also be a challenge for the NCAA policymakers. One of the biggest hurdles would be to determine how the current bowls can best be factored into the playoff equation.

REFERENCES

Brewington, Peter. "Women's Leaders Target Sport: Coaches Say Enough on Cuts." *USA Today*, November 7, 1995, pp. 1C, 2C, 4C; November 9, 1995, p. 8C.

Cady, Edwin H. *The Big Game: College Sports and American Life.* Knoxville: University of Tennessee Press, 1978.

Knight Foundation Commission on Intercollegiate Athletics. "Keeping Faith with the Student-Athlete: A New Model for Intercollegiate Athletics." March 1991.

Layden, Tim. "Who Needs It?" *Sports Illustrated*, August 29, 1994, p. 128.

Lucas, John A., and Ronald A. Smith. *Saga of American Sport.* Philadelphia: Lead Febigev, 1978.

Chapter 12

Structure of the National Collegiate Athletic Association

O n January 8, 1996, the National Collegiate Athletic Association (NCAA) passed historic legislation at its ninetieth annual convention. This legislation, in the form of Proposal 7, dramatically changed the way the association conducts its business. Essentially, it was a restructuring plan that provided for a federated association and placed university presidents and chancellors in all the top decision-making positions.

The plan was developed by the Oversight Committee on the NCAA Membership Structure. After 18 months of study and debate, the core legislation was overwhelmingly supported by a vote of 777–79–1, to be effective August 1, 1997.

The NCAA Council and Presidents' Commission were replaced by a 16-member executive committee and three separate boards representing the three divisions within the NCAA. Twelve members of the executive committee are from Division I, including eight from the major football schools. These schools are also most prominent on the Division I board. Eight of the 15 seats on that board are held by representatives of the eight major conferences, encompassing 95 schools. Chief executive officers are the members of both the executive committee and the division boards or councils. Every division also has a Management Council, composed of athletic administrators, that is overseen by the presidents. All of this also replaces the one-school, one-vote convention system of the past. Most important the new structure gives each division autonomy in conducting its business.

Prior to the convention, the restructuring plan also received support from leading higher education associations. These included the American Council on Education, the Association of American Universities, the Association of Governing Boards of Universities and Colleges, the National Association of Independent Colleges and Universities, and the National Association of State Universities and Land-Grant Colleges. In a letter to institutional executive officers, the presidents of these associations stated their reasons for supporting the legislation.

"Restructuring will place presidents in control of the NCAA and end the awkwardness of having two bodies, the Presidents' Commission and the Council, each of which can act independently," the letter stated. "While the Presidents Commission has been effective and the Council has been cooperative, we believe the time has come for presidents to assume direct control of NCAA policy." (*NCAA News*, January 8, 1996, p. 1)

The letter also referred to the value of maintaining the integrity of the NCAA as a whole, even though the restructuring plan gave a high degree of autonomy to each division. This was a valid point because Division I institutions, particularly those with large football programs, had threatened to withdraw from the NCAA if major changes were not made in the structure. In spite of such external support, Proposal 7 was highly controversial before passage. Even after the large vote for approval, this major change in structure was viewed with apprehension by some.

But even though the legislation was approved by more than 90 percent of those voting, it was not uncommon in debate to hear lingering concerns. In particular, speakers revealed apprehension about access to the governance structure, especially in Division I which chose to set aside the Association's one-institution, one-vote principle in favor of a more representative form of governance.

Christine H. B. Grant, women's athletic director at the University of Iowa, said that the Association and Division I in particular should not turn away from the one-school, one-vote principle, "which has served us so well for so long."

Tanya Yvette-Hughes, student-athlete chair of the NCAA Student-Athlete Advisory Committee, noted that student-athletes were assured of representation on the Division II and III Management Councils but not in Division I.

Edward B. Fort, Chancellor of North Carolina AT&T State University, supported the proposal but repeatedly emphasized that Division I must develop a plan to assure access to the structure for minorities.

University of Nevada President Joseph N. Crowley, chair of the Oversight Committee on the NCAA Membership Structure, acknowledged the significance of the access questions and assured the membership that they would be addressed further over the 18–month transition period.

To the Student-Athlete Advisory Committee, Crowley said, "I can assure the members of that committee and others that their role will be enhanced in restructuring."

As for gender and minority access, Crowley said that 1996 Convention Proposal No. 9 "will help us down the road." That proposal directs the Division I transition team "to develop a specific written plan for achieving the stated goals of representation in a restructured Association and to submit appropriate recommendations" for consideration at the 1997 Convention.

Crowley also attempted to allay concern about faculty athletics representative access in the Division I governance structure.

Ultimately, many comments centered on the need to have faith in one another. (*NCAA News*, January 15, 1996, pp. 1, 7)

THE ISSUE

The principal issue is one that has persisted in the NCAA for some time: To what extent should the balance of power reside with the large, powerful athletic programs, particularly those that play I-A football? Prior to the 1996 Convention, Patricia Viverito, commissioner of the Gateway Football Conference, succinctly expressed the sentiment of some regarding the Division I-A institutions: "We're already handing them the keys to the castle. . . . Why do we have to give them their own wing?" The truth of the matter is that NCAA Division I athletics has relatively little in common with Divisions II and III. A further complication is the differences between the I-A and I-AA institutions. They have the common denominator in all sports except football, but the football programs in I-A tend to be worlds apart from those in I-AA. Also, as noted earlier, I-A institutions hold the balance of power on the executive committee and the Division I governing board. Furthermore, Division I-AA football programs are between the proverbial "rock and the hard place." More about that will be said later.

In spite of the significance of the issue, one can see why Proposal 7 was passed in such a convincing manner. To begin with, Division I institutions received a large degree of autonomy, which they had been seeking for years. Among the schools in that division, only Texas voted against the restructuring package. Divisions II and III also received greater autonomy. However, more importantly, the restructuring format preserved the NCAA in its traditional form even though autonomy was given to each division. If Division I institutions had withdrawn from the NCAA, Division II and III schools would be left with very little support from the association. The NCAA is largely financed through funds from the Division I men's basketball tournament. If those funds were not available it would be a very different modus operandi for Division II and III. Thus, the opposition to restructuring had to come largely from Division I-AA schools, which had the most to lose in a division dominated by the I-A football powers. As mentioned earlier the other concerned constituencies were minorities, women, student-athletes, and faculty representatives, all seeking sufficient access in the Division I structure.

THE UNDERLYING SIGNIFICANCE

The passing of the restructuring legislation involved much more than appears on the surface. In so doing, the NCAA membership gave tacit recognition to the fact that college athletics is not college athletics. Aside from the differences among sports, there are two major forms of college athletics. One is truly amateur sport, with true student-athletes, exemplified in the Division III philosophy and operation. The other is professional or semi-professional sport, with athlete-students, as exemplified in Division I men's football and basketball. With the new legislation in place, Division I now has more freedom to proceed further in the direction of highly commercialized sport. Once again, Christine Grant, Iowa women's athletic director, sounded the alarm for those who resisted the major change in structure: "They've got the power to move I-A even farther away from the rest of the organization. . . . I hope they don't. I suspect they will. They could increase scholarships . . . increase coaching staffs. They can literally do what they want" (Wieberg, p. 9C). On the other side of the fence, as one might expect, Pacific 10 Commissioner Tom Hansen provided reassurance from the Division I perspective: "There's no intent to affect any radical change. . . . I can't tell you two things anybody wants to do Aug. 2, 1997 (the day after restructuring goes into effect)" (*USA Today*, January 9, 1996, p. 9C). At the time of this writing no one really knows what the effect of restructuring will be. More may be known when this book is in print. At any rate, the NCAA took a major step in recognizing a major difference among its membership.

Elsewhere in this book (chapter 2), reference is made to the statements of Howard Swearer, then president of Brown University in 1982:

May not the time have arrived when it would be desirable to recognize openly this symbiotic relationship between the big athletic powers and professional sports, and make the necessary structural changes?

The factions are wearing thin. I for one, see no harm in associating a professional or semi-professional team with a university; and I do see a number of benefits. It would help clarify what is now a very murky picture. Athletes should, of course, have the opportunity to take courses and pursue a degree, if they wish; but they would be regarded as athletes first and should be paid accordingly. By so doing the regulatory and enforcement burden and the temptations for illegal and unethical practices would be dramatically eased. The clear separation between the academic and athletic purposes of the university would be beneficial to both. . . .

The possibility I have sketched out is not a choice that I believe Ivy League and similar institutions should or would take. However, I hope that the Ivy League will also take a positive and active role in the long-term restructuring of intercollegiate sports. (Swearer, p. 52)

Fourteen years later some of the restructuring that Swearer envisioned was closer to reality. It may not have been as drastic or extreme as Swearer might hope, but at least it was a step in that direction. One also has to wonder whether the restructuring effort was the right one for the Ivy League schools with their I-AA status.

CONCERNS

Following the 1996 Convention, the concerns expressed earlier continued to exist. For the most part these concerns centered around the idea that there might not be a means to keep the big-time programs in check. Following was a fairly typical reaction among the skeptics: " 'I support the idea of giving I-A what they think they are due,' says Edward H. Hammond, president of Fort Hayes State University, referring to the NCAA's Division I-A, which includes 108 of the colleges that spend and make the most money on sports. 'But I don't support abdicating our ability to have some say in critical issues that regard the principles of this association' " (*Chronicle of Higher Education*, p. A33).

Here were some of the more specific concerns. Will Division I raise its limits on the number of scholarships that can be offered? If so, the "haves" would have more at the expense of the "have nots." In other words the major powers in Division I football would become that much more powerful. Likewise, will these same schools be free to pay stipends to athletes who play on teams that generate cash?

As noted in chapter 11, the restructuring also had very significant implications for the I-A football playoff idea. The profits from such a playoff, estimated at $100 million annually, would no longer have to be shared with the other NCAA schools. Does that mean the Division I-A football playoff will finally become a reality?

On the other side of the fence, Division I-A leaders tended to dismiss the concerns as overreaction. They quickly pointed out the override provision of the 1996 restructuring legislation. Actually there were two possibilities. The 338 members of Division I could overturn any decision by a five-eighths vote. Also the NCAA executive committee could call a vote of the full membership on the action of any division. If so, the 991 members of the association could override the action by a two-thirds majority.

Yet, there are others outside of Division I-A who seriously questioned the viability of the override provision. They quickly pointed out that half of the NCAA executive committee would be from Division I-A, and four more members would also be from Division I. Under that structure, is the executive committee likely to call a vote to override a Division I decision? From his perspective as president of Fort Hays State, a Division II school, Edward Hammond once again sounded the warning for those institutions in Divisions II and III. "Here we have a body that will act as the protector of our constitution, and yet we still are conceding control to one part of the association. . . . That's an awful lot of power to give to 16 people when 12 of them are from Division I" (*Chronicle of Higher Education*, p. A33).

The issue involving the most appropriate structure for the NCAA was by no means settled as a result of the 1996 legislation. This merely reinforced the idea that there is no single entity called college athletics—the differences between Division I institutions and those in Divisions II and III are enormous. Furthermore, conference re-alignment and expansion, involving I-A football schools, will only continue to enhance the disparity in the NCAA membership.

CONFERENCE REALIGNMENT

Within recent years, conference realignment has been the "name of the game" in college athletics at the Division I level. One can only assume that this movement and expansion will continue, at least for the foreseeable future. There is absolutely no doubt that television is the driving force in this movement of schools from one conference to another or major independent schools now having a conference affiliation. Ten years ago who would have thought that Miami would become a member of the Big East or that Penn State would join the Big Ten? Actually, the latter action represented one of the more dramatic changes and signaled the beginning of much that has taken place in the interim. Notre Dame is the only independent I-A football school that can afford to remain independent. The reason is simple; Notre Dame has its own television contract. By contrast, the fact that Notre Dame chose to join the Big East in basketball is also not surprising. That conference has one of the best television markets.

In terms of conference expansion, the earliest of the more significant actions was the reconfiguration of the Southeast Conference by forming two divisions with six schools in each division. Furthermore this ended the traditional rivalry between Texas and Arkansas when the latter school became part of the new, Southeast Conference. Similarly, another traditional rivalry, Pittsburgh-Penn State, went by the boards when Penn State joined the Big Ten.

Perhaps the strongest break with tradition was the elimination of the Southwest Conference after the 1995–1996 academic year. The defection of Texas, Texas A&M, Texas Tech and Baylor to the Big Eight (thus forming the Big Twelve) marked the end of a major conference and a Cotton Bowl with a 60-year history. The reaction was mixed when this dramatic change was announced in 1994:

Progress has come to college football in the form of reconfigured conferences and bowl coalitions, but not without a price. A sport that, much like
baseball, lives as much in the past as the present and thrives on a rich
tradition, has had to give some away.

"It's a fine line to walk," says Nebraska coach Tom Osborne. "I don't think
there's been so much upheaval yet that a lot of violence has been done to
tradition. But you can see a whole lot more being damaging."

"There are two ways to look at it," says Big East Commissioner Mike
Tranghese, whose basketball only league turned to football in 1991. "Things
are being ripped apart. But if they're ripped apart, is it being done for
something better?"

Says the Pacific 10's Tom Hansen: "A lot of this change has been set in
motion by things that were not illogical." (Wieberg, p. 9C)

There is little doubt that the lack of a sufficient television market
was the principal factor in the demise of the Southwest Conference.
At present there are six major I-A football conferences, and all of
these have the television market needed to survive under the present
set of conditions. These dominant groups in I-A football are the
Southeast, Big Twelve, Big Ten, Pacific 10, Big East, and Atlantic
Coast conferences. They will also be the key players in the restructured NCAA Division I.

One can now begin to see the scenario unfolding. The bowl
coalition is on shaky ground due to the uncertainty of being able
to consistently match the top two teams. For example, in 1996, the
Nebraska-Florida matchup would have lost its luster if Ohio State
had not been upset by Michigan in the last game of the regular
season. Otherwise, Ohio State would have gone to the Rose Bowl
as a third undefeated team (in addition to Nebraska and Florida).
Furthermore, the coalition arrangement has had an adverse effect
on the other bowl games in terms of attendance and television
arrangements. Continued realignment of conferences could result
in seven large conferences and Notre Dame as a major independent. This would provide eight teams for a I-A football playoff.
The revenue from the playoff could be shared by only Division I
members. One of the provisions of the 1996 restructuring legislation was that any new NCAA revenues need not be shared by the
membership at large.

THE DILEMMA OF I-AA FOOTBALL SCHOOLS

As noted earlier, the Division I-AA football schools have been in a sticky situation for some time, and the restructuring legislation only enhanced the problem. These schools have existed in the shadow of I-A football from their very inception. The 1996 legislation gave further power to the I-A institutions, and thus further widened the gap between I-A and I-AA.

The basic problem is that I-AA football schools lose a considerable amount of money through their football programs. The number of athletic scholarships offered, size of the coaching staffs, travel costs, poor spectator attendance, and lack of television contracts result in substantial deficits in general. One I-AA athletic director in 1996 stated that Marshall University was the only school in that division currently showing a profit through its football program.

For the I-AA schools at large the only real solution would seem to be that of significantly reducing the number of athletic scholarships that are allowed. That might not solve the entire problem, but at least it would alleviate the financial loss. Individual schools might attempt to move to Division I-A, but that is easier said than done. First there is the problem of finding a conference that can and will accommodate a new I-A member. In some cases this would be easier than with others. For example, the University of Connecticut is currently attempting to make the move from I-AA to I-A. One big advantage of UCONN is that it is already a member of the Big East in all sports except football. Therefore, the move to the Big East in football could be easily accommodated.

Aside from the possible obstacle of conference acceptance, there is also the money factor. Even though I-AA football is generally a losing proposition, it also takes considerable funds to move to I-A. In many cases a new stadium must be built or the current stadium needs to be enlarged. There is also the need to fund the additional scholarships for I-A football as well as the additions to the coaching staff. The recruiting costs will also increase significantly.

Of course I-AA schools also have the option of moving in the other direction, but that too has its limitations. Division II schools share the similar problem of being caught in the middle without a true identity. Division III football is not the best option for a large institution that plays at the Division I level in other sports. The final choice would be to drop the football program altogether. Villanova University is a good example of the problem in making that choice. For historical reasons, football is typically an integral part of the American college scene.

CONCLUSION

College athletics in the United States is currently at the crossroads. The restructuring legislation at the 1996 NCAA Convention represented one of the most significant changes in the history of that association. It was also legislation that was much needed to keep pace with other changes in the nature of college athletics. Television has accentuated the highly commercialized nature of Division I football and basketball and made those activities very different from the rest of college athletics. Will the restructuring plan be successful in improving the overall quality of college athletics? The next century will provide the answer.

REFERENCES

Chronicle of Higher Education, February 2, 1996, p. A33.
NCAA News, January 8, 1996, p. 1; January 15, 1996, pp. 1, 7.
Swearer, Howard R. "An Ivy League President Looks at College Sports."
   New York Times, February 21, 1982, p. 2S.
USA Today, January 9, 1996, p. 9C.
Wieberg, Steve. "Progress Seen in Realignment of Conferences, Bowl Alliance." *USA Today*, August 25, 1994, p. 9C.

Chapter 13

Facility Funding

Facility funding for sport programs is a broad topic because one finds a wide scope of facilities utilized by diverse sport organizations. These facilities range from large arenas and stadiums for major spectator sports to small, specific facilities for recreational participation. The organizations using these facilities may be professional sport teams, individual professional sport organizations, private clubs, corporations, the military, community recreation programs, schools, or colleges. In this chapter, we will focus on two major categories of facilities: college athletic facilities and professional sport facilities. Policies for funding college athletic facilities are particularly critical due to the frequent need to compete for institutional funds. Although the focus is on colleges, much of the consideration applies equally to high school facilities. Policies for funding professional sport facilities are also most critical due to the impact on the city and public funding for such facilities.

COLLEGE ATHLETIC FACILITIES

The Process

Funding athletic or sport facilities is a complex process that requires careful organization and planning. It involves identifying and justifying needs, locating the sources of funds, preparing a financing plan, and finally, mounting a drive to secure the funding.

The first step may often be overlooked. Policymakers must review the institutional policy toward sport, athletics, and physical education to ascertain the goals or objectives of the institutions in this area. To a large extent, this will determine the necessary facilities and the possible funding. Such a review would include emphasis on different kinds of activity, participation of specific groups, potential community participation, and possible relationships with neighboring institutions.

With respect to funding for a facility, one of the steps is the formation of a development team. The development program is a two-stage operation requiring a preliminary survey to establish funding potential followed by a formal funding campaign. The team charged with mounting a development program should comprise individuals who will administer all phases of the project, including a member of the institution management/planning unit, a marketing/public relations person, a financial consultant, and one or more administrators from the athletic department.

When there is a need for a specific fund-raising campaign, it is often desirable to use one or more consultants to assess the funding potential, develop a financing plan, and orchestrate a drive for funds. George Casey presented guidelines as to when, why, and how professional counsel should be used in a fund-raising campaign.

Seeking professional counsel should be considered when the objective is in the range of $200,000 or more. While this figure is somewhat arbitrary, it should be recognized that the costs per dollar raised will be higher for a campaign at this level than for a much larger objective. . . .

Professional counsel normally conducts a fund-raising appeal more speedily and economically than the client's staff. Wide experience and training equip the fund-raising professional to determine the most effective and cost-efficient procedures for a campaign. . . .

A major advantage of employing a firm specializing in fund-raising counsel is "back-up," service. If, for any reason, the campaign director becomes incapacitated, a competent replacement is available, avoiding a delay should the institution be forced to seek a substitute. . . .

The presence of accredited professional counsel with a known record of success tends to create an air of confidence. . . .

It is better practice to select professional counsel early in the planning process than wish later that more time were available. If your organization is not ready for a campaign, you will be so advised. The professional firm can assist you in getting ready. (pp. 70, 73–74)

Another early organizational step is to evaluate the need for either new or improved facilities within the institution's total operation. There are relatively few occasions when a totally new facility is clearly mandated from the outset. Most institutions will begin by carefully assessing existing athletic facilities to determine whether they are adequate to meet the needs of the program. (This tends to be particularly critical for recreational sport facilities at institutions that are trying to meet increased demands for space.) Many existing facilities have become obsolete due to the greater participation of women in all sports and the necessity to meet the needs of special groups, especially participants with handicap conditions.

David L. Finci, director and senior vice president of the Eggers Group, which specializes in sports facilities planning, offered the following advice regarding the bottom line, cost data, financing, and project budget estimate.

The information gathered must be translated into cost data, which must go beyond the actual costs of initial alterations to the physical structures or new construction and include operations and maintenance costs over the projected planning period.

While alterations to existing mechanical and electrical systems may ultimately result in more efficient operations, these economies must be weighed against the costs of making such changes and compared with the life cycle costs of building anew. Assessing the costs of alterations is a complex business. Generally speaking, one can assume that if the costs of alterations approaches 50 percent to the cost of new construction, then it does not make sense to embark upon them. (p. 26)

Other information must also be obtained during the preliminary planning. There should be a survey of the attitudes of students, faculty, staff, administrators, and other users regarding the existing facilities and programs. The extent of such a survey will largely depend on the specific nature of the projected facility. Research into future programs and trends is also needed. What is being done by other institutions in terms of facility development? What kind of changes are taking place locally, regionally, and nationally in terms of program development and sport popularity? Finally, and most importantly, the preliminary planning or organizational process is completed by identifying the possible sources of funding and assessing the intensity of competition for funds. This includes marshaling support for the programs from units inside and outside the institution. Such groups would likely be the student government association, the alumni office, faculty senate, related cultural groups, and various community organizations.

Possible Sources of Funding

When competing for funds, an athletic department must justify the need for a facility and demonstrate a viable plan for financing. The potential sources of funding vary greatly, depending on the nature of the institution. Generally speaking, the following sources may be available:

1. *Institutional Funds:* These are funds specifically appropriated for facilities. The appropriation would come from the state in the case of a public college or university, from the school district for a public school, or from the trustees for a private institution.
2. *Revenue from Intercollegiate Athletic Events:* This source applies to relatively few institutions in terms of the entire collegiate spectrum.
3. *Special Fund-Raising Drive:* In many cases, this is basically in the form of alumni support. However, this source is by no means limited to alumni for most institutions.
4. *Student Fees:* As noted later, this is a growing source of funding particularly for recreational facilities.
5. *User Fees:* This was typically used more frequently outside the school and college environment, but the potential for development is also there in this setting.
6. *Corporate Funding:* This may also be tied in with the special fund-raising drive.

There are other possibilities, depending on the institution. The above appear to be the more viable alternatives. Nevertheless, the situation has changed considerably in recent years. Robert Bronzan, an athletic facilities consultant for APER Consulting Services in Danville, California, identifies what appears to be the major change.

Until some 12 years ago, two major sources existed for funding athletic, recreation, and special spectator event facilities on state college and university campuses. The nation is dotted with institutions who received state monies to construct stadiums, arenas, gymnasiums, natatoriums, tracks and other types of sports-related facilities. This source has virtually disappeared, however, except for Sun Belt states currently experiencing population and economic explosions. Economic and political signs point to continued austerity programs for most states.

The other major funding source in the past was the Department of Intercollegiate Athletics (Men). Some institutions, private and public, enjoyed profitable athletic programs in football and basketball. Surplus funds were channeled to construct facilities which have been used also for recreation and fitness programs. However, during the past decade a limited number of athletic programs have realized a profit. The causes are many, but leading are inflated operational costs, increases in the number of intercollegiate sports sponsored, particularly the addition of women sports, and the issuing of grants-in-aid to more students. (p. 18)

Student Fees

Bronzan said that the real answer for many institutions, particularly for recreational sport facilities, is to provide facility funding through student fees. Even though construction for athletic and physical education facilities has lagged because of budget cuts, there has been a surge in recreational facility construction. Incoming college freshmen, reflecting a societal trend, have become more involved in sports, exercise, and fitness programs. Thus, they are willing to dig into their pockets to fund such facilities. On an increasing number of campuses, students have voted to assess themselves additional fees to fund the construction of recreation centers. The facilities are usually financed through long-term notes.

Programs financed by these self-assessed student fees also reflect a change in terms of an emphasis on "open recreation," as opposed to intramural sport or club sport. Again, this reflects societal trends away from the more highly structured sport activities to individual exercise and fitness pursuits. The shift also affects the role of administrators who recognize that when students fund a facility, they also expect to have a direct voice in determining design, operational policies and practices, and program content.

Bronzan cautioned that the groundwork must be carefully laid if facilities are to be funded from the student fee source. Approval is usually by means of a referendum, but there are many earlier steps. A referendum campaign should probably begin at least three years before the voting year. This provides time to identify and nurture the facility need with three successive freshmen classes, using selected student leaders who recognize the need and favor student financing. This is largely accomplished through a Central Campaign Committee, which includes representation from various components of the institution. Strategy and tactics are very important in planning such a campaign, including the timing of the referendum. Bronzan suggests two time periods that may prove to be advantageous. One of these is six to eight weeks after the registration for the fall term, a time during which students tend to be enthusiastic and are more likely to have a feeling of financial security. At this point in the academic year, there is also less time for the opposition to get organized. The other time might be about three to four weeks prior to the end of the academic year. Seniors are thinking about graduation, and the fees will not apply to them. The students generally are more likely to be thinking about final examinations than mounting opposition to a fee structure.

User Fees

Another type of fee structure is increasingly employed in providing funding for recreational sport facilities. This is the user fee, which may also be called the "pay as you play" or "pay as you go" fee. In the educational setting, the essential difference between the student fee and the user fee is that the former is an across-the-board assessment of all students, regardless of the extent to which any individual or group may use the sports facilities. Within the past ten years, the user-pay concept has been implemented frequently in municipal recreation programs, but there is potential for utilizing this kind of fee in the school and college context.

Perhaps the most significant factor in this form of facility financing is to have definite policies that determine the fee structure and are applied consistently. For example, this kind of fee is particularly applicable to private groups who wish to rent the facility. Beyond that, various questions arise. Should students be assessed through a general fee structure? Should faculty and staff be required to pay a user's fee? If so, should the fee structure be set at a different level than it is for other users? Some groups or programs may receive preferential treatment in using the facilities. Should the fee structure be set accordingly? An institution may also decide that it should charge lower rates for beginners programs than it does for advanced programs, working from the assumption that it has an obligation to introduce people to various sport activities.

Aside from the differences among users, there is one other complication in having user fees as a source for funding: to determine the amount of the assessment for any given group. What are the real costs in providing and operating the facility? The number of users has to be related to the total costs. That can be most difficult to determine, particularly in the school or college setting. Facility costs must be assessed in order to establish an appropriate scale of fees.

Corporate Funding

The two previous funding sources particularly apply to recreational sport programs, even though student fees are also assessed to fund spectator sport facilities. Another possible option for major funding of spectators sport facilities is corporate funding, although this is also very much related to the special fund-raising drive and alumni contributions. Of course, either of the latter two possibilities extend beyond corporate funding per se.

There is little doubt that corporate funding is one of the more effective means of promoting and generating revenue in the sport enterprise generally. With respect to facility funding, the potential is enriched by the possibility that the business firm may have the opportunity to support and have its name identified with a specific, permanent project. One cardinal rule of thumb more or less applies to any form of corporate involvement—the company is likely to get involved, if it has the money.

There is a cloud on the horizon, however, in terms of the future possibilities for corporate support. Reductions in tax incentives may hurt college athletic fund raising. The 1986 IRS decision (Ruling 86–83) limits tax deductions to athletic programs if the contribution is tied to the donor's ability to gain preferential seating at athletic contests. Furthermore, the 1986 Tax Reform Act limited the tax deduction for business entertainment expenses to 80 percent. Most threatening, in terms of its impact on new stadium construction and renovation, is the three-year phaseout of tax deductions for skyboxes. By 1989 annual leases on skyboxes were no longer deductible. The situation at the University of Oregon provides a case in point in terms of how tax reform might severely limit corporate funding.

Bill Byrne thought he had it all figured out: 54 skyboxes at $25,000 a year for 10 years would bring in enough extra revenue to give the University of Oregon's Autzen Stadium a facelift, and add 13,000 needed seats to boot.

That was B.T.R. (Before Tax Reform), when a skybox lessee could blithely write off the cost of his or her box as a tax-deductible business expense. Under the Tax Reform Act of 1986, those deductions were phased out by 1989. Today, the Oregon athletic director's plans are considerably more restrained. The skybox plan has been scaled back to 22, and only 11 of them are spoken for, although Byrne originally had 20 commitments. For now, a shell large enough to contain all 22 skyboxes will be constructed, but the future is uncertain enough that Byrne says he will finish each box as it is needed. . . .

Other revenue will be generated by setting aside reserve preferential seating for supporters who contribute at least $1,500 to the Oregon athletic program.

Even that strategy—a tried and true method of fund-raising—is not as simple as it once was. Under IRS Ruling 86-83, contributions to athletic programs may not be tax deductible if the contribution entitles the donor to purchase game tickets that would not be available to him or her otherwise.

The IRS ruling requires the recipient institution to determine how much, if any, of the contribution is deductible.

In Byrne's case, he has a number of long term season ticket holders already occupying seats in the preferential-seating section. Those patrons will be able to keep their seats under a grandfather clause. In the meantime, Byrne will have supporters who paid $1,500 to $2,000 for the right to buy tickets sitting next to people who paid for nothing but the ticket itself. Out of that, Byrne is expected to come up with a coherent policy under which donors can claim their tax deductions. "It's been an administrative nightmare," says Byrne. ("A Legacy Lives On," p. 22)

Overall, there tends to be some difference of opinion among athletic directors regarding the impact of the change in tax legislation. In general, the private institutions depend more on fund raising than the state colleges and universities. However, their alumni may also be more loyal and may continue to contribute without the tax incentive. A further complication is adverse publicity for college athletics, resulting from scandals in certain programs. In the final analysis, whether it be corporate funding or broader means of fund raising, the bottom line is to develop and maintain good personal relationships with the supporters of an athletic program.

CASE EXAMPLES

There is no single formula for facility planning or facility funding. Although all college athletic departments face a continued need to upgrade their sport or athletic facilities in some way or another, the common ground ends there. Probably the only other similarity is that there is always some resistance to providing money for new athletic facilities, due to the belief that classrooms, laboratories, and libraries should have priority on college campuses. Beyond that, planning and funding sport or athletic facilities depend on the nature of the program and the institution. The following case examples illustrate some of the differences and complexities.

The Ohio State University

Starting in 1984, the athletic department developed a 25-year master plan to provide up to $79 million worth of facility improvements by adding new facilities and renovating existing facilities. This master plan, completed in January 1986 at a cost of approximately $200,000, called for a two-phase construction schedule: the "Scarlet Phase," to be completed by 1990, at an estimated cost of between $41 million and $45 million; and the "Gray Phase," to begin in 1991, projected to cost between $27 million and $34 million. Facility renovation would include about $15 million to $20 million for the Ohio State stadium, which was completed in 1992.

The funding for all these new or renovated athletic facilities will come from a university-wide capital campaign aimed at raising $350 million for a variety of academic, athletic, and extracurricular facilities. Prior to this development, the athletic department had not undertaken a major facility project in 20 years.

The principal-in-charge of the facilities plan was architect Dennis Wellner, vice president of Hellmuth, Obata, and Kassabaum Sports Facilities Group (HOK). He noted that the funding for the athletic facilities was facilitated by the tie-in with the $350 million for academic and service facilities for the entire university. Another member of the department (master planning) team was Robert Bronzan, who also had the valuable background as a teacher, coach, and athletic director ("Masters of Their Fate," pp. 18–23).

UCLA—The Wooden Center

The university's major spectator arena, Pauly Pavilion, was built in the late 1960s. At that time, the plan was to add two complementary buildings in the future. One of these, a building for athletic department administrators, was built. The second, a recreational sport building, did not materialize as planned.

Another feasibility study for this second building was conducted in 1977 at a time when funds for the University of California system were being constricted by the state government. State funding would not be available. The only real possibilities for funding this building were private financing through a fund-raising effort and student-assessed fees.

It was also apparent that a fund-raising drive was not likely to be successful if the building was only intended for recreational purposes. Potential donors preferred to support the intercollegiate athletic program. The answer was to extend the Wooden Center building project to include additional athletic facilities. That stimulated the support of the boosters, who contributed $2.5 million. The remainder of the total cost for the building was financed by bonds underwritten by the student assessed fees. After the first student referendum failed in 1977, a second referendum passed overwhelmingly the following year.

Ground for the Wooden Center was broken in late 1980. The building was completed in 1983 at a cost of $80 per square foot or $8 million. It is a facility that includes two gymnasia, racquetball and squash courts, a gymnastic room, recreation and intramural office space, activity rooms, and underground parking for 450 cars ("A Legacy Lives On," pp. 38–45).

Gustavus Adolphus College—The Lund Center

This comprehensive facility is an excellent example of funding through alumni support. The building includes a multisport forum, an ice arena with seating for 1,200, a natatorium, gymnastics studio, five handball/racquetball courts, a weight room, wrestling room, and various support facilities. The forum also has spectator seating for 3,000. The 10.8 million, 222,000 square-foot complex was completely funded with private funds. Short-term financing of $3 million at 8 percent was used to get started. The remainder of the funds was generated through foundations and personal gifts. There were 5,000 individual gifts. These included a $1 million contribution from the Russell T. Lund family as well as three other private donations of more than $600,000.

Even the operational funds are not derived from student fees. There is an ongoing alumni solicitation program with pledges from those who support this kind of campus activity.

The athletic department increased the number of varsity sports from 7 to 23, many of which were for the women's program. In addition, the building has become a social center for the campus, with a strong interest in open recreation. The building was designed to put particular emphasis on separating intercollegiate events from intramural and open recreation activities ("Comprehensive Facility," pp. 34–37).

University of California at Berkeley—
Recreational Sports Center

This $13.5 million facility was completed in 1984. As early as 1958, the need for such a facility was recognized. However, it was not until 1981 that the regents authorized interim financing during construction after 61 percent of the voting students (51 percent of the student body), in a campuswide referendum, voted to assess themselves an annual fee to amortize the cost of building construction. The requirements for approval were that at least 25 percent of the students must vote, with at least 55 percent voting in favor of the mandated fee.

An extensive promotional campaign was used to gain student support for the referendum. This included two campuswide surveys to determine student interest in the proposal and the possibility of student financing. During the final three months preceding the referendum, student leaders and staff members from the department of recreational sports intensified the promotional effort.

The construction costs of the building were entirely funded from the student fees with the students being assessed $28.50 per semester. The fee collection began when the facility was completed and will remain in effect for the duration of the 30–year revenue bonds used to provide the funds for the project.

The multiuse concept was central in designing the facility. However, this did not include provisions for a major spectator facility. The building was clearly established to have recreational programs as the functional priority. As with other facilities of this type, the recreational sports center also serves as a social gathering spot for students.

Due to the source of funding, students had a major role in determining the type of building that was constructed. They also had input in developing policies and continue to be a major voice in the operation (Manning, pp. 42–46; "A Place of Their Own," pp. 24–27).

Concordia College—Outdoor Track

This NCAA Division III college had conducted a track and field program for several years without having its own outdoor track facility. The base project for an outdoor track was completed in 1979, but the college was unable to add a quality synthetic top surface due to other priorities in the general budget.

In January 1983 the college administration gave approval for a special fund-raising drive to finance the completion of the track through the Letter Club. The club was not the typical booster club, but rather an organization of alumni athletes.

This special fund-raising project for the track was designed not to conflict with the regular fund-raising efforts of the college's development office. The drive was targeted toward letter receivers and other supporters of the athletic program who were more than likely to support this kind of project. The idea was to obtain relatively small contributions from as many people as possible. The initial goal for the drive was set at $200,000. This could be reached by obtaining a $500 pledge from each of 400 people. The pledge was called a "meter," to relate to the 400 meters of the track circumference. Potential donors were encouraged to at least buy a "meter" for $500. Further incentive was to buy two "meters" and thus become a member of the college's C-400 Club. (The latter had been established in 1955 for the purpose of college development generally. Under this plan, a member of the club pledges to contribute $1,000 to the college over a four-year period.) Either type of pledge could be paid over a four-year span. Of course, pledges of all amounts were accepted, and these ranged from $5 to $1,000.

A special letter, outlining the needs for an all-weather track, was sent out to the target group of alumni. This was followed by a phone-a-thon during which local alumni contacted other alumni through long-distance calls.

The results were very successful. By the end of May 1983, $146,000 had been pledged. The total cost of the track was projected at $173,000, and construction began in August. The track was completed and dedicated at Homecoming on October 1, 1983. At that time, the amount pledged had risen to $163,000 (Pipho, pp. 104–106).

Babson College—The Babson Recreation Center

Babson College, a small college with an undergraduate enrollment of only 1,250, was able to build a $1.5 million multiuse recreation center and athletic complex in the mid-1970s through unique financing.

The 92,000 square foot facility includes an ice hockey rink with a seating capacity of 1,500, eight indoor tennis courts, saunas, locker rooms, pro shop, snack bar, a first aid room, and a nursery.

The idea for the center arose from the need for a hockey rink both for Babson College and the Wellesley, Massachusetts, community where the college is located. The college had more than 200 acres of unused land, jointly owned with Babson Reports, Inc. In searching for a location for a hockey rink in Wellesley, the Babson Recreation Center, Inc. (BRC) approached the college with an offer to buy or rent a 26-acre piece of land.

The decision was to rent the land with the following financial arrangements for the center. The stock in BRC was distributed three ways: (1) 25 percent is owned by the college from its endowment; (2) 25 percent is owned by the Babson Organization, Inc. holding company for the business interests of the late Roger Babson, the founder of the college; and (3) 50 percent is owned by sports-minded investors in the community. The center was expected to realize a profit by the second year of operation through memberships in the tennis facilities and rental of the ice rink.

For the college, the plan was advantageous. It built an athletic complex on the campus for only a 25 percent investment in the common stock. The college also receives rent for the use of the land and dividends as a stock holder. The investors made a profit. There was even a benefit for the taxpayers in Wellesley because the land for the center was previously tax exempt.

The circumstances surrounding the case may be somewhat unique to Babson, particularly with the availability of so much land and the corporate relationship that existed. Nevertheless, the case offers a stimulating example of what can be done through innovative facility funding (Bauman, pp. 63–64).

Fredericktown, Ohio—High School Field House

The field house on the high school grounds in Fredericktown, Ohio, was recognized as a Facility of Merit in 1982. The complex is valued at $175,000, but the cost was about $85,000.

No school or taxpayer funds were used in building the facility. Funding was through the Fredericktown Boosters Club. This began in the mid-1970s with the creation of the 200 Club, which contributed $4,000 a year to the Booster Club. The boosters also operated a concessions trailer at the county fair, local produce shows, and home football games. Other funds were generated through donations from individuals and business organizations. For example, one firm matched any donation of $25 or more from an employee.

The key to the low construction cost and the value of the facility was donated materials and labor. Total construction time was four months, and all the labor, except for block and brick work, was donated.

This 4,700-square-foot complex is used for all spring sports and football. Also included in the building are a training room, a large concession area, ticket rooms, and locker rooms ("A Community-Built . . . Center," pp. 44–46).

PROFESSIONAL SPORT FACILITIES

For the past twenty years, North American cities have been on a frenzy of constructing professional sports stadiums or arenas. New Orleans, Chicago, Toronto, Baltimore, Charlotte, St. Petersburg, and Miami are a few of the cities that built or renovated over 200 arenas during the past two decades, whether or not there was a team to occupy the facility. Funding for these facilities ran the gamut from mostly private to completely public, with most combining some private contributions with a hefty dose of public money, bonds and tax incentives, and abatements.

The enormous amount of money and political capital spent to acquire these stadiums or arenas poses several questions: Why is there this intense interest and competition in attracting or keeping professional sports franchises? How do municipal governments deal with the financing of their stadiums? What is the effect on the city, the taxpayers, and the team itself? And, how can cities develop policies to keep and attract teams without abusing the public trust or giving in to the whims of franchise owners?

The Issue of Value

The value of a professional sports team to a city is debatable. Franchise owners see their teams as creating jobs and bringing in fans who have money to spend, which benefits local radio and television stations as well as restaurants, hotels, theaters, and other merchants.

Municipal governments see professional teams as conferring major-league status on their cities, putting smaller cities on a par with the likes of New York, Los Angeles, and Chicago. For example, the city of Charlotte, North Carolina, built a new basketball arena in 1987 because the city had "an identity crisis of sorts." It believes it is being confused with other 'Ch' cities in the region: Charleston, South Carolina, Charlottesville, Virginia, and Charleston, West Virginia. Having a pro basketball team raises your profile in the convention and trade-show business. People want to go to a place they have heard of (Recio). When the baseball Giants were threatening to move from San Francisco, Angela Alioto, a member of San Francisco's Board of Supervisors, said, "Losing the Giants would be like losing the symphony, the opera, or the ballet" (Fimrite, p. 50).

Peter Creticos, a Chicago-based consultant specializing in the economics of facilities, argues that prestige alone is enough to justify the expense of a stadium: "They may not be obvious, you may not be able to put a dollar to it, but I do think they play an important part in marketing an area" (Baker and Harris, p. A1). Others see stadiums as pure ego. Says Moon Landrieu, former mayor of New Orleans when the Superdome was built, "The Superdome is an exercise in optimism, a statement of faith. It is the very building of it that is important, not how much of it is used or its economics" (Barnes, p. 25).

Most importantly, and more tangible, cities believe that teams are a spur to the local economy. An early 1980s study concluded that Pittsburgh's benefits from the baseball Pirates totaled $37 million annually and the football Steelers added an additional $11.8 million to the city. In Indianapolis, the figure from the football Colts has been estimated at $21 million a year. Even if the stadium itself loses money, they say, "it is more than made up for by the development it attracts, the jobs it creates and the taxes it collects—the so-called multiplier effect" (Barnes, p. 25).

The evidence, however, is not so clear-cut. Many believe that "stadiums don't create wealth, they just redistribute it" (Barnes, p. 25). Since sports is entertainment, it competes with, rather than complements, other entertainment forms such as movies, theater, and even the zoo. If there is no sports team, people will spend their money elsewhere. For most people, the discretionary income spent on entertainment is limited, so it is a matter of either one or the other, but not both.

The economic benefits to a city are disputed as well. "Teresa Serata, San Francisco's budget director, says she can document only a $3.1 million annual net gain from the [baseball] Giants; the city's gross economic product is $30 billion, or 10,000 times as large" (Corliss, p. 50). Although stadiums can attract tourists and their dollars, there are not enough games during a year or other events using the otherwise empty stadiums to make up for the money spent to build them. "The domes may bring in some business, but offsetting that is the operating deficit," said Bruce Bingham, a consultant with Peat, Marwick, and Mitchell Co. (Barnes, p. 25). As for supporters' assertions that stadiums create jobs, Robert Baade, a professor a Lake Forest College in Illinois, has studied the situation and concludes that the employment created are mostly low-wage and part-time jobs and does little to expand the tax base.

Competition for Teams

The dubious economics of building and maintaining stadiums have not deterred most cities from competing for teams to move to their towns. In sports-mad America, cities will go to almost any length to lure or keep a big-league ball club, and owners know it. Team owners have the advantage in negotiating for a new or renovated facility and will willingly play off one city against another to obtain their goal regardless of past ties to a particular locality.

A June 1992 study of NFL franchises by the Senate Finance Committee of the State of Virginia concluded that a professional football team "seems to have the upper hand" when negotiating with its host city over financial arrangements for a stadium. Furthermore, the study found, "If the teams don't get the desired stadium replacements, renovations, or revenue enhancements they desire, they threaten to move when their leases expire." Cities about to lose a team have past examples to frighten them into conceding to an owner's wishes. "The threat of losing a major league team cannot be taken lightly by a city leader who knows what happened to Brooklyn after the Dodgers left and has to fear that the same loss of sense of community and identity might occur if a similar calamity befell his city" (Barnes, p. 25). This most often means tax breaks and the granting of ancillary rights to the team owner and especially for the funding of the stadium itself.

Many cities, including St. Petersburg and Indianapolis, built stadiums before there were teams to occupy them. St. Petersburg spent $138 million on the multipurpose Suncoast Dome in 1987, most of it coming from revenue bonds residents never got to vote on. Indianapolis was able to lure the Colts away from Baltimore largely due to the Hoosier Dome and the city's promise of minimum ticket sales, favorable loan rates, and a new training facility. Putting the stadium before the team was a major factor in the National Basketball Association's decision to expand in the mid-1980s. The NBA might not have considered expanding this soon if it weren't for the ample supply of new facilities. Says NBA Commissioner David J. Stern: "The arena construction boom clearly influenced the decision to expand" (Recio, p. 90). Without an adequate stadium, a city may be left out of any future expansion plans in the four major league sports.

The prospect of moving to St. Petersburg's Suncoast Dome was used by the owners of baseball's Chicago White Sox, Seattle Mariners, and San Francisco Giants to scare their original hometowns into renovating or building a new stadium for their respective team. This tactic works well. For example, rather than see the White Sox move to Florida, the Illinois State Legislature approved using $125 million in public funds to build a new Comiskey Park. Similarly, the prospect of losing the football Falcons convinced Atlanta to propose the $210 million Georgia Dome.

In the late 1980s owner Al Davis of the football Los Angeles Raiders made a deal with the city of Oakland, home of the Raiders a decade ago, for the city to finance, through tax-exempt bonds, $57 million in improvements to the Oakland-Alameda County Coliseum. Davis was to get a guaranteed percentage of gate receipts plus more than $600 million extra in fees and payments. The agreement fell through when Los Angeles offered an even more agreeable package for Davis to stay put.

Public versus Private Funding

As in Chicago, St. Petersburg, and Oakland, the vast majority of the financing of stadiums is underwritten by taxpayers. Few professional sports stadiums in North America are privately built or owned. Wrigley Field in Chicago, Busch Stadium in St. Louis, Dodger Stadium in Los Angeles, Fenway Park in Boston, and Arlington Stadium in Arlington, Texas, are all owned by the baseball teams that occupy them. But they are the exceptions. Most stadiums are built and operated with a generous amount of public resources. Even those team owners who can afford to build arenas with large scale government funding turn to the city and state for tax abatements, property tax relief, and nondirect government aid. For example, in the 1980s, wealthy developer Donald Trump proposed building a privately financed domed stadium in Flushing, New York, for his New Jersey Generals of the U.S. Football League; however, he wanted New York City to build the access roads to the stadium and improve nearby subway stops and demanded property tax abatements. Due to Trump's personal financial problems, and the failure of the League, the project never got off the ground.

Taxpayers can have input in the decision whether to fund a new stadium when city officials put bond issues that would pay for the facility on the ballot. Frequently, especially as the recession in the late 1980s worsened and municipal funds dwindled, voters have not been willing to spend the money. Joe Robbie built his stadium with his own money only after voters turned down bond issues to pay for renovating the Orange Bowl, former home of the Dolphins. Spending his own money was not as simple as it sounds, since Robbie put up the Dolphins as collateral on a $100 million loan to get construction started and, as building continued, he had to put up much of his fortune as collateral on a second loan.

In 1988 New Jersey voters, who had financed the enormously successful Meadowlands sports complex a decade earlier, rejected a state bond issue to build a baseball stadium on Meadowlands property. The bond issue included not only the stadium and parking lots, but construction of an exit off the New Jersey Turnpike, its own commuter rail stop, and a guarantee of 2.2 million in annual attendance for each of the first five years. Since an expansion team at the Meadowlands would infringe on the New York Mets' and Yankees' territorial rights, New Jersey would have had to lure one of those teams to the new facility. This stadium proposal was used by New York Yankees owner George Steinbrenner to extract $100 million in renovations to the present Yankee Stadium—including a new parking garage, luxury boxes, and a restaurant—from New York State and City. If the renovations were not completed at taxpayer expense, he warned, he would leave the Bronx for New Jersey when the lease on Yankee Stadium expired in 2002. New York spent the money and, at least for the near future, the Bronx Bombers will stay in the Bronx.

The story of the baseball Giants provides an example of the tortuous path a franchise owner must follow if he chooses to rely on the taxpayer dollars to fund a stadium. Owner Bob Lurie was turned down twice by the citizens of San Francisco, in 1987 and 1989, in his efforts to replace Candlestick Park, despite having had the support of the mayor and other officials, largely out of fear by the voters that a new stadium would become a tax burden. In 1990 he looked to the southern suburb of Santa Clara, only to be rejected by voters there as well.

In early 1992, Lurie announced an agreement with the city of San Jose, just south of San Francisco, to construct a stadium. San Jose would pay $155 million, through an increase in the city's utility tax, and Lurie would pay $30 million plus any additional costs and overruns. San Jose Mayor Susan Hammer enthusiastically pushed for the stadium, saying that not only would the Giants deliver to San Jose between $50 and $150 million annually, but she believed that a major league baseball team would bring her city the recognition it was due as a big league metropolis. The voters denied Lurie his stadium in a June referendum. Lurie then sold the Giants to a Florida investment group for $115 million, but the sale was nullified by the other National League owners when a San Francisco group came forward to buy the team from Lurie for $100 million. However, the stadium issue has yet to be settled. Says new managing general partner Magowan:

I do not believe baseball can be a long-term financial success in the Bay Area if we do not have a new stadium. We need to solve the problem of Candlestick Park. . . . I think each of the four attempts [to find a new stadium] failed because each one placed too great a premium on financing the stadium through public resources. I think the climate for approving . . . is much better today because Bob Lurie finally carried out his threat to move the team if he couldn't get a stadium. Before, he was thought to be a rich San Francisco businessman who would never abandon baseball in the Bay Area. I think the people now know if we don't get a stadium, the team will be forced to move. ("Chronology," p. 3C)

In other words threats work, and the city of San Francisco probably has not seen the end of the Candlestick Park saga.

The SkyDome in Toronto provides one of the most well-known and current examples of a stadium conceived by municipal officials and funded with a mix of private and public money. The SkyDome's financing is a model of how, even when public resources are carefully used and the government works closely with private investors, problems still arise. In addition, it presages what could be a new concept in stadium design: located in Toronto, it is a multiuse facility with a hotel, a health club, restaurants, and a shopping mall. It can be used for trade shows, conventions, and concerts as well as sporting events and thus be open for business for at least 200 days a year.

The SkyDome was envisioned in 1982 when then Ontario Premier William Davis decided that the baseball Blue Jays and CFL football Argonauts needed a new home to replace the poorly designed and situated Exhibition Stadium. But any old stadium would not suffice. Toronto not only needed a dome, but the most modern and technologically advanced dome available. The reason? "Toronto had to make a statement, put itself on the map" (Hawkins, p. 136). Davis turned to Toronto businessman John Trevor Eyton after the province of Ontario agreed to fund the stadium for up to $50.4 million if private investors could be found to contribute an additional $40 million. Eyton persuaded 28 companies to put up to $4.2 million apiece. In return, the companies, which included Coca-Cola, Ford Motor Company, McDonald's, Exxon, and RJR Nabisco, were promised luxury boxes and parking at no charge, guaranteed advertising space inside the SkyDome, and exclusive supplier deals. For example, Coca-Cola holds the exclusive soft drink contract in the Sky-Dome, and McDonald's built its largest restaurant in North America there and operates all of the stadium's concession stands. The Stadium Corporation of Ontario, the municipal organization that originally ran the SkyDome and until recently owned 51 percent of it, got a hefty 38 percent share of the revenues generated by these concessions.

Other private sources of financing included the sale of private boxes, season tickets and advertising rights. Ten-year leases on luxury boxes generated $50 million in sales before the SkyDome was completed. The final money was raised through a public sale of stock and bank loans.

Critics of this financing deal charge that Eyton should have opened the process to the highest bidder, and that the agreement gave the corporations too many benefits at the taxpayers' expense. Yet, many of the contributing corporations will never realize a return on their investment and even those that will, took a gamble in underwriting the SkyDome when it was still in the planning stages. The idea of building something for the community may have been lost amid the commercial aspects. Clearly, the civic virtues of the SkyDome were as important as the monetary ones throughout the realization of the stadium.

Unfortunately, the SkyDome has been losing money since it opened in June 1989. Despite record attendance at Blue Jays games and strong turnouts for other events, it lost $18 million in 1990, even though it met its revenue target of $39 million. Enough money was initially raised to meet its original budget of $360 million, but it quickly ran into cost overruns and unforeseen events. Although hailed as the wave of the future, the hotel and health club were not in the original plans, were expensive to build, and have lost money since the SkyDome opened. The partners failed to provide contingency money, and, after a strike during construction, the final cost of the stadium hit $496 million. The SkyDome was $288 million in debt two years after it opened. Interest payments on that debt created the majority of the annual losses. Says Tony Tavares, chairman of SMG, a stadium management organization, "They got caught up in the glitter and excitement and lost sight of what this thing would look like as a business" (Symonds, p. 40).

The taxpayers of Ontario were footing the bill for the debt. That, combined with the overwhelming Canadian recession, led to calls to sell the SkyDome to a private company to relieve the government of the expense of owning and operating the facility. In November 1991, the SkyDome was sold to a consortium of eight private companies for $110 million, thereby ridding the government of its share of the debt.

In the end, the SkyDome project shows that no matter how successful in design and diligent in execution, a project as large as a stadium holds risks that often cannot be foreshadowed, and the public will usually end up paying for those risks. "The SkyDome should serve as a warning to other cities about the dangers of getting carried away with showcase projects. In the end, someone has to pay the bill, and it's usually the taxpayers" (Symonds, p. 40).

CONCLUSION AND POLICY FRAMEWORK

Although there are different opinions as to the economic benefits of a stadium to a particular city, it is generally acknowledged that stadiums and the professional sports teams they attract add to the overall quality of living in or near a city and are as beneficial and important to an area as any other civic enterprise. Still, there is great controversy as to how much, if any, a franchise owner should be compensated to keep or move a team. In a time of deep financial trouble for cities and states across North America, questions arise as to the wisdom of what is in essence subsidizing very wealthy people.

Even when a stadium project is carefully planned and budgeted, or when an owner promises to pay for the entire venture, the taxpayers will ultimately be forced to foot at least some of the bill. Each stadium-building city may have its own motives and its own price, but two results are almost assured. The city will lose money, and the team owner will gain. The owner gets a home with very little liability. Taxpayers get a bond issue that will dog them for a generation.

Nevertheless, local officials will continue to compete for the opportunity to have a pro sports team and claim that their city will be better off with a franchise than without one, no matter what the cost. The overriding point is that teams are advantageous to a city, adding to the many community institutions that make a place unique. Sports teams are a civic amenity, along with museums, theaters, symphony orchestras, restaurants, shops, universities, great architecture, botanic gardens, and zoos, and should be regarded as such. If they boost the local economy, so much the better. That sports teams are profit-making operations, unlike most of the above, and are owned by wealthy individuals, should be taken into account but not used to disqualify teams and stadiums from being a part of the total civic picture. The difficulty is in trying to devise a consistent policy to anticipate and deal with team owners who know that they usually have the upper hand in negotiations. As can be seen in San Francisco, Toronto, and other cities, each situation is different, depending on such disparate themes as politics, the economy, personal rivalries and personality conflicts, the mood of the voters, and so on. In order to keep or lure a team, city officials have to formulate policies that accommodate team owners to a reasonable extent. If lucky, events can turn out advantageously; if not, most cities will mourn the loss of their erstwhile teams for years to come.

Unfortunately, accommodation means that taxpayers will end up financing stadiums to some degree, probably at a greater level than a lesser one. The realities of America's lifelong love affair with sports and the fact that even multibillionaires are not willing to fully finance a project if they can wrest money from the public ensures that stadium financing will continue to be a public burden. As stated above, each situation and the personalities involved play a large part in negotiations and can determine the extent of concessions, enticements, tax breaks, and such, but the final determination rests with the owner. It is up to local officials to keep the process open to the public at every step, to make the plan as tolerable and fair to the citizenry as possible, to work with instead of against the franchise owner, and to make the building of a stadium a matter of community pride, not animosity.

REFERENCES

"A Community-Built High School Athletic Center." *Athletic Purchasing and Facilities*, Vol. 7, No. 8, August 1983, pp. 44–46.

"A Legacy Lives On: The John Wooden Center." *Athletic Business*, Vol. 10, No. 5, May 1986, pp. 38–45.

"A Place of Their Own." *Athletic Business*, Vol. 9, No. 12, December 1985, pp. 24–27.

Baker, Donald P. "Cooke Would Get Good Deal after He Pays for Stadium." *Washington Post*, August 22, 1992, p. C1.

Baker, Peter, and John F. Harris. "Stadium Deal Called 'Giveaway.'" *Washington Post*, July 19, 1992, p. A1.

Barnes, John A. "Home Sweet Dome." *Washington Monthly*, February 1988, p. 25.

Bauman, M. "Unique Financing Provides Babson College with a New Athletic Complex." *Athletic Purchasing and Facilities*, Vol. 2, No. 5, October 1978, pp. 63–64.

Bronzan, R. T. "Student Fees: A New Source for Funding Facilities." *Athletic Business*, Vol. 8, No. 3, March 1984, pp. 18–22.

Casey, G. R. "Using Professional Counsel in Your Fund-Raising Campaign." *Athletic Purchasing and Facilities*, Vol. 6, No. 3, March 1982, pp. 70–74.

"Comprehensive Facility Is Pride of Small College." *Athletic Business*, Vol. 10, No. 1, January 1986, pp. 34–37.

Fimrite, Ron. "Oh, Give Me a Home . . . " *Sports Illustrated*, June 1, 1992, p. 50.

Finci, David L. "Need New Facilities? Don't Overlook the Old." *Athletic Purchasing and Facilities*, Vol. 5, No. 3, March 1981, pp. 24–30.

Hawkins, Chuck. "After SkyDome, Stadiums Will Never Be the Same." *Business Week*, March 20, 1989, p. 136.

"How to Work with a 'Corporate Partner.' " *Athletic Purchasing and Facilities*, Vol. 5, No. 3, March 1981, pp. 24–30.

"How Will You Fund Your Athletic Facility?" *Athletic Purchasing and Facilities*, Vol. 4, No. 6, June 1990, pp. 31–36.

Manning, B. "Creative Planning: Berkeley's Recreational Sports Complex." *Athletic Purchasing and Facilities*, Vol. 5, No. 6, June 1981, pp. 42–46.

"Masters of Their Fate." *Athletic Business*, Vol. 11, No. 1, January 1987, pp. 18–23.

McCuaig, K. "Seeking Facility Fees that Make Sense." *Athletic Business*, Vol. 8, No. 11, November 1984, pp. 36–41.

Pipho, A. "New Track Fund-Raiser Targeted Athletic Alumni." *Athletic Business*, Vol. 8, No. 6, June 1984, pp. 104–106.

Recio, Maria E. "Build an Arena Now, Get a Team Later—Maybe." *Business Week*, April 20, 1987, p. 90.

"Recreation on Campus: The New Building Boom." *Athletic Business*, Vol. 9, No. 4, April 1985, pp. 10–16.

"Scandals and Taxes." *Athletic Business*, Vol. 11, No. 5, May 1987, pp. 20, 22, 24–25.

Symonds, William C. "Take Me Out to the Cleaners." *Business Week*, May 6, 1991, p. 40.

"Throwing a Curve Ball at City Hall." *U.S. News & World Report*, October 23, 1989, p. 20.

Chapter 14

Professional Sport Franchise Expansion and Relocation

W ithin recent years, professional sport franchise expansion and relocation is the "name of the game." This has not always been the case. Prior to 1953, very few professional teams relocated, and there was hardly any expansion. For example, from 1903 to 1953 not one major league baseball team moved to another city. If new stadiums or arenas were built, they were constructed in the general location of the franchise.

The Boston Braves moved to Milwaukee in 1953, the St. Louis Browns to Baltimore in 1954, and the Philadelphia Athletics relocated to Kansas City in 1955. Yet, the major league baseball teams, as well as other professional sport teams, were still largely concentrated in eastern United States and specifically in the Northeast. It was not until the Brooklyn Dodgers and the New York Giants moved west that cities realized the tenuous position regarding their professional sport teams. For the first time, politicians and fans came to the realization that professional sport franchises are strictly a business, a result of capitalism and free enterprise. Keeping a franchise in place could no longer be taken for granted. Money will likely outweigh any loyalty to the current location.

Although possible relocation is always a reality today, professional sport expansion has been even more evident. Nevertheless, there is variance among the four major professional sport leagues. Historically, baseball has been the most sluggish when it comes to expansion. Until Colorado and Florida were added in 1993, there had been no additions to major league baseball franchises for 16 years. However, these additions were rather quickly followed by franchise expansion in Phoenix and Tampa-St. Petersburg.

Even these four additions do not mean that baseball expansion has kept pace with the other major sport leagues. Baseball economists suggest that the sports' anti-trust exemption is a major reason for relatively slow expansion in baseball. Rival leagues have pushed the expansion in other sports. The anti-trust exemption restricts the possibility of a rival league forcing expansion in baseball. In addition, baseball has had difficulty finding adequate stadiums and faces the increased marketing demands of a 162-game schedule.

Expansion has been prominent in the other major professional sports. Since 1967 the number of hockey teams has increased from 6 to 26 and basketball from 10 to 29. The National Football League expanded from 16 to 30 teams. This includes the merger with nine American Football League teams in 1970. More recently, there has been speculation about further expansion. In the NHL, Atlanta and Milwaukee have been mentioned as possible, franchise sites. The NBA is considering Mexico City by the year 2000. NFL Commissioner Paul Tagliabue has identified Mexico City, Toronto, and Vancouver as expansion possibilities.

In analyzing some of the complications involving expansion and relocation, it is helpful to begin by considering the nature of franchises in general. From there, the particular characteristics of professional sport franchises should also be noted. The other key consideration is the differences among the four major professional sport leagues.

FRANCHISES

According to *Webster's Ninth New Collegiate Dictionary*, a franchise is defined as "the right or license granted to an individual or group to market a company's goods or services in a particular territory." The terms of a franchise agreement grant the right to sell the franchiser's name within a designated area. Typically, when people think of franchises, the first things that come to mind are fast food restaurants and hotels, not sport teams. However, when one considers the scope of the definition of a franchise, professional sport teams clearly qualify as being franchises. The teams, the franchises, pay the leagues, the franchisers, a fee to be allowed to market the other teams and the league itself within the home team's designated territory. In other words, the Boston Red Sox, through their franchise rights, can market Major League Baseball and its teams in the greater Boston area.

Professional sport leagues maintain firm control over the individual teams. Most importantly, the league has control over who can acquire a franchise. At one time the league also had more control as to where that franchise can be located. It is in the best interest of the various franchises to protect the integrity and the image of the league and the sport itself.

Nevertheless, it is also important to note that leagues have power only at the discretion of the owners. The league is the central, administrative unit that sets and administers rules about team composition, schedules, and playing conditions. However, the powerful owners really guide the ship. Leonard Koppett drives home this point most succinctly:

So, it is impossible to understand or interpret how a league works without realizing that club owners, and only club owners, make decisions about things that matter. Commissioners are allowed independence only on issues that matter less, or along lines tacitly agreed upon. . . .

Only the club owners "own" anything; and leagues are merely the agencies through which their collective assets are managed. They hire and fire commissioners at will, and since the players have formed strong unions of their own, the ability of the owners to use the commissioner to discipline players or control their movement has been eroded.

What really rules every league, therefore, is a consensus among the more powerful (or more respected) club owners in the group. (Koppett, p. 80)

MONOPOLISTIC TENDENCIES OF
PROFESSIONAL SPORT

These owners are very much aware of and willing to protect the monopolistic tendencies of the leagues they control. Thus, they also strive to control the number of teams within a league even though there are proceeds from league expansion. Expansion can also negatively affect the financial status of certain franchises.

The professional sport industry has been very fortunate that Congress has historically held a laissez-faire-type attitude toward the industry as a whole. The area in which this attitude is most prevalent is that of anti-trust law, which is a preeminent factor in other segments of the business world. For some reason, Congress has not felt the need to change past judgments that sports are exempt, in varying degree, from anti-trust legislation. Although the other major sport leagues have been allowed to deviate from the anti-trust legislation to some extent, only baseball has held complete immunity from that legislation.

The focus of the immunity or exemption is the Sherman Anti-trust Act of 1890. The legislation contained two clauses that, on the surface, seemed applicable to baseball:

Section I. Every contract, combination in the form of a trust or otherwise, or conspiracy, in restraint of trade or commerce among the several states, or with foreign nations is hereby declared illegal. Every person who shall make any such contract or engage in such combination or conspiracy, shall be deemed guilty of a misdemeanor. . . .

Section II. Every person who shall monopolize, or attempt to monopolize, or combine or conspire with any other person or persons, to monopolize any part of the trade or commerce among the several states, or with foreign nations, shall be deemed guilty of a misdemeanor. (Scully, pp. 26–27)

There are three areas of professional sport league operation that would appear to be related to that legislation. These are league membership regulation, transactions with players, and negotiation of national television broadcast rights. The first of these, league membership regulations, is particularly applicable to professional sport expansion and relocation.

Baseball received its immunity in 1922 when Justice Holmes delivered the court's opinion that baseball was not subject to the anti-trust statutes. The basis for the decision was that baseball was not commerce. That was later reaffirmed in other legal cases. During the course of years, the other professional sports have not fared as well in the courts. Nevertheless, all of professional sport has received some degree of exemption. Thus, the monopolistic tendencies tend to be prevalent. The basic argument always remains that a strong league is essential to individual franchise welfare.

Economists and lawyers have consistently stressed that the principal objective of American anti-trust law is the maximization of consumer welfare. Thus it can be argued that consumer welfare will increase as a result of team collusion through a strong league. In other words, consumers, as well as individual teams, stand to benefit from a strong league that develops and promotes the sport. So, once again, we have further reason why professional sport leagues continue to function in somewhat of a monopolistic fashion. Unlike other industries where it is possible for one sector to seek its own market, the professional sport franchise cannot simply walk away from the league.

Territorial exclusivity is one way an individual franchise can benefit from control by the league. Basically, this means that the league protects the franchise by ensuring that it will not be in direct competition for fans and broadcast rights if another franchise is brought into the particular geographic territory. There are very few cities that are large enough to accommodate two professional teams in the same sport. Exceptions are the Yankees and the Mets in New York, the Cubs and the White Sox in Chicago, and the Lakers and the Clippers in Los Angeles. As one example on the other side of the spectrum, the Green Bay Packers benefit considerably from territorial exclusivity.

This function of a league in protecting the territory of a franchise is an important consideration in decisions involving expansion and relocation. Today it continues to be an important factor in expansion of franchises. Relocation is now a more complicated matter. When Al Davis chose to move the Raiders from Oakland to Los Angeles, the role of the league changed. The NFL failed in that effort to protect territorial exclusivity.

LEAGUE EXPANSION

Thus, we find that territorial exclusivity is one of the reasons why leagues use restrictive methods of expansion. Another reason certainly is to ensure that there is a sufficient supply of player talent to compete at the highest level in that sport.

On the other hand, an expansion franchise pays a hefty fee to gain entry into a league. Furthermore, that figure is continually rising within each league. The question is, when does a given league reach the saturation point? Some economists have suggested that the vigorous age of sport franchise expansion has passed. This is partially based on the premise that many of the current owners may seek to "unload" their teams in the future. These owners will look at the exorbitant prices the league is charging for an expansion team and arrive at an inflated figure for the worth of their team.

One also cannot ignore the fact that new franchises directly and indirectly affect the rest of the teams in the league. For example, scheduling is definitely affected. It is possible that the number of contests between traditional rivalries may be reduced, thus causing a loss in some revenue. As noted earlier, the pool of available, qualified player talent is also directly affected by expansion. In a given sport, this can be particularly critical at certain positions. As a case in point, there is typically a shortage of high quality left-handed pitchers in baseball. When major league baseball decides to add one or more expansion teams, the shortage of talent becomes that much more severe.

Nevertheless, the current league owners have obviously reached the conclusion that the financial benefits of expansion outweigh the negative results of adding one or more franchises. This is evident as we consider the leagues individually, even though the range of differences among the four major professional sport leagues should also be noted.

National Hockey League

The NHL has experienced some difficulty in recent years due to its relative lack of national exposure, particularly in television. This may also partially account for the fact that the league has dramatically changed with regard to its approach toward expansion. During the 24-year period from 1943 to 1967, the NHL was made up of the same six teams. Since then, the league has grown by over 400 percent. The current 26 teams include the most recent additions in Anaheim, Tampa Bay, and Ottawa.

When it comes to expansion, the NHL has one of the more difficult decisions. Should the league expand to more underexposed areas in southern United States or within northern United States and Canada where hockey is already very popular? There are a plethora of arguments for each side. Sometimes bidders are merely selected because they can meet the league's entry fee without qualifications. Nevertheless, the decision to expand to Edmonton as well as relocation in Calgary was geographically based.

Corporate ownership has also been a key factor in NHL expansion. This matter of corporate ownership was controversial when Anaheim was awarded its franchise. The Mighty Ducks are owned by the Walt Disney Company. There was a confilict of interest in the awarding of territorial fees to the Los Angeles Kings.

Aside from the Anaheim situation, the NHL has had the most corporate proliferation with six teams having corporate owners. The others are the Toronto Maple Leafs, Tampa Bay Lightning, St. Louis Blues, New York Rangers, and Montreal Canadians. The latter provides an excellent, early example of a corporation running a successful professional franchise.

The Canadians were bought by Molson Companies, Ltd. from Edward and Peter Bronfman in 1978. The club has been the league's most successful franchise since its formation in 1909, winning 23 Stanley Cups, 17 of them coming after 1944. The team does just as well off the ice, generating an extensive profit each year. The Molson Company takes pride in the ownership of the franchise and runs it like any other business. That means keeping expenses low and profits high. Of course, it took some time to get to the present position. Like any business, it takes a while to obtain the footing. As late as 1989, the team announced losses. The players are well paid, and the Canadians also have a large staff for a professional sport franchise. They have invested heavily in marketing, scouting, and their farm system.

Molson can afford to be patient with its hockey franchise as it is a small part of its total business venture. This is a major benefit corporate owners can offer a team. If a single owner was to experience losses season after season, chances are he or she would sell the team.

National Basketball Association

Among all the professional sport leagues, the NBA has had almost a fairy tale type of existence in recent years. Although the association was founded in 1946, it was not until the 1980s that the NBA really gained the popularity it has today. Much of this can be attributed over the years to the presence of superstars such as "Magic" Johnson, Larry Bird, Michael Jordan, Shaquille O'Neal as well as the leadership of Commissioner David Stern.

The success of the NBA is also reflected in the expansion of franchises. A number of cities has taken chances with millions of tax dollars to build arenas in the hope of attracting teams. Currently, there are 27 teams in the NBA. The newest members are the Toronto Raptors and Vancouver Grizzlies. However, the Minnesota Timberlines, Orlando Magic, Miami Heat, and Charlotte Hornets were also added in the 1990s. The latter is a classic example of municipal support. In the drive to obtain a franchise and then gain "big city" recognition, the taxpayers of Charlotte approved $68 million in bond financing for the coliseum.

National Football League

The National Football League was founded in 1920. For many years it consisted of relatively few teams with only a small amount of support and recognition: the Chicago Bears, Cleveland Browns, Detroit Lions, Green Pay Packers, New York Giants, Pittsburgh Steelers, and Washington Redskins. Today there are 30 teams. A significant step in expansion was the merger with the American Football League teams in 1970. However, the expansion has continued in recent years with the addition of the Carolina Panthers and Jacksonville Jaguars in 1995. Currently, there is further speculation about expansion with Mexico City identified as one of the possibilities.

A spokesman for the league says there are no set guidelines for choosing a location for an expansion team. As with expansion in the other professional sport leagues, the decisions usually involve politics, personalities, and whims of team owners in lieu of demographics. Nevertheless, all expansion decisions do take into account the population of the prospective franchise site, television markets, and the overall economy of the site. More recently, the willingness of companies to purchase skyboxes is also an important factor in selecting a site for NFL expansion.

Major League Baseball

As noted earlier, major league baseball has been the most reluctant to expand, at least until recent years. The Colorado Rockies and the Florida Marlins were added in 1993; Phoenix and Tampa-St. Petersburg were awarded franchises in 1995.

The additions of the Florida Marlins and Tampa-St. Petersburg were logical in view of the fact that they have large television markets. The geographic locations of Colorado and Phoenix were also favorable. In order for Florida and Colorado to be admitted, they had to receive a unanimous vote from the owners of the National League. By contrast, entry into the American League requires only a three-fourths vote by the owners. This only points to the realization that policies involving major league baseball are particularly complicated due to differences between the two leagues.

RELOCATION

When a sport franchise decides to move, it causes an uproar that is virtually unmatched in any other aspect of the business world. The reason is that municipal government and public policy play a large role in team relocation. Government and taxpayers are willing to spend their money financing stadiums and arenas to attract and keep sport teams. This is partly a result of a general perception that the city itself becomes a major player when it is home to a sport team. For example, local politicians are obsessed with having their cities recognized as "major league" status. The thought is the city needs a sports team to achieve that status.

Government officials and their constituents are quick to react to their team's leaving because finding a replacement team is extremely difficult. There are many classic examples. Baltimore did not have an NFL team for many years after losing the Colts. Washington, D.C. still lacks a baseball team after losing the Senators.

The classic case of relocation is that involving Al Davis and the Raiders. Davis moved the Raiders from Oakland to Los Angeles in 1982 and then back to Oakland in 1995. The first move was made after the NFL lost a lawsuit filed by Davis when the league attempted to block the move. This case actually established a precedent in professional sport and probably explains in part why relocation has been so prevalent in recent years.

Nevertheless, the number-one reason for moving is strictly money, and more specifically, luxury suites. In 1995 *Sports Illustrated* reported that 39 of the 109 major league franchises were considering a move if they did not get a new arena or stadium or a more favorable deal with the government that owns the facility. This included 14 baseball teams, 14 football teams, 8 NBA franchises, and 3 NHL clubs. The oldest facilities are Fenway Park in Boston and Tiger Stadium in Detroit, both opened in 1912. However, some of the venues are quite new. For example, the Charlotte coliseum and

Miami arena were opened in 1988. Yet, by 1995, they were seeking a more favorable arrangement.

Much of the attempted movement has been stimulated by the financial benefits of attractive new stadiums such as Baltimore's Camden Yards and Cleveland's Jacobs Field. The former was planned in the 1980s when the Orioles then owner, Edward Bennett, refused to sign more than a one-year lease for Memorial Stadium. It was feared that he would move the franchise to Washington, D.C. This forced the city to yield to the pressure and build Camden Yards. Similar pressures led to the construction of Jacobs Field.

When a city refuses to yield to the pressure, the relocation may materialize. The financial benefits can be considerable for the franchise that moves. The St. Louis Rams are a classic case in point:

The Rams became one of the NFL's highest-grossing teams when they moved from Los Angeles to St. Louis in 1995. This resulted from stadium revenue, including luxury boxes, advertising, and personal seat licenses (paying for the right to buy a season ticket).

As with expansion, there is considerable variance among the four major professional leagues with respect to relocation. The NHL and NFL have had more movement than the other two leagues. However, the NBA did have considerable movement in the earlier years. The Atlanta Hawks moved from the Tri-Cities to Milwaukee, St. Louis, and then Atlanta. The Philadelphia 76'ers originated in Syracuse as did the Detroit Pistons in Fort Wayne; San Diego lost teams to both Houston and Los Angeles.

In recent years, the NFL has been the most volatile in terms of relocation. Following is a listing of the NFL franchises that have left their metropolitan arenas since the merger of the NFL and the All-American Football League in 1950:

1960	Chicago Cardinals moved to St. Louis
1961	Los Angeles Chargers (AFL) moved to San Diego
1963	Dallas, Texas (AFL) became Kansas City Chiefs
1982	Oakland Raiders moved to Los Angeles
1984	Baltimore Colts moved to Indianapolis
1988	St. Louis Cardinals moved to Phoenix
1995	Los Angeles Rams moved to St. Louis
1995	Los Angeles Raiders moved back to Oakland
1995	Cleveland Browns moved to Baltimore

1997   Houston Oilers moved to Nashville

(*USA Today*, November 8, 1995, p. 2c)

Even more recently, the NHL has seen franchises on the move. The Winnipeg Jets became the Phoenix Coyotes in 1996, and the Hartford Whalers became the Carolina Hurricanes in 1997.

Once again, major league baseball has been the most resistant to relocation, probably due to its anti-trust exemption. In early 1990, four teams were told by the league owners that they could not move. These were the Montreal Expos, Seattle Mariners, Houston Astros, and San Francisco Giants. As noted in chapter 13, the latter is a classic case of control by the other baseball owners. Bob Lurie actually sold the Giants to a group in Tampa Bay for $115 million. Then the sale was nullified by the other National League owners. Even though a San Francisco group came forward to buy the team for $100 million, Lurie lost $15 million when the relocation was blocked by the league owners.

CONCLUSION

Franchise expansion and relocation certainly represents one of the key issues in professional sport today. The records show that very little can be taken for granted concerning the stability of a franchise or a league. This topic also points to a larger question: How much power should reside with a league over the individual franchises? There seems to be little doubt that the league structure is somewhat unique to sport. It is the league structure that makes the entire operation what it is today. The league is naturally the controlling point for expansion, relocation of a franchise is another matter.

REFERENCES

Koppett, Leonard. *Sports Illusion, Sports Reality*. Boston: Houghton Mifflin Company, 1981.

Scully, Gerald W. *The Business of Major League Baseball*. Chicago: University of Chicago Press, 1989.

USA Today, November 8, 1995, p. 2c.

Webster's Ninth New Collegiate Dictionary. Springfield, MA: Merriam-Webster, Inc., 1988.

Chapter 15

Professional Sport Playoffs

During the past decade all the professional sport leagues have expanded the number of playoff teams and changed the playoff structure. The National Basketball Association expanded to a 16-team playoff format, while the NHL restructured its playoff format to copy the NBA model. The National Football League changed its playoff format and added one more wild card team to each conference. Finally, Major League Baseball realigned the divisions within each league, changed its playoff format, and doubled the number of playoff teams from four to eight, including wild card positions.

It is quite clear that the number of playoff positions is a real issue because there are legitimate arguments for and against expanding the number. More about that will be said later, but it might be useful to begin by looking at the history of the playoff situation.

HISTORY

As is true with history generally, the history of the playoff policies in professional sport sheds some light on why the policies exist as they do today. The 1970s were somewhat of a turning point in professional sport because it was a period of expansion. For example, the NBA grew from 8 teams in 1960–1961 to 17 teams by the beginning of the 1970s. Likewise, the NHL was made up of only six teams until 1967. Similarly, MLB underwent a four team expansion in 1969. Also, 1970 marked the completion of the merger between the National Football League and the American Football League. In all four leagues the result of the expansion was increased competition for a limited number of playoff slots. This led to changes in policy to accommodate more participation in the post-season. However, differences among the four major professional sports should also be noted.

MAJOR LEAGUE BASEBALL

Baseball is a sport rich in tradition, and this is reflected in the way Major League Baseball has conducted post-season play. Basically, this has meant that a premium has been placed on the regular season record with the goal of reaching the World Series. Only recently have we seen some departure from that traditional approach.

The first World Series was played in 1903, following a two-year war between the National League and its rival, the American League. This basic concept of regular season play followed by "the series" was more or less followed until 1995. The two leagues were divided into two divisions each. At the end of the long season, the teams in first place in each division (pennant winners) qualified for the league championship series (LCS) while all the remaining teams ended their seasons. If two teams from the same division finished in a tie for first place, a one-game playoff decided the division championship. Home field advantage in the LCS was awarded to the team with the best overall record. In 1985, the LCS was changed from a best three-of-five series to a best four-of-seven format, the same as for the World Series.

The most significant change in the playoff structure was made on September 9, 1993, when the baseball owners approved the current playoff policy. Three divisions were established in each of the leagues, and one wild card team from each league also advanced to post-season play. Thus, the number of playoff teams was doubled from four to eight. The wild card team in each league is the one with the best season record among those teams that did not win a division championship. For example, in 1995, Cleveland, Boston, and Seattle were division champions and New York was the wild card team after having the best record among the remaining teams in the American League. This was the first year the playoffs were conducted under this new structure. The change was scheduled to take place in 1994, but did not materialize due to the strike and the curtailment of the season.

Prior to the 1995 playoffs there was considerable discussion through the news media that the playoff changes were not for the better. However, after some very exciting playoff games, much of the sentiment seemed to swing in the other direction. Nevertheless, many people still contend that baseball threw away its heritage and tradition for a quick fix to the public's waning interest in the game. They argue that there is nothing so exciting as a close pennant race. For example, in 1994, NBC Sportscaster Bob Costas had this to say about baseball's new playoff policy: "Yes, you will have additional mediocre teams alive for diluted playoff spots in an ersatz pennant race—but never again will you have the feeling you got from the genuine race between the Braves and the Giants last season" (Costas, p. 14).

Baseball owners and the players agreed to this new, expanded playoff policy for a minimum of four years. This will serve as a trial period for the new format. In other words the new policy will have to face the true test of time before it is fully accepted. As noted before, part of this is related to the traditional stance of baseball. What Branch Rickey said in 1994 still holds true: "Baseball people—and that includes myself—are slow to change and accept new ideas" (Wulf, p. 93). Certain changes to baseball are still hotly contested by opponents. More than two decades have passed since the designated hitter rule took effect in the American League. The opposition to this policy has not abated. One can be assured that the expanded playoff format will continue to be viewed with contempt by the traditionalists.

NATIONAL HOCKEY LEAGUE

From the very beginning, the emphasis in the National Hockey League has been to win the Stanley Cup. That cup is named after Governor General Frederick Arthur Stanley who developed the idea of a hockey championship for Canada in 1893, when the silver cup was first awarded to the Montreal Athletic Association. The following year a formal championship format was developed for six teams that competed for the valued Cup. From that time on, the emphasis in professional hockey has focused on the importance of the post-season play. To some extent this is true of all professional sports, but hockey has dramatized the significance of the post-season through its playoff format.

In 1967 the National Hockey League expanded the number of teams in the league from 6 to 12. With the expansion, the NHL doubled the number of playoff teams from 4 to 8. The top four teams from each of the two divisions advanced to the playoffs. These were the teams with the highest point totals, based on two points for a victory and one point for a tie. Should there be a tie, the team with the highest number of goals would get the playoff spot. Each division had a best-of-seven series, and the winners met in the finals of the best-of-seven series for the Stanley Cup.

By 1980 the NHL had expanded to 21 teams, and the number of playoff teams again doubled from 8 to 16. A new policy also involved seeding the top 16 teams, based on points during the season, regardless of conference or division. The playoff policy rewarded the teams that performed well during the season with relatively easy first-round opponents. However, a problem with this playoff system was that it ignored conference geographical boundaries. This created a problem because of the great distance some of the teams traveled to compete in the first round. For example, in the 1980 playoffs, the Los Angeles Kings faced 3,000 miles of jet lag in its best-of-five series against the New York Islanders. As a result, criticism led to another change in the playoff policy.

The first and second rounds of the playoffs were then held within each division with the top four teams from that division. In the third round, the division champions battled for the conference title. Then the conference champions met for the Stanley Cup Finals. However, this change also had its problems, centering around the matter of inequity. A division could be very weak and still automatically qualify four playoff teams. More importantly, under that playoff format, teams with losing records in one division displaced winning-record teams from another division.

The current playoff policy became effective during the 1993–1994 season and is designed to address the problems associated with the earlier policies. Under this structure, the two division champions in each conference and the next best six teams from each conference qualify for the playoffs. The division champions receive the top two seeds, based on point totals. In other words, the top seed goes to the division champion with the most points at the end of the season.

Again, the points are based on two points for each victory and one point for each tie. The six other teams are seeded three through eight. Therefore, equity is created within each conference because no losing-record team can replace a winning-record team in the conference playoffs. Also, the travel distance is reasonable for the first three rounds of the playoffs because teams within the league are split by Eastern and Western conferences. There is the Eastern Conference with the Northeast Division and Atlantic Division. Likewise, there is the Western Conference with the Central Division and Pacific Division.

Nevertheless, many people still criticize the NHL playoff policy because it qualifies too many teams for post-season play. There has been some improvement in that regard. In 1986, 16 of 21 teams qualified for the post-season. Since then five new franchises have been added to the NHL so the league now qualifies 16 of its 26 teams for the playoffs. Yet, the final few playoff spots are typically occupied by relatively weak teams with losing records. The large number of playoff teams tends to dilute the importance of the NHL's 84-game regular season. Some observers suggest that the league should consider limiting the number of playoff teams to no more than a minority of teams.

A positive aspect of the NHL regular season is the President's Cup. This is awarded to the team with the best record (highest point total) in the regular season. The players earn a handsome bonus, and the team has home advantage throughout the playoffs. This establishes a reason for the leagues' best teams to strive for winning at the end of the season. Yet, there is no denying the fact that the focus is always on the post-season play. The NHL has capitalized heavily off the fan's illusion that their team (no matter how weak) can triumph in the post-season. This can be true. For example in 1991, the Minnesota North Stars were seeded fifteenth among the 16 playoff teams. Yet, they reached the Stanley Cup Finals. On the other hand, the North Stars success that year was clearly an exception to the rule. By and large, the weaker teams are eliminated in the first round.

Outside the NHL, undoubtedly there is consensus that the league has too many playoff teams and, consequently, a playoff schedule that is too long. So why does the NHL persist in qualifying too many playoff teams? The simple answer is economics. Many of the franchises depend on the revenue received in the post-season. For that reason, the NHL's basic, playoff policy is not likely to change in the near future.

NATIONAL BASKETBALL ASSOCIATION

Although the sport of basketball was originated by Dr. James A. Naismith in 1891, it was not until the late 1930s that the sport was professionalized. There were two professional basketball leagues, the Basketball Association of America and the National Basketball League. These two leagues merged in 1949 to form the National Basketball Association. In 1967, the American Basketball Association (ABA) also merged with the NBA to increase the NBA teams from 17 to 22. Currently the NBA has 29 teams, an 82-game schedule, and (like the NHL) an extended playoff format.

When the playoffs were originally established, the league qualified 12 teams. The four division champions were awarded first round byes, and the four teams with next best records in each conference qualified for the first round of playoffs. The NBA changed its playoff format for the 1983–1984 season. The number of teams was increased to 16, and, thus, the first round byes for conference champions were also eliminated. This revised policy still remains in place. The format is similar to that of the NHL, and this is not by coincidence. Gary Bettman, the NHL commissioner, helped develop the NBA's playoff policy when he was the senior vice president of the latter league.

One of the distinguishing features of the playoff policy is an elaborate tie-breaking provision. There is a multiple-team tie-breaker, and a two-way tie-breaker. The latter has five points of comparison in this order:

1. Results in head-to-head competition
2. Winning percentage within conference
3. Winning percentage within division (used only if teams tied are from the some division)
4. Winning percentage against playoff teams in own conference
5. Point differential in the games between the two teams

One might question why there is a need for such an elaborate tie-breaker provision. A look at a case study from the 1992–1993 season provides the reason why it is needed. The Orlando Magic and the Indiana Pacers finished the season with identical records of 41–41 (.500). Thus, the NBA turned to its tie-breaker procedure to determine which team would qualify for the playoffs. The first factor could not be used because Orlando and Indiana split the four games they played during the regular season. The second comparison also had to be precluded because both teams had the same winning percentage within the Eastern Conference, 27–29 (.482). The third factor was not applicable due to the fact that Orlando and Indiana are not in the same division. Even the fourth comparison did not break the tie as the two team's records against playoff teams in the Eastern Conference were identical. Finally, the fifth tie-breaker determined the playoff qualifier. The Indiana Pacers obtained the playoff spot because they had cumulatively out-scored the Orlando Magic 444–439 in their four meetings. So, by a factor of two baskets, the Orlando Magic lost out on obtaining the eighth playoff spot in the Eastern Conference in 1993.

Although the NBA's tie-breaker provision is carefully conceived, it also points to a possible flaw in the playoff policy of that league. The policy rewards the team that played consistently against its opponents, with an emphasis on games within its division and conference. However, there is no accountability for team performance at the end of the season. In the case study cited, there were four days between Indiana's and Orlando's final regular season game and the first game of the playoff. It seems as though these teams should have met in a one-game playoff to determine the true winner of the tie-breaker. That would have been fairer than the determination by the differential of two baskets scored during the regular season.

Again like the NHL, the NBA allows too many teams into post-season play. There has been some improvement in this regard when the league expanded from 27 to 29 teams, with the addition of Vancouver and Toronto in 1995. Yet, 16 of the league's 29 teams still qualify for the playoffs. There have been cases when even losing record teams qualified for post-season play. Even if a team has a .500 or slightly better record, there is no good reason to believe that it is of playoff quality. The record shows that the lowest seeded teams really do not belong in post-season play. Since the NBA instituted its current playoff policy in 1984, there has not been a single upset of the number-one seed by the number-eight seed. Similarly, there have been only a few times that the number-seven seed defeated the number-two seed. Therefore, elimination of the bottom two seeds in each conference would make the playoffs more competitive and place a greater premium on regular season victories. Why this is not likely to happen can be summarized in one word: money!

NATIONAL FOOTBALL LEAGUE

In 1921 a professional football league was formed in Canton, Ohio, that became known as the National Football League. The league expanded in 1946 when it absorbed several teams from the All-American Conference. However, it was during the 1960s and 1970s that the NFL really began to flourish and reach a high level of popularity. In 1960, another rival league, the American Football League (AFL) was formed. The two leagues agreed to merge in 1966. Part of the merger agreement included the champions from each league meeting in a final championship game, the Super Bowl. Needless to say that agreement established one of the largest championship playoff games in all of sports.

The basic playoff policy of the NFL was established in 1970. This is the addition of wild card teams in the playoffs. This was also the year that the AFL merged with the NFL to form one league with two conferences, the NFC and AFC. Each of the conferences consisted of three divisions (West, East, and Central). The three division champions from each conference automatically qualified for the playoffs. One wild card team from each conference with the best runner-up record also qualified for the playoffs. Thus, there were eight playoff qualifiers, four from each conference.

In the first round, the division champion with the best record played at home against the team with the worst record among the four playoff teams in the conference. In the other conference game, the home field advantage went to the division champion even if the wild card team had a better season record. For example, in 1970, Miami was the wild card team with a record of 10–4. Oakland received home field advantage over Miami because Oakland was the AFC West division champion, with a record of 8–4–2. The two winners of the first round games then faced each other in the AFC Conference Championship with the winner advancing to the Super Bowl against the NFC champion.

In 1988 the National Football League expanded the number of regular-season games for each team from 14 to 16. The league also added one more wild card team for each conference. In the first round, the two wild card teams played each other while the three division champions received a first-round bye. The home field advantage throughout the playoffs went to the team with the best won-lost-tied percentage in the regular season.

The current NFL policy for playoffs was adopted in 1990. The major change was the addition of a third wild card team for each conference. The three wild card teams are the three nondivision champions with the best overall records. Tie-breaker policies establish procedures in case teams have equal records. The six playoff teams are seeded according to their regular-season records. The division champion with the third-best record has the home field advantage against the lowest-seeded wild card team. The other two wild card teams (fourth and fifth seeds) also play against each other in the first round. Thus, only the top two seeded teams have byes in the first round. The second round matches the first seed against the winner of the four-five wild card game. The second seed plays the winner of the three-six playoff game. From there, the playoff procedures are the same as in previous playoff formats.

One of the strong features of the NFL's policy is that only 12 of the league's 30 teams advance past the 16-game regular season. This helps considerably in maintaining the importance of every game in the schedule. The league has also been able only to qualify teams that have winning records. The result has been competitive match-ups in the post-season. On the other hand, the wild card teams have had limited success in winning playoff games. From 1970 to 1992, only 12 wild card teams advanced to the conference championship, and only three advanced to the Super Bowl. The 1980 Oakland Raiders were the only team to win a Super Bowl as a wild card. Thus, the wild card teams have an opportunity for success, but overall the teams with better records prevail in the playoffs.

Even though the NFL's playoff policy seems to be basically sound, there is one possible flaw. Several teams can have equal records going into the last week of the regular season. A playoff-bound team entering the final game has a fairly good idea of their match-ups in the post-season depending on whether they win or lose their final game. As an example, in 1992, the Houston Oilers defeated the Buffalo Bills in the last regular season game and then lost to the Bills the following week in a very cold Buffalo. If the Oilers had lost the first game against the Bills, they would have played in sunny San

Diego in the first game of the playoffs. The Oilers knew this before the game was played. Obviously, they put forth an all-out effort in spite of the known consequences. Nevertheless, there is always the concern that the integrity of the NFL could be threatened by this kind of playoff scenario.

THE ISSUE

In professional sport generally, the key playoff issue whether there are many teams in the playoffs. Many sport journalists argue that qualifying more teams for the playoffs has diminished the value of the regular season. Consequently, many fans hold the same opinion because they are largely influenced by what the journalists have to say. Why are there so many playoff positions? The simple answer is money! The playoffs have consistently generated considerable revenue for the participating teams. For example, gate receipts for two home games in a best-of-five NBA first round playoff series can generate an extra $1 million for a team that just "squeaks" into the playoffs. Much the same applies to the NHL playoffs with the financial stakes rising as a team advances in the playoffs. Some of the franchises have reported that as much as 30 percent of the revenue from gate receipts is earned during the playoffs.

The added revenue from ticket sales is just the beginning of the windfall. Teams that consistently make the playoffs are able to negotiate larger broadcast rights fees with their local television contracts. This is because pricing for commercials doubles for playoff games due to the sharp increase in ratings. The national television networks also have a strong interest in expanded playoffs because they too benefit from higher ratings and advertising revenues. In some cases, more than half of the television revenue is from post-season play.

There are also more indirect, financial benefits from the playoffs. Stadium and arena concessions are often run by companies that operate independently from the professional sport franchises. Yet, the financial growth of these companies is dependent on whether a team in their venue makes it to the playoffs. Not only do the extra playoff games translate into added business days, but sales of food and beverage are greater than for a regular season game. For example, customer spending at concessions was up 20 percent over a regular season game during the 1993 NFL playoffs at Miami and San

Francisco (Waddell, January 25, 1993, p. 19). Likewise, in the NBA playoffs in 1993, beer sales broke all records. According to Chuck Ridge, manager of San Antonio Concessions, "it must be the excitement, because it's the same people—the season ticket holders" (Waddell, May 24, 1993, p. 18).

Another party that indirectly benefits from a team making the playoffs is the city. In 1992 the *Philadelphia Business Journal* reported that a home team in the playoffs can bring in up to $4.5 million in direct taxes for the city. The city of Philadelphia receives amusement taxes from tickets, wage taxes from visiting players' paychecks, and sales taxes from concessions (Lehren, p. 1). As a matter of fact, sometimes cities become too dependent on these revenues and are severely hurt when their professional teams do not qualify for the playoffs.

Even though the financial benefits of the playoffs are most evident, this does not necessarily mean that having more playoff teams is necessarily better for all concerned. Sometimes there is a fine line between not having enough and having too many playoff qualifiers. It seems reasonable to assume that a playoff team should have a regular season record at least above .500. Otherwise, anyone would have to question the integrity of the playoff structure and the legitimacy of the playoff competition. The regular season has to have some value other than just working toward a top seeding in the playoffs.

In this regard, the NFL has an advantage over the other professional sport leagues. The 16-game schedule means that each game has some importance, and some of the games have tremendous importance. The latter is particularly true during the last week of the regular season schedule. It is not at all uncommon to have 10 to 20 teams still in competition for 4 to 6 playoffs spots during the last week. For example, in 1995, 11 games affected the NFL playoffs on the last weekend of the regular season.

The situation is quite different in the other three major professional sport leagues due to the length of the seasons. Baseball, of course, has the longest season with its 162 game regular season schedule. Ironically, baseball also has the fewest playoff teams even though two wild card teams were initiated in 1995. As noted before, this can be attributed to the traditional stance of baseball with its emphasis on the excitement of the pennant races in each league.

The NHL and NBA also have long seasons, but they also have the most playoff teams. In fact it can easily be argued that both of these leagues have too many playoff teams although there has been some improvement in that regard due to league expansion. In 1991, when the NHL consisted of only 22 teams, 16 of those teams qualified for the playoffs. Thus, the purpose of the NHL's 80-game season was to eliminate just six teams from the playoffs. Since that time the league has expanded into four cities while maintaining the same number of playoff teams. Nevertheless, more that half of the teams still qualify for the playoffs. A very similar scenario exists in the NBA. As noted previously, there was improvement in 1995 when the league added Vancouver and Toronto. Yet, 16 of 29 teams are in the playoffs.

In terms of providing better competition both during the season and the playoffs, the NFL also has an advantage over the other leagues. This is the parity generally found among the NFL teams year after year. In the other three leagues there are usually a few teams that stand out above the other teams in the league. This whole matter of parity is an issue in itself. Some people argue that too much parity is not good for a league because it lowers the standard of excellence found among top teams. On the other hand nobody can deny the fact that parity results in close games. Furthermore, spectators tend to like the excitement of close games. When the outcome is in doubt, the competition becomes that much more intense.

CONCLUSION

The debate about the right number of playoff teams for professional sport will probably be around for a long time. There is no magic formula except there seems to be little justification for having more than half of the teams in the league playoffs. One cannot deny the fact that money will be the determining factor because a professional sport league is in the business of that sport. At the same time, the value of regular season games also has to be preserved to the greatest extent possible.

Differences among the four professional sport leagues should be taken into account when assessing the merits and limitations of the playoff formats. On the surface, it appears that the NFL has the most sound policy, one that balances economics and competitiveness. Yet, it could be that the same policy would not be as effective in the other leagues due to the differences from sport to sport. The NHL and NBA will continue to be subject to criticism with the current ratio of playoff teams. Furthermore, the debate over wild card teams in baseball is not likely to disappear readily.

REFERENCES

Costas, Bob. "Will Baseball's Divisional Realignment Make for Better Regular Season Play? No." *Inside Sports*, April 1994, p. 14.

Lehren, Andrew. "Lackluster Play of Sports Teams Hits City's Wallet." *Philadelphia Business Journal*, December 21, 1992, pp. 1–4.

Waddell, Ray. "Concessionaires Big Winners at NFL Playoffs in Miami, Frisco." *Amusement Business*, January 25, 1993, p. 19.

Waddell, Ray. "Sales at NBA Playoffs Top Regular Season." *Amusement Business*, May 24, 1993, pp. 18–19.

Wulf, Steve. "Scouting Reports." *Sports Illustrated*, April 4, 1994, p. 93.

Chapter 16

Conclusion

W e have examined the policies involving 14 different areas in college athletics or professional sports leagues. A review of those policies leads to the following conclusions.

First, there are some major differences between the scope of policies in college athletics and those in professional sport. The differences are also manifested in the way in which these policies are developed. College athletics tend to have more policy considerations. Part of this may be attributed to the delicate balance between academics and athletics in institutions of higher education, particularly those at the Division I level.

The other key factor in the proliferation of college athletic policies is the role of the National Collegiate Athletic Association (NCAA). Since its inception in 1905 this organization has been the dominant force in establishing policies for the control of intercollegiate athletic programs. Furthermore, this control has been exercised through an endless stream of legislation. Some of the legislation is of minor nature, involving details and procedures. Nevertheless, significant policies have also been developed from that source. Proposition 48 is a classic example in the policy realm.

Professional sport leagues may have fewer policies per se, but those that exist are not less significant. It can easily be argued that policies involving free agency are the dominant force in professional sport today. Many of the changes in professional sport during the past 20 years can be attributed to the effect of the free agency. Inflated player salaries is the most obvious change. However, beyond that, increased ticket prices, luxury boxes, lack of competitive balance, and even franchise relocation are by-products of free agency.

Among the chapters on college athletics, at least three stand out from a major policy prospective. One of these is the topic of Title IX. This has had a monumental impact on college athletic programs during the past 25 years. For many reasons, the administration of college athletic programs has changed drastically due to the existence of the Title IX policy. Aside from any other considerations, the financial effect of Title IX is significant to identify it as one of the most significant policies.

Those policies related to the restructuring of the NCAA also stand out as being particularly important. When restructuring legislation was passed in 1996, the association drastically changed the way it had done business for 90 years. Much of the future direction for college athletics will be determined by the policies providing for a new structure for the NCAA.

The recruitment of college athletics also has to rank as one of the big policy areas in the college sector. The reason for this should be quite clear. Admissions, academic standards for freshman eligibility, and satisfactory degree progress are all dependent on the quality of the athlete who is recruited. If the recruitment policies are sound, there is good reason to believe that many other things will fall into place for the establishment of a solid athletic program.

A final conclusion is that some of the topics in this book are subject to considerable change. A good example would be college football playoffs at the Division I-A level. This has been discussed for years but has yet to materialize. Nevertheless, there could be a major change in policy down the line. Much the same could be said about some of the other topics such as professional sport franchise expansion and relocation and professional sport playoffs. By contrast, the topic of evaluating coaches tends to be a more stable consideration. We noted at the outset that policy development is the continuous process of making significant decisions from a long-term perspective. Nevertheless, sport managers must also have the flexibility to cope with changing conditions.

Index

About the Author

HAROLD J. VANDERZWAAG is Professor Emeritus, Associate Department Head and Graduate Program Director of Sport Studies at the University of Massachusetts at Amherst. He is the author of six previous books, is a past president of the Philosophic Society for the Study of Sport, and is a former editor of the *Journal of the Philosophy of Sport*.

ISBN 0-275-96089-7

90000>

EAN

9 780275 960896

HARDCOVER BAR CODE